AL HANISSIM

MEIR LAMBERSKI

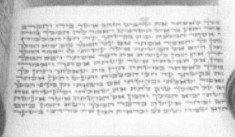

THE COMPLETE STORY OF PURIM

Translated from the **Hebrew Al Hanissim**
by Rabbi Meir Lamberski

Published and distributed by:
Shanky's Judaica, Jerusalem
Tel 02-538-6936
Fax: 02-538-6921
sales@shankysjudaica.com

Printed in Israel

PREFACE

I am deeply grateful to the Creator for enabling me to reach this day, when I hold my first completed work in my hands describing the wonders of Divine Providence and the miraculous sequence of events that took place in the days of Mordechai and Esther.

My abilities are certainly not responsible for this accomplishment. More than just siyata dishmaya, Heavenly assistance, this book is an undeserved gift from Hashem.

Therefore, at this moment, I turn heavenward in gratitude and prayer to my Father in heaven: gratitude – for His granting me this valuable gift, and prayer – that His kindness should continue to accompany me throughout my life.

Every year, we make sure to hear the megillah read twice, as Mordechai and Esther ordained. We are careful not to miss a single word of the reading, not even a syllable, so as to properly observe the mitzvah. Each year anew, we strike at the name and memory of Haman and proclaim, "Cursed is Haman who sought to annihilate me, blessed is Mordechai the Jew, cursed is Zeresh, the wife of the one who terrorized me, blessed is Esther, who was on my side, cursed are all the wicked, blessed are all the righteous, and Charvona as well is remembered for the good!"

But let us stop and ask ourselves: Do we know clearly what role each of the characters just mentioned played in the sequence of events? Do we appreciate the depth of the miracle, the extent of Divine Providence that was expressed in the annals of our people at that time? Do we really feel the great kindness of Hashem that accompanied the Jews at every step and brought about the miraculous salvation?

I have tried to give a clear picture of the events according to the words of Chazal and our great Rabbis through the ages, revealing the clear line of Divine control that directed matters, and attempting to bring the ideas to life to deepen the reader's emotional connection to the story.

Therefore, I offer my fervent prayer that this book should be of benefit to all who read it and should rouse in them a love of their Creator.

There is not a single point in this book that I invented. Everything described in these pages is based on Midrashim of Chazal and the words of the great Rabbis; all I added was some colorful description in places where I felt it would better rouse the reader's emotions.

The main consideration that guided me in consolidating this book was the degree to which each point would clarify the story and show Hashem's kindness. Therefore, in certain areas of the text, I adhered mainly to the descriptions of Chazal in the Gemara and Midrashim, while in others, I followed the approach of the great Rabbis of the generations. The order in which the opinions are cited does not indicate their centrality or importance. The readers are advised to look into the footnotes, find the source of the various opinions, and keep each one in the proper perspective.

Many people assisted me in bringing this book to print with their good advice, encouragement, and enlightening remarks. It would be impossible to list all of them, but I offer them my deepest thanks. May Hashem fulfill all their requests for the good, and may they enjoy success in all their endeavors.

However, I cannot refrain from specifically thanking my dear mother, who raised and educated me, and stood at my side devotedly from the moment I was born until this very day. May the Creator endow her with robust health, a long life of prosperity and happiness, and much nachas from her children and grandchildren.

I will also take this opportunity to thank my father-in-law, who is like a father to me, Rav Sholom Hakohen Klein, shlit"a, and my mother-in-law, for bringing blessing to my home, and for their encouragement and support for this book and in general. May the Creator bless them with only nachas from all their descendants.

And of course, to my dear wife, I give my heartfelt blessing for her encouragement, for the sacrifices she had to make, and for her patience. May we merit to bring up upstanding children from whose lips the Torah shall never depart.

In conclusion, I wish to thank my cherished friend, Rabbi Yitzchok Hershkowitz, shlit"a, without whose help this book would never have reached publication.

❖

My one request of Hashem is that just as He helped me bring this book to its successful conclusion through His kindness, so may He generously grant me the opportunity to continue further. May my work please the readers, and may Hashem enable my words to bring the readers spiritual benefit.

Meir Lembarski

Table Of Contents

IN THE DAYS OF ACHASHVEROSH

*"And it came to pass in the days of Achashverosh,
the Achashverosh who reigned from Hodu to
Kush, over one hundred and twenty seven
provinces." (1:1)*

These words open the story of the *megillah* and introduce us
to King Achashverosh.

When we read *Megillas Esther* we might get the impression
that Achashverosh was a fine, upstanding personality since
the king had Haman hanged and also handed his ring over
to Mordechai so that he could write whatever he wanted
concerning the Jews. We may have assumed that it would never
have occurred to Achashverosh to hurt the Jews, were it not for
Haman's smooth talk and power of persuasion.

But this impression could not be further from the truth.
Chazal teach us that Achashverosh was just as much of a *rasha*
as Haman himself, though he cleverly concealed his wickedness
under the veil of diplomacy.

Achashverosh – "the Brother of Rosh"

The first thing to know about Achashverosh is that he was
the one who halted the construction of the *Bais Hamikdash* in
his time. Chazal explain the etymology of the king's name as,
"Achashverosh – the brother of *Rosh* and the colleague of *Rosh*.
The brother of *Rosh* because he was the brother of the wicked
Nevuchadnetzar who was called *Rosh*. The colleague of *Rosh*

because just as he (Nevuchadnetzar) killed, he (Achashverosh) sought to kill, and just as he destroyed, he sought to destroy."[1]

The first chapter in the book of Ezra fills in the background. Koresh granted the Jewish people permission to return to Yerushalayim and erect the new *Bais Hamikdash*. During his lifetime the foundations were laid down, but the construction was not completed. In the fourth chapter of Ezra, we discover why the building was stopped. King Artachshasta (another name for Koresh)[2] received a letter from a man by the name of Mitredas Tav'el and his cohorts, the ten sons of Haman,[3] warning the king that the people of Yerushalayim were rebelling.

"If you think that the Jews are going to continue sending their taxes up to you after they finish fortifying the walls of

---

[1] Megillah 11a

[2] There are a number of approaches among Chazal regarding this matter. In the regular text above, we followed the version of Rashi, identifying King Artachshasta as Koresh, who, after originally granting permission to build the *Bais Hamikdash*, later rescinded his authorization and ordered the construction stopped. Achashverosh, on the other hand, (according to this version) did not stop the construction of the *Bais Hamikdash*, since it had already been halted in the time of Koresh. Rather, he hampered renewal of the construction and also sought to destroy the foundations that remained from the days of Koresh.

However, according to many authorities, and as we find explained in the words of Chazal in several other places including the Yalkut cited in the next footnote, Artachshasta is actually King Achashverosh himself. He was the one who halted the building of the *Bais Hamikdash* as a result of the letter of indictment sent to him. According to this version, Koresh died before the work was completed, but he was not responsible for its cessation.

A third approach is that brought by the Maharzu (Esther Rabbah 1:1), also based on the words of Chazal in several places. According to this version, King Artachshasta is actually both Koresh and Achashverosh! This approach bridges the two prior ones, maintaining that Koresh and Achashverosh are one and the same. Consequently, it turns out that Koresh - also known to us as Achashverosh - ordered the building of the *Bais Hamikdash* and later stopped its construction.

[3] Yalkut Ezra 1065

their city, you are gravely mistaken!" read the missive. The writer went on to further depict the financial doom that would befall the empire. "They will not carry out the labor assigned to them by the king, nor will they make use of the elaborate theaters and circus arenas that you erected for the benefit of the residents, so you will also lose out on all the income you expected from these entertainment centers!"

King Artachshasta accepted the words of the letter and promptly halted the construction of the city of Yerushalayim. However, he left intact the foundations of the *Bais Hamikdash*. Chazal tell us that just as Nevuchadnetzar sought to actively destroy the *Bais Hamikdash*, so did Achashverosh seek to demolish these foundations from Koresh's rule, though he did not succeed!

Similarly, just as Nevuchadnetzar killed Jews, so Achashverosh sought to do. From a superficial perusal of the *megillah*, we might conclude that King Achashverosh had no personal interest in harming the Jewish people and merely agreed to "sell" the Jews to Haman for ten thousand silver talents. However, Achashverosh's malicious intentions are spelled out in the following *moshol* regarding the partnership of Achashverosh and Haman:[4]

A man had a heap of dirt in his field that interfered with his work. His friend had a pit in his field that was an obstacle to his work.

Each day, when the one with the pit would pass by the field of his friend, he would think wistfully, "If only I could buy that pile of dirt and use it to fill up my pit!" And each day, when the

---

[4] Megillah 14a

owner of the heap would pass by his friend's field, he would sigh to himself, "If only I could buy this pit and empty my heap of dirt into it!"

One day, the two met. The owner of the pit turned to his friend and said to him, "Perhaps you would agree to sell me the pile of dirt in your field?" The owner of the pit was certain that he would have to pay a hefty sum for the privilege, but to his surprise, the other fellow responded, "If you want this dirt, it's yours for free, just take it! I don't want anything in return. I have been hoping for ages to find someone who will get rid of it for me!"

The *nimshol* is clear. Chazal teach us that Achashverosh was just as interested in getting rid of the Jewish nation as was the wicked Haman. Therefore, when Haman suggested that Achashverosh sell him the Jewish nation, Achashverosh readily agreed.

Achashverosh didn't change his attitude towards the Jews even after he became aware of Esther's origins. Chazal stress,[5] "*Hu Achashverosh* – he was the very same Achashverosh in his wickedness from start to finish!" The same dastardly Achashverosh who joined forces with Haman remained steadfast in his villainy to his dying day. Even when he handed his signet ring over to Mordechai and raised him to a glorious position, in his heart he still wished he could wipe out the Jews. He only restrained himself because he understood that doing so was not worth his while.

---

[5] Megillah 11a

The One Who Reigned – Who Took the Reign on His Own

Let us examine now the circumstances that led him to rule over 127 provinces.

Unquestionably, Achashverosh was not slated to be the next king after Koresh. First of all, he was not of royal lineage. Secondly, the *posuk* indicates that he simply announced himself as the ruler of his own accord, and his reign was accepted.

Chazal[6] differ regarding the enigma of how Achashverosh succeeded in gaining control over the vast empire of Paras and Madai. Some explain it to his merit, that he was the most worthy to rule. Others explain that Achashverosh was in fact not worthy, but gained control by paying hefty bribes to the ministers so that they would choose him as king. Other commentaries[7] maintain that Achashverosh attained his position by virtue of the lineage of his wife, Vashti, the granddaughter of Nevuchadnetzar.

One Hundred and Twenty Seven Provinces

Either way, Achashverosh succeeded in sitting on the royal throne. At first, Achashverosh did not rule over all 127 provinces, but over Madai and Paras alone. The other provinces were conquered over the course of time. First he captured seven provinces, followed by an additional twenty, and only later, the final hundred. Of these countries, one hundred were on the continent, while the remaining twenty seven were islands.[8]

---

[6] Ibid

[7] Malbim

[8] The Gra finds a hint to this in the words of the *posuk* (Esther 10:1), "The King Achashverosh placed a tax on the land and on the islands of the sea." The word *mas*, tax, has the numerical value of one hundred, a hint to the hundred

How did Achashverosh manage to conquer 127 provinces? The king used a clever strategy.[9] First he conquered seven provinces, using the armies of Madai and Paras. After they were conquered, he drafted additional soldiers from the new countries under his rule to bolster his army. With this strengthened battalion, he was able to conquer another twenty provinces. Once he controlled twenty seven provinces, he was able to call a general draft from his growing empire and put together a powerful force that was capable of conquering one hundred additional provinces.

One Hundred and Twenty Seven Provinces – in the Merit of Esther

In what merit did such a foe of the Jews gain power over such a mighty empire? The reign was granted to him from Heaven in the merit of his future queen, Esther.[10] The merit of Sarah Imeinu, who lived 127 years, allowed Esther to be queen over 127 provinces,[11] and in the zechus of his future wife, Achashverosh reigned. It is ironic how deeply Achashverosh hated the Jews when it was only in their merit that he ruled!

From Hodu to Kush

Interestingly, Chazal point out that the distance from Hodu to Kush was not great. In fact, Hodu and Kush were two

---

provinces that were on land, while the word *v'iyay*, the islands, amounts to twenty seven, a hint to those provinces that were in the sea (Perush HaGra).

[9] Esther Rabbah 1:7

[10] Esther Rabbah 1:8, and Megillah 11a. The Maharsha (ibid) explains that Achashverosh merited to rule over 127 provinces only after he took Esther as his queen. However, the simple understanding of the words of Chazal in the Gemara and Midrashim does not imply as such.

[11] Yefei Anaf on Esther Rabbah 1:8

neighboring provinces. The term "Hodu to Kush" is explained, therefore, in one of two ways.[12]

One approach interprets this choice of words as an indication of the stability of Achashverosh's reign. Just as Achashverosh was able to exert total control over these two adjacent lands, so was he able to exert a full and stable rule over his entire empire.

Others[13] explain the term from another angle. Since the world is round, though Kush and Hodu abut each other from one side, they are on two opposite ends of the world from the other side. Thus, when we say "from Hodu to Kush," we are actually saying that Achashverosh ruled over all the provinces between these two – that is, the whole world.

Achashverosh is mentioned among the few sovereigns who ruled "b'kippa," over everything beneath the heavens,[14] or, alternately, over half the world,[15] 127 out of 252 provinces around the globe.[16]

---

[12] Megillah 11a; Esther Rabbah 1:4
[13] Yefei Anaf on Midrash Rabbah ibid
[14] Megillah 11b
[15] Esther Rabbah 1:5
[16] Indeed, even though Achashverosh ruled over only half the world, all the Jews of that generation – without exception – lived within the limits of his empire, a fact that would have enabled him to carry out the decree of decimation plotted by the wicked Haman (see Perush HaGra 3:8).

UPON HIS ROYAL THRONE

"In those days, when King Achashverosh sat upon his royal throne which was in Shushan the capital." (1:2)

The *megillah* places particular emphasis on King Achashverosh's royal throne. This throne was a replica of the throne of King Shlomo, which Achashverosh had a deep desire to possess.

King Shlomo's throne was certainly magnificent in its wondrous design. However, the uniqueness of King Shlomo's throne did not lie in its splendor; rather in its remarkable qualities.[1]

The Structure of King Shlomo's Throne

King Shlomo's throne was made of special, high quality gold and multi-colored marble, and set with pearls and precious stones, including topaz and emerald.

Six steps led up to the throne,[2] an allusion to the six days of Creation and the six *mitzvos* incumbent upon the king. The

---

[1] The expanded description is brought in Targum Sheini. The Midrash (Esther Rabbah 1:11) presents a more concise discussion of the throne's design, although it differs from the Targum regarding certain details. Since the Targum's version is more detailed, we will base our description of King Shlomo's throne on that source, while in regard to King Achashverosh's throne, we will mention the words of the Midrash as well. In the footnotes, we will relate to some of the points in which the two sources differ.

[2] The Midrash Ponim Acheirim states that there were six accesses to the throne, each one with six steps.

seven heavens were also hinted at in the structure of the throne, with the six stairs corresponding to the six lower heavens, and the seat of the king to the seventh heaven, the "seat" of the King of Kings – Hashem.

On each of the steps of the throne, twelve golden lions stood directly opposite twelve golden eagles, giving us an idea of the massive dimensions of each step! Aside from the lions and eagles, a variety of other animals, all made of pure gold, crouched on the stairs, representing the king's command over all living beings in the world.

On the first step, an ox crouched opposite a lion. On the second step lay a wolf across from a sheep. The third step held a leopard facing a camel, the fourth, an eagle opposite a parrot, the fifth, a cat across from a rooster, and on the sixth step stood a hawk facing a dove.

Above the king's throne stood a golden dove[3] holding a golden hawk in its claws. The dove alluded to the future rule of Moshiach, the king of Israel, over the nations of the world, the hawk.

In position above the throne was a pure gold *menorah* with fourteen arms, each engraved with a different face, seven per side. On the seven arms on one side were engraved the seven "fathers of the world" – Adam, Noach, Shem, Avraham, Yitzchok, Yaakov and Iyov. The arms on the other side were embellished with the forms of the seven "pious ones of the

---

[3] The Midrash explains that the dove's role was to hold the king's crown in her beak so that it would look as if it was perched on his head, while not actually weighing on him.

world" – Levi, Kehos, Amram, Moshe, Aharon, Eldad and Medad.

In addition, a pitcher of pure olive oil, with a basin filled with oil beneath it, stood at the head of the *menorah*. The oil in these vessels served for lighting the *menorah*.

There were two golden chairs attached to the sides of the throne, for the *kohen gadol* and the king's viceroy.[4] Above and behind the throne, seventy golden chairs were set up for the Sanhedrin to sit in judgment.

Two golden *bnot yam* supported the king's head as he sat upon his throne, while twenty four golden grapevines provided him with shade.

Unique Qualities

The true uniqueness of the throne did not lie in its outer splendor, but rather in its exceptional powers.

First of all, King Shlomo's throne was not immobile, but would carry the king everywhere he had to go – without any human being directing or moving it![5]

The golden animals perched on the steps were also animated. When the king would climb to the first step, the golden animals would move him from step to step.[6] Once the king

---

[4] The Midrash Ponim Acheirim states that one chair was set aside for the prophet Gad, while the other was for the prophet Nosson.

[5] It should be stressed that both the Yalkut and the Midrash Ponim Acheirim point out that the throne worked by way of an inner mechanism, not through supernatural powers of some kind.

[6] The Midrash maintains that the lions and eagles were the ones to stretch their hands out to the king as he climbed the steps to his throne, and does not mention the other animals at all.

reached the top step, the eagles would lift him directly onto his royal seat!

In addition, as the king was raised from step to step, the golden lions would sprinkle perfumed water, suffusing the air of the royal palace with a pleasant aroma.

Once the king reached his seat, the great eagle would arise and place the golden crown upon him, and the lions and eagles would take position to shade his head. The golden dove would then descend from its perch above the throne, open the *aron kodesh*, take out the *sefer Torah* written by Torah command especially for the king, and present it to the monarch.

In addition, in King Shlomo's chambers, it simply was not possible to say a mistruth! Any word that veered from the truth roused a fierce response from all the golden animals positioned at the sides of the throne, as each emitted its own angry growls and howls. They would not resume their calm silence until the perjuring witnesses would retract their false words.[7]

Travails of King Shlomo's Throne

This throne of King Shlomo was captured from its native land, passing through the palaces of several kings, among them Nevuchadnetzar, king of Bavel, and Pharaoh, the king of Mitzrayim.[8] Eventually, the throne reached the treasuries of

---

[7] This is according to the version of Targum Sheini. However, the Yalkut and Midrash Ponim Acheirim differ and say that the animals would roar when any witnesses would arrive in order to threaten and frighten them, preventing them in advance from offering false testimony.

[8] On this point we also find disagreement between the version of the Midrash and that of the Targum. The Midrash explains that Pharaoh took possession of the throne after King Shlomo's death, justifying himself with the claim that he was merely collecting what was promised in the *kesubah* to his daughter, one of King Shlomo's

King Achashverosh, but opinions differ regarding the precise sequence of events.

One opinion[9] claims that Nevuchadnetzar was the first one to try and sit on King Shlomo's throne, misconstruing the throne as a magnificent piece of art. He paid the price for his error soon enough. The golden lion perched on the first step rose from its place and slapped the king's thigh with his paw, leaving Nevuchadnetzar with a lifetime deformity – a serious limp in his left leg.

Shishak, king of Mitzrayim,[10] was the next in line to try his luck,[11] and suffered a similar fate. The moment he set his foot on the first step, the lion struck at him, leaving him a cripple. From that day on, he was universally referred to as "Pharaoh *Necho*" – Pharaoh the cripple.

The one foreign king who was given Divine permission to sit on King Shlomo's throne was Koresh, king of Madai, in the merit of his having granted the Jews license to rebuild the House of Hashem.

This opinion complements the view[12] that Achashverosh and Koresh were one and the same and that the throne mentioned

---

wives. After making the rounds to a number of other locations, the throne returned to the kings of Yehuda. Only afterwards was it captured by Nevuchadnetzar. Targum Sheini, on the other hand, explains that the throne was captured by Pharaoh only after it was carried down to Bavel by Nevuchadnetzar, leading us to conclude that this version is referring to a different Pharaoh. Targum Yonasan presents a third approach, stating that the throne was captured twice by kings of Mitzrayim – once by Shishak, and then, after it had made its way back to Yerushalayim, by Pharaoh Necho. After he had it, it fell into the hands of Nevuchadnetzar.

[9] Targum Sheini

[10] All kings of Mitzrayim were called "Pharaoh."

[11] As mentioned, some authorities maintain that Shishak's rule preceded that of Nevuchadnetzar.

[12] Cited above (Ch. 1, FN 2).

in *Megillas Esther,* "when King Achashverosh sat upon his royal throne," was the authentic throne of King Shlomo. At the same time, it would indicate that Achashverosh merited to sit on King Shlomo's throne even after he rescinded his permission to build the *Bais Hamikdash.*

However, there is another opinion in the Midrash that Achashverosh never merited to sit on Shlomo's throne, though Nevuchadnetzar did. According to this view, only someone who ruled over the entire world, as Nevuchadnetzar did, was entitled to sit on the throne of King Shlomo.[13] Since Achashverosh's rule did not extend that far, he was denied the right to sit on this throne.[14]

Since Achashverosh was not permitted to sit on the actual throne of King Shlomo, he ordered the construction of an imitation, which would resemble Shlomo's throne on the outside, but would lack the unique qualities described above.

Even the creation of this pale replica was not easily accomplished.[15] The only place where such a throne could be constructed was in Shushan, the international center of expert goldsmiths. From the seat of his empire in Bavel, Achashverosh turned to the craftsmen of Shushan to create for him a throne similar to that of King Shlomo.

When the work on the throne was completed, all that remained was to transfer it to the palace in Bavel. It was then

---

[13] The words of the Midrash match the version cited earlier in the discussion of Achashverosh's rule which stated that Achashverosh did not rule over the entire world, but only half of it.

[14] The Yalkut brings a third opinion, which states that neither Achashverosh nor Nevuchadnetzar sat on King Shlomo's throne.

[15] Perush HaGra on *Megillas Esther*

that the king discovered, to his deep disappointment, that transporting the throne was simply an impossibility.

And so, Achashverosh found a solution. He moved his capital city from Bavel to Shushan in the land of Elam. Everything – the palace, servants, furnishings, treasuries – was relocated, to a different capital city in a different land. This entire uphval was initiated just so that the king could sit on his pitiful replica of King Shlomo's throne.

In fact, however, there was a deeper reason why Achashverosh ended up in Shushan. Mordechai lived in Shushan, and since the salvation of the people of Israel was destined to come about through him,[16] it was necessary to move the capital. In order to do so, the ridiculous idea took root in Achashverosh's mind to build himself a throne like that of King Shlomo, the technical problem stood in the way of transporting the throne, and the entire royal court followed the throne to Shushan.

The king was absolutely thrilled with his new throne. Achashverosh ignored the significant differences between the original throne and the copy,[17] and publicly expressed his satisfaction with the new, elaborate throne by announcing a colossal feast – the well known feast of Achashverosh.

---

[16] As we shall explain, he had to correct the sin of his great-great-grandfather, Shaul, who left Agag, king of Amalek, alive, thus facilitating the continued existence of the Amalek offspring, Haman among them.

[17] Esther Rabbah 1:14

THE FEAST OF ACHASHVEROSH

*"In the third year of his reign, he made a feast
for all his ministers and servants, the army of
Paras and Madai, the nobles and officials of the
provinces being present, at which he displayed the
riches of his glorious kingdom and the splendor
of his magnificent grandeur for many days – one
hundred and eighty days. At the conclusion of
these days, the king made a seven day feast for all
the people present in Shushan the capital, great
and small, in the courtyard of the garden of the
king's palace. There were hangings of white and
blue fine cotton, fastened with cords of fine linen
and purple, upon silver rods and marble pillars.
The couches of gold and silver stood on flooring
of green and white, and shell and onyx marble.
The drinks were served in golden goblets, each
one different from the other, and there was royal
wine in abundance, bountiful as befits a king. The
drinking was according to law, without coercion,
for so the king had ordered all the officers of his
household, to serve each person according to his
pleasure." (1:3-8)*

The *megillah* describes the feast that Achashverosh decided
to make in the third year of his reign. During the first two years[1]
of Achashverosh's reign, he was not at ease. At the forefront of

---

[1] Megillah 11b

his mind dangled the prophecy of Yirmiyahu, "At the end of seventy years in Bavel, the people of Israel will be redeemed!"

"For the time being, I rule over all the people of Israel, and the vessels of the *Bais Hamikdash* adorn my treasuries. But any day now, the picture can change completely!" Achashverosh said to himself in deep dread. "If the prophecy of Yirmiyahu comes true, the Jews will surely found their own empire and throw off the yoke of my rule and even take the holy vessels of the *Bais Hamikdash* with them!"

But once the third year of Achashverosh's rule arrived, he felt calm. According to his erroneous calculations, that year marked the end of seventy years since the Jews had been exiled to Bavel. "If they have not been redeemed by this point," he assured himself, "Yirmiyahu's prophecy was meaningless. From now on, I have nothing more to fear from his words." With a happy heart, he decided to celebrate with a grandiose feast, using the holy vessels of the *Bais Hamikdash* that were in his treasure houses.[2]

Achashverosh chose this particular date[3] for his feast because it marked the removal of the threat of Yirmiyahu's prophecy,[4] but there was another, more insidious, reason for his celebration.

---

[2] The Radal explains that this feast was in essence a somewhat delayed coronation ceremony for Achashverosh. He adds that it was common practice in those days for a king to hold his coronation ceremony only after some time had elapsed since he stepped up to the throne, after his rule had been proven to be stable. According to the words of the Radal, we can certainly understand that Achashverosh would carry on the coronation even later, after three years, since only then did he feel that his reign was well established and not endangered by the threatening prophecy of Yirmiyahu.

[3] Esther Rabbah 1:14

[4] See Maharzu ibid. Others explain that the date was intentionally set at the end of the years of *chazoka*, the established fact, of the suspension of work on the *Bais*

Achashverosh actually wished to celebrate the third anniversary of his decision to halt the construction of the *Bais Hamikdash*.[5] The words "*b'shnas shalosh l'molcho*," the third year of his reign, are interpreted by Rabbi Nechemiah to mean "*b'shnas shalosh l'm'lachto*,"[6] the third year of his *m'locho*, his work, referring to the suspension of work on the sanctuary which Achashverosh had announced three years earlier, when he took the throne.

The downfall of the people of Israel, represented by the frustration of their plans to reconstruct Hashem's holy abode, was good reason in Achashverosh's opinion to throw a series of gala parties, the feasts described in the *megillah*.

According to a third opinion,[7] the celebrations took place to mark the completion of the construction of the king's throne.[8] Construction of the throne began immediately after Achashverosh became king, and took three full years to complete. When the work was done, the king announced the

---

Hamikdash. As is well known, such *chazoka* is set after three years (Etz Yosef, Esther Rabbah 2:1).

[5] This version fits in well with the view that the letter of indictment that halted the construction of the *Bais Hamikdash* was sent to King Achashverosh, and that it was he who suspended the work. According to those opinions that state that Koresh was the one to suspend the construction while Achashverosh only prevented its resumption, it is harder to understand what point there would be in marking three years since he "did not resume construction." See footnote above, where all the opinions on this matter are cited (Ch. 1, FN 2).

[6] This *drasha* fits in well with the opinions that Achashverosh and Koresh were one and the same. According to these views, the parties did not take place at all in the third year of *malchuso*, his reign, but rather in the third year of *m'lachto*, his work, which can be understood to mean either the work on the *Bais Hamikdash* that was suspended or the work on the throne that was completed.

[7] Ibid

[8] Rabbi Yehuda also interprets the words "*b'shnas shalosh l'molcho*," the third year of his reign, as if it was written "*b'shnas shalosh l'm'lachto*," the third year of his work, but according to him, the *posuk* refers to the construction of the throne that was completed at this time.

feasts at which he planned to boastfully display the special throne.

Furthermore, since, as we pointed out, the technical difficulty involved in transporting the throne forced Achashverosh to move his capital city to Shushan, the close of three years marked not only the conclusion of the throne's construction, but also the arrival of Achashverosh in Shushan.[9]

In addition to the three approaches for the timing of the feast, Rabbi Avraham Ibn Ezra brings two more opinions:

According to the first opinion, the king was busy during the early years of his reign conquering all the provinces from Hodu to Kush. Only after finishing all his battles, in the third year of his reign, was he able to turn his attention to holding the grand feast described in the *megillah*.[10]

The second opinion maintains that the parties took place in honor of the marriage of the king with Queen Vashti.

Duration of the Feast

The king held two separate feasts. One feast was meant for the king's ministers,[11] his servants,[12] the elite armies of Paras

---

[9] Indeed, the Radal points out that the *posuk* specifically mentions that the celebrations took place in "Shushan the capital," i.e., to mark the transition to the new capital city.

[10] The Targum on this *posuk* implies the same. In the Yalkut as well (1056), the implication is that Achashverosh just returned then from conquering the provinces. However, in this source, it sounds as if there were nations that rebelled against him and that he only now succeeded in subjugating them. See also another opinion cited there, which states that the feast took place to celebrate the king's birthday.

[11] Ibn Yichyeh explains that the king held the party for his "ministers," i.e., the kings of the provinces under his rule, who are considered no more than ministers in contrast with King Achashverosh, the king of kings, and for his "servants," the viceroys who came with each of those kings, who are considered like humble

and Madai, the governors of the various districts,[13] and the ministers of his provinces. The second party was geared for the ordinary citizens. [14]

There are different opinions regarding the duration of the feasts.[15] Some maintain that the seven days of the second feast were included in the 180 days of the first one; the masses joined the honored guests for the final seven days of the celebration.[16] In contrast, others state that after the 180 days came to an end, the king threw a separate party for an additional seven days, exclusively for the common citizens.[17] Either way, it is clear

---

servants in regard to King Achashverosh. Also participating in this feast were *"chayl Paras u'Madai,"* the important people from each and every city in Paras and Madai, as well as *"sarei Madai u'Paras,"* the officials of the various cities in Paras and Madai itself. According to this explanation, we find that from Achahverosh's own home province, Paras and Madai, he invited the heads of every city and town, while from each of the other provinces, he summoned only the king and his viceroy.

[12] Obviously, all the servants of the kings of each province could not possibly have come to the party.

[13] Rashi. However, Chazal explain that the word *"part'mim"* refers to the esteemed families who were authorized to coronate the kings (Esther Rabbah 1:18), while the Ibn Ezra says that the reference is to members of the royal family.

[14] Another opinion cited in Chazal maintains that there was only one feast. However, for 180 days the king displayed his vast treasures to his more honored guests, after which he held a joint party for them together with the residents of the capital city of Shushan (Etz Yosef Esther Rabbah 2:2).

[15] Esther Rabbah 2:6

[16] The Radal explains that the purpose of the first feast was in order to take counsel with the dignitaries of the various provinces against the Jews, while the second feast was the result of their counsel: They claimed that it was necessary to lead the Jews to sin so that their God would decree their destruction. Later on, we will see that this was actually Haman's idea, and he may have been the one to propose this plan by the first feast.

[17] In Y'aros D'vash, Rabbi Yonasan Aibschutz explains that the feast commenced on Rosh Chodesh Nisan, continuing for 180 days and concluding on the third of Tishrei (six months – three full months of thirty days and three short months of twenty nine days – as well as three additional days, to complete the calculation). On the fourth of Tishrei began the general feast for the residents of Shushan, which lasted for seven days, concluding on Yom Kippur, the day of Vashti's downfall (cited in Anaf Yosef, Esther Rabbah 2:2).

that the first feast was mostly dedicated to the distinguished members of the royal entourage.

Displaying the Riches of His Glorious Kingdom

The purpose of the first feast was to display the king's riches before the officers and dignitaries, in order to find favor in their eyes. Since this was Achashverosh's objective in throwing the party, the central attraction of the party was tours of the king's treasuries.

On each of the 180 days of the feast, the dignitaries were given a guided tour through six treasury rooms.[18] The *posuk* hints at this when it states that Achashverosh displayed "*'osher'* *'kvod'* *'malchuso'*" and "*'y'kar'* *'tiferes'* *'g'duloso'*"[19]– six separate terms describing the king's treasures.

Each of these rooms did not hold just one solitary item. Every such treasury room held vast and beautiful treasures, beyond imagination! Examining the contents of the six treasure rooms provided the guests with more than enough entertainment for a full day, and this activity repeated itself for 180 days. With a simple mathematical calculation, we arrive at the conclusion that Achashverosh possessed no less than 1080 rooms filled with marvelous treasures – fabulous, indescribable wealth!

In fact, the duration of the party – 180 days – was determined by the amount of treasures that the king wanted to show his

---

[18] Esther Rabbah 2:2

[19] According to this opinion, the Gra explains why the *posuk* veered from the accepted syntax, according to which the *posuk* should have mentioned the length of the feast, "180 days," before elaborating on the details of the party, "at which he displayed the riches of his glorious kingdom and the splendor of his magnificent grandeur." He states that since these words do not only describe the party but indicate its purpose and the reason for its length, the syntax is correct; the king showed these treasures, six rooms each day, until he finished displaying them all after 180 days.

officers.[20] Because he had 1080 treasure rooms, 180 days were necessary in order to display them all, six a day. The king wanted to prove "*kvod malchuso,*" literally, the honor of his kingdom. In other words, he wanted everyone to know that he was the most worthy to rule.

In what way would vast treasures convince the people he was a commendable ruler? A rich king is less likely to accept bribes. He also has the resources to plot out superior strategies and achieve his goals![21]

Nevuchadnetzar's Treasures

These treasures were an inheritance from Koresh, his predecessor to the throne. Achashverosh himself did nothing to amass them.

The source of all of Koresh's wealth was the wicked Nevuchadnetzar. The riches underwent many vicissitudes[22] until they reached Koresh, and finally Achashverosh.

When Nevuchadnetzar conquered the world,[23] he amassed amazing treasures from all the lands he captured and gathered the wealth of the world into his coffers. Nevuchadnetzar was

---

[20] On the other hand, the Radal explains that the length of the party was an outcome of the king's desire to allot one day for each of the dignitaries of the provinces and for the king's close servants. Since he ruled over 127 provinces, that means that 127 officers (kings under his rule) attended the feast. And since a different servant was responsible to serve the king each week, that means that there were also fifty two honored servants – one for each of the fifty two weeks in a solar year – present at the feast. The total number of all the servants and foreign dignitaries amounted to 180. Based on this number, the king planned the party for 180 days, one day for each honored guest.

[21] Ibn Yichyeh

[22] Esther Rabbah 2:2

[23] Nevuchadnetzar is one of the three kings who ruled *b'kippa,* over the entire world (see Megillah 11a).

so selfish that he could not bear the thought that someone else would enjoy his riches after his death, even if that person was his own son, Evil Merodach.[24]

Nevuchadnetzar loaded all of his treasures into great ships built of heavy copper. He then carved out a channel parallel to the riverbed of the Euphrates River, digging deep into the soil, and hid the valuable ships in the depths of the ground. After, he redirected the river so that the water would cover the buried ships and eliminate any possibility of locating them.

Nevuchadnetzar did not suffice with sinking the ships in the depths of the Euphrates. Had he done so, a determined individual might dive deep into the river and extricate the treasures. The only way he could make sure his plan would be successful was by first burying the ships in the ground and only afterwards channeling the river to flow over them. Digging up soil in the depths of a mighty river was definitely an impossible task. Therefore, the king felt assured that his treasures were safe.

It seems most reasonable that this was carried out by Nevuchadnetzar while he was still alive, a fact that indicates the extent of his selfishness. After all, after hiding his treasures in the depths of the river he himself could no longer enjoy them either! Nevertheless, it was worth it to him in order to ensure that no one else would benefit from his wealth after his death.

Nevuchadnetzar certainly did not take into consideration the possibility that Hashem had already designated his treasures for someone else.

---

[24] Ponim Acheirim

It was Koresh who earned the right to these fabulous treasures, when he granted the Jewish nation permission to return to their land and rebuild the holy sanctuary. After Koresh announced his intentions to allow the construction of the *Bais Hamikdash*, Hashem revealed to him the treasures of Nevuchadnetzar.

The wealth of Nevuchadnetzar, who razed our *Bais Hamikdash*, was handed over to the very man who sought to rebuild what he had demolished. King Achashverosh, in turn, inherited all this wealth when he succeeded him to the throne, and he showed it off for the 180 days of his feast.

Treasures of Hashem's Abode

Among the treasures secreted by Nevuchadnetzar and subsequently inherited by Achashverosh were the holy vessels of the *Bais Hamikdash* and the *bigdei kehuna*, the special garments of the *kohanim*.

Chazal[25] perceive the words *"tiferes g'duloso,"* his magnificent grandeur, as a hint to the fact that Achashverosh displayed the eight garments of the *kohen gadol* that were made *"l'chovod u'l'siferes,"* for honor and glory.[26]

Achashverosh did not suffice with displaying the garments; he donned the holy garments of the *kohen gadol* himself and strutted about, proudly showing them off.

In fact, an international incident almost erupted surrounding these holy vessels and the *bigdei kehuna*. The Jews among the officials, who were compelled to be present at the feasts, refused

---

[25] Megillah 12a; Esther Rabbah 2:2
[26] Shmos 28:2

to participate in the festivities that were staged in front of the vessels of the *Bais Hamikdash.*

"How can we sit back and revel, eating delicacies and drinking fine wines, when before our very eyes we see the vessels of the holy sanctuary that was destroyed because of our sins?" the Jews asserted painfully. Their complaint was brought before the king and was accepted. In his attempt to appear enlightened and liberal, the king graciously allowed the Jews to dine separately in special rooms, so as not to mar their enjoyment.[27]

Nevertheless, during the days of the feast, Achashverosh could not resist teasing his Jewish guests.[28] "So, what do you say?" he sneered. "Could your God serve you more sumptuous meals than those I set before you now?"

But the Jews had a ready response. "The prophet Yeshayahu[29] said, 'No eye but Yours, Hashem, has seen what He shall provide for those who await Him,'" they quoted to him, adding pointedly, "If Hashem's feast would not be finer than yours, we would be able to claim that we *did* see a feast like the one that awaits us, and that would contradict the prophet's words! Therefore, we are fully confident that in the future our God will serve us a meal so elaborate that no one will be able to claim that he ever saw anything like it!"

Despite this uncomfortable incident, the festivities went on as scheduled, with all the officers and dignitaries taking part – including the Jews among them.[30]

---

[27] Targum Sheini

[28] Esther Rabbah 2:6

[29] Yeshayahu 64:3

[30] According to the version of Rabbi Chanina bar Papa in the Midrash, even *gedolei hador* were counted among the guests, but they beat a hasty retreat as soon as they saw the vessels of the *Bais Hamikdash* and the *bigdei kehuna.*

Since the feast was attended by monarchs from all corners of the world, it was necessary to tailor the menu to each one's eating habits. The Parsi guests would not enjoy Madai style food, and the ones from Madai would refuse to touch Parsi dishes. Therefore, Achashverosh adapted the menu to accommodate the tastes of each and every one of his guests, even providing each guest with special wine imported from his native land.

The king did not entrust all the logistical details that were entailed in preparing the feast to his servants, but was involved personally in all the details. As the *posuk* states, he was the one who "made a feast," and he himself made sure that everything went smoothly.[31]

Furthermore, the king made sure that the last day of the feast would be as exciting as the first.[32] Ordinarily, as an event progresses, the enthusiasm fades away. The host, too, generally becomes more lax with his hospitality and the attention he lavishes on his guests.

In contrast, by the feast of Achashverosh, there was no discernible difference between the first day and the last! Achashverosh introduced new attractions every day, to make sure his guests would fully enjoy the celebrations without becoming bored.

In the end, the king's efforts effectively achieved their goal. The feast was a rousing success, the guests were satisfied, and the king began the next feast geared for the common people.

---

[31] Etz Yosef Esther Rabbah 1:16, in the name of Yefei Anaf.
[32] Esther Rabbah 2:4

The Seven Day Feast

The second feast took place in the courtyard of the garden of the king's palace, among lovely orchards emitting fragrant scents and upon carpets of lush grass and flowers.

The *posuk* defines the location of the party at three levels: "*Chatzer,*" courtyard, "*ginas,*" garden, and "*bisan hamelech,*" the king's palace. The "*ginah*"[33] was the royal garden. At its center was the "*bisan,*" a closed, protected structure, and before it was the "*chatzer,*" a broad square through which one would pass to reach the garden.

Chazal[34] explain the location of the feast in several ways.

Some understand that the guests were divided into three groups, with one group dining in the *chatzer*, another in the *ginah*, and the third in the *bisan*. The division was based on the status of the guest, who was seated with people of similar standing.[35]

Others explain that, at first, the feast was scheduled to take place in the *chatzer*, the courtyard of the king. However, when huge numbers of guests poured into the palace grounds, the courtyard could not hold them all. To accommodate the crowds, the *ginah* was drafted into use as well. When that too was not enough to contain the many celebrants, the area occupied by the feast was extended to include the *bisan*.

---

[33] Perush HaGra
[34] Megillah 12a
[35] The Tosafos point out that this arrangement did not cause jealousy at the meal, a concern which was later raised regarding the couches of gold and silver, since the people of one group neither encountered nor even saw the ones from the next group.

A third opinion maintains that the main party took place in the *chatzer*, but the guests were permitted to enter the *ginah* and the *bisan* as well, if they wished to rest a bit or to stroll through the magnificent gardens of King Achashverosh.[36]

Opinions differ also in regard to whom the second feast was geared for. Some state[37] that the party was meant for all the residents of the capital city of Shushan, while others maintain that it was intended only for the assimilated Jews in the city.[38]

One thing is clear. The invited guests were allowed to bring all their family members, even their small children. We can assume that King Achashverosh arranged special activities for the little ones as well.

Chazal[39] disagree as to whether the king acted wisely by inviting the commoners to the festivities only after the feast for the dignitaries had been concluded.

Some assert that he did the right thing. He knew he could pacify the people of the city at any time, but it was urgent to

---

[36] The Megillas S'sorim explains that since the objective of the feast was to lure the Jews into violating serious transgressions, the king enabled them to enter the privacy of the little *bisanim*, booths, that were scattered throughout the *chatzer*, so that they could sin there as they wished without anyone seeing them. The open air *ginah*, on the other hand, was made available by the king for mixed strolls that were likely to rouse them to sin. The actual meal took place in the *chatzer*. The words of the Megillas S'sorim seem to agree with this opinion, that the meal took place in the *chatzer*, while entrance was allowed into the *ginah* and the *bisan*.

[37] This opinion emerges from the section of Gemara Megillah 12b, where we are told that a discussion arose between the king and those present regarding the people of Madai and Paras. The same also seems to be implied in other details of the feast, for example, in the fact that the *kashrus* of the food at the feast was "*k'r'tzon ish va'ish,*" each person according to his pleasure, which the Gemara interprets as "according to the desire of Mordechai and the desire of Haman."

[38] That is the understanding that emerges from the language of Targum Yonasan, even though some explain his words to mean only that Jews *also* participated in the feast.

[39] Megillah 12a

curry the loyalty and favor of the distant dignitaries, who could easily rebel against him, as soon as possible. Others believe that King Achashverosh acted foolishly. First and foremost, he should have secured the loyalty of the residents of his capital city so he could rely on them to stand at his side in the event of a rebellion by distant provinces.

In any case, the regal palace had always been off limits to the regular population. The common folk never imagined they would be able to wander freely through its rooms for seven days, while being served elaborate meals! And even in their wildest dreams, they would never have been able to imagine the dizzying wealth, luxury and splendor of the palace.[40]

In the courtyard itself, where the feast took place, fruit trees and fragrant spice trees whose scent wafted to great distances lined the area. The king ordered their branches tied one to the other, creating a canopy of living branches[41] over the heads of his elated guests.[42]

King Achashverosh even ordered some of the trees, which would never have been used elsewhere for furniture, cut down altogether and made into seats for his many guests. These chairs emitted the intoxicating fragrances of the exclusive spice trees they were made of.

Valuable fabrics that were only used for fine clothing were draped across the area between the trees. These were fabrics of "*chur*," lacework or costly white material, "*karpas*," green material, and "*t'cheiles*," a light blue color fabric.

---

[40] From this point on, our description of the details of the feast is based on Esther Rabbah 1, Megillah 12a and the Targums.

[41] The Ralbag explains that the fabrics of white and blue fine cotton were used as an overhanging to protect the heads of the guests.

[42] Targum Sheini

Generally, no one is particular about the quality of the threads used to sew fabrics together or to embroider on them. In this case, however, the threads were of "*butz*," fine linen, and "*argaman*," royal purple strands.

The fabrics were supported by silver rings, and were connected to pillars made of precious stones. On the periphery of the courtyard, illustrated ropes were draped across in a stunning display. The finest royal designers were enlisted to design the setting of the affair, and they did a masterful job.

The pillars which supported the precious fabrics[43] were not even to be found in the possession of the wealthy King Shlomo. They were made of a stunning marble imported from far-flung quarries known only to Achashverosh. These pillars were so massive that one could lie atop them with his limbs stretched out, yet they were formed of one unhewn piece of solid marble. Even solid gold would have been less expensive than the importing of these monumental pillars. The main point of the feast was to impress his subjects with the magnitude of his wealth, and so the pillars were specially imported.

The feast area was not lit by the dim glow of candles, but from a spectacular light that radiated from a special precious stone. The luster of this enormous, rare diamond provided light bright enough to compete with daylight.

If the guests were impressed at first by the intoxicating scents, the beauty of the arbors or the exclusive design, the moment they set eyes on the magnificently set tables they forgot their original excitement. They were overwhelmed by the precious stones and pearls scattered on the tables, spreading their glint in all directions.

---

[43] Esther Rabbah 2:8

In the courtyard of Achashverosh, they did not dine at ordinary wooden tables; the tables themselves were made of gold and silver!

As we can imagine, simple glass vessels would not appear on such tables, not even crystal. The entire meal was served on an array of dishes of pure gold.

When a guest finished drinking the contents of his golden goblet, he would not put it down on the table and pour himself another drink. Instead, an elegantly dressed waiter circulating about the tables would collect the used cups and set down fresh ones, also fashioned of pure gold, but of a different design from the first.[44]

Gold, a form of metal, is not the ideal material to drink out of. Still, Achashverosh felt impelled to use golden vessels alone, preferring to compromise a bit on the comfort of his guests in order to impress them with his wealth.

Still, Achashverosh made sure that the golden goblets would not mar the sweet taste of the expensive, royal wines. He ordered the wine to be poured every few minutes from one vessel to another, so it would not absorb an aftertaste from sitting in golden vessels.[45]

There is another opinion that the drinks were not literally served in golden goblets, but rather in cups made of a rare and valuable glass, so costly that its value exceeded that of gold. These goblets were used for the meal, even though surely many broke during the course of the seven day feast.[46]

---

[44] The design was expressed in the shape of the cups as well as in the different types of diamonds that were imbedded in them (Ralbag).
[45] Commentary of the Radal.

Vessels of the **Bais Hamikdash** *at the Meal*

The king also had the audacity to use the vessels of the *Bais Hamikdash* that were in his possession during the feast.

Achashverosh did not learn a lesson from the experience of his father-in-law Belshatzar, who used these vessels and died that same night.[47] He did understand, though, that it was no simple matter to start up with the holy vessels of the *Bais Hamikdash*. However, he erroneously surmised that Belshatzar's sin lay in using these vessels for a party in which intoxicating drink served as the central component.

"A feast that is totally based on drunken revelry is indeed a degradation of these honorable vessels!" Achashverosh said to himself. Therefore, he planned out his own feast in a different manner, placing the emphasis on much eating and less drinking. Use of the holy vessels at such a feast, he figured, would not be

---

[46] In fact, the Midrash (Esther Rabbah 2:11) asks how Achashverosh could have used golden vessels, for the reason we pointed out. The same question is posed by the Midrash regarding the golden goblets used by King Shlomo, but the commentaries explain that the question of the Midrash is primarily about the goblets at the feast of Achashverosh, where the motto was "each person according to his pleasure." "Since you are so concerned for your guests, why don't you provide them with the pleasure of drinking from goblets that do not mar the taste of the wine?" Chazal 'ask' King Achashverosh, and they immediately answer that he indeed used goblets of highly valuable glass.

According to the words of the Midrash as explained by the commentaries (Matnos Kehuna), King Shlomo, in contrast, indeed used golden vessels. He was compelled to do so because of the honor of his position, even though drinking from glass goblets would certainly have been more pleasing to the taste.

However, according to the approach of the Radal cited above, which stated that they did use golden goblets at the feast of Achashverosh, but that the wine was poured from vessel to vessel so that its taste should not be affected, the words of the Midrash can be explained in a different manner. We can say that the explanation cited regarding the use of glass vessels is regarding the goblets of King Shlomo, which were indeed made of precious glass, while Achashverosh insisted on displaying his wealth, and therefore used real golden vessels, as we wrote in the text above.

[47] Daniel 5:30

considered a disgrace for them, and therefore, he wouldn't be punished.[48]

The Midrash[49] tells us that the vessels of the *Bais Hamikdash* were more beautiful than the finest vessels of King Achashverosh. Further, when Achashverosh's goblets stood near the vessels of the *Bais Hamikdash*, they changed colors and turned the ugly, grayish hue of lead.[50]

Wine as the Enticement to Sin at the Feast

There was also another new practice introduced at this feast in regard to the drinking of wine.

Until the time of this feast, it was accepted practice in Paras to set a large goblet called a *piska*[51] before each of the guests, and not to remove it until he had finished drinking its contents to the last drop. Even if he was already intoxicated, even if he felt he was ready to choke, even if he sensed he was about to lose his mind or die, he had to drink the wine in the goblet until it was finished. If not, it would be interpreted as a mortal insult to the host. Nobody knew where this strange practice had originated, but it was universally practiced.

The ones who gained most from this practice were the wine stewards at every feast, since whoever felt they just could

---

[48] Maharsha Megillah 12a

[49] Esther Rabbah 2:12

[50] It is possible that this transformation was an actual, miraculous change, or it may be that they just appeared like leaden cups in contrast with the stunning vessels of the *Bais Hamikdash*. In any case, this Midrash gives us an idea of the incomparable beauty of these vessels, and leads us to raise our eyes in *tefillah* that we will merit to see the glory of Hashem's home rebuilt speedily in our days.

[51] Esther Rabbah 2:14, elaborated on in Targum Sheini.

not drink the full goblet of wine as expected would bribe the stewards to ignore their incomplete drinking.

At the feast of Achashverosh, the wicked king sought to provide his guests with a relaxed drinking experience, "each person according to his pleasure." He ordered the wine stewards not to bring the oversized goblet to the feast at all. Each of the guests would be permitted to drink just as much as he desired – no more and no less. Achashverosh adopted the persona of a democratic monarch – no compulsion, no force![52]

The insistence on "freedom of drink" was not by chance. The underlying intent of Achashverosh's feast was to lure the Jews into sinning. Achashverosh was afraid that the Jews would later be able to defend themselves as having sinned while inebriated, without realizing what they were doing. To forestall that possibility, Achashverosh publicly announced that there was no obligation to drink to excess. In this way he ensured that when the Jews would sin, it would be with full possession of their faculties and out of their own free will.[53]

Aside from the amount of drink, the guests were also not forced to compromise on *kashrus*. Achashverosh did not compel the Jews[54] to drink wines that were forbidden to them by Jewish law. In fact,[55] Mordechai, along with Haman,

---

[52] The accepted understanding of the words "*ein onais*," without force, is that the king did not force anyone to drink against his will. However, the Ralbag explains that these words imply that no one was forced to *refrain* from drinking. The Malbim, on the other hand, states that each of the guests had a personal carafe of wine set before him, from which he could pour for himself whenever he wished, so that no one should compel his friend to rush his drinking so as to pass the decanter on to the next person.

[53] Megillas S'sorim

[54] Esther Rabbah 2:14

[55] Megillah 12a, and see Rashi ibid, section beginning "*k'r'tzon Mordechai v'Haman.*"

was a wine steward at the feast of Achashverosh. Mordechai himself had to attend and serve as the *kashrus mashgiach* on the premises.[56]

But, once again, even when Achashverosh announced that no one is obligated to drink wines forbidden to him by his religion, his announcement stemmed from his wicked intentions.[57]

Achashverosh knew that if he would compel the Jews to drink from his forbidden wines, their sin could be excused as done under coercion and would avoid Divine punishment.

Therefore, Achashverosh preempted this excuse by eliminating any element of compulsion from the feast, even regarding the choice of wines. He was confident that the Jews would not be able to resist the tantalizing fragrance of the fine wines, and would taint their souls with forbidden beverages of their own free will!

The king's dastardly plans notwithstanding, there were kosher wines at the feast as well, and we can infer the same regarding the food. In fact, a brand new kitchen was built in the king's palace, for the express purpose of preparing delicacies for the Jewish guests, and every detail and nuance of *halacha* was strictly observed there.[58]

---

[56] The commentaries state that Mordechai agreed to fulfill this role in order to save the Jews from sins that could be avoided, such as the drinking of *yayin nesech*, forbidden wine.

[57] Etz Yosef; Esther Rabbah 2:12

[58] The commentary Minchas Erev on Megillas Esther writes that Mordechai was indeed responsible for the beverages at the meal, and in that regard, there really was no compulsion and the *kashrus* arrangements were meticulously observed. Regarding the food, however, the Minchas Erev maintains that the wicked Haman himself was responsible, and the menu included *neveilos* and *treifos* – absolutely non-kosher meats. The rule of "without force" did not apply in regard to the food,

Now, going back to the wines, no ordinary, simple wines were served at this feast, nor even the usual fine wines, but rather royal wines that, under regular circumstances, would appear only on the table of kings.

The waiters set up a fancy bar, where they provided every thirsty guest with top quality wine that was older than he was. If a twenty year old asked for a drink, he would get twenty one year old wine. If the request came from a forty five year old, he would be given wine aged for forty six years, and so on. Even the elderly among the guests were able to take pleasure in drinking extremely aged wines, older than they were.

Achashverosh made sure to serve each guest wine from his province of birth, knowing that every person is accustomed to the taste and fragrance characteristic to his country's wine.

In addition, there are places were the practice is to drink after eating, while in others, the aperitif opens the meal. There are places where the wine is preserved in a goatskin receptacle, while in other lands, wine is stored only in clay vessels.[59] At the feast of Achashverosh, each of the guests could choose a wine processed according to his country's customary practice,[60] and to drink it at the time it was accepted to drink in his land. Achashverosh provided the most perfect hospitality possible at his feast.

---

since refraining from eating would be considered a mortal offense against the king's honor, and the offender would be liable to the death penalty. Left with no choice, the Jews were forced to partake of the loathsome dishes, since refusing to do so would endanger their lives. The Yalkut (1048) seems to understand it the same way.

[59] Similarly, some take their wine straight, while others are accustomed to drinking it blended, some like their wine weak, and others prefer strong wine. At the feast of Achashverosh, each one received wine precisely as he liked it.

[60] Esther Rabbah 2:14

Even the floor the guests walked on was special. The entire floor was made of precious stones and pearls, arranged in a unique, spectacular design.[61] Imagine – an ordinary citizen, the kind who copes each day with the pressures of eking out a meager living, suddenly found himself walking on diamonds! Rows and rows of diamonds were set out to be trampled by the feet of the guests – just to prove the inconceivable magnitude of the royal host's wealth.

Eventually, the celebrants ran out of energy. After all, even when a person is surrounded by wealth beyond anything he has ever seen and is enjoying all the pleasures of the world, he can't go without sleep for too long a time.

The king prepared couches[62] of gold and silver[63] for his guests to rest on. Some say the body of the couches was silver with gold plating, while others explain that the visible outer part was of gold, while the inside was silver. Yet others maintain that the body of the couches was made completely of pure gold, while the silver served only for connecting pieces. Or, the body was made of silver, while the legs that protruded from beneath the bed linens were made of pure gold.[64] Whatever the precise combination, we can safely assume that none of those present had ever had the opportunity to rest his weary bones on such a luxurious bed. Each couch was probably more costly than their entire house.

---

[61] Ralbag

[62] Esther Rabbah 2:9; Megillah 12a

[63] One opinion in the Gemara states that each of the guests was awarded a bed according to his status. The more esteemed guests slept on golden beds, while the simpler folk, on silver beds. However, this opinion is rejected, since it does not make sense that Achashverosh would discriminate in a way that was likely to rouse jealousy among the guests and spoil the pervasive festive atmosphere.

[64] Maharsha Megillah 11b

According to some opinions,[65] the couches also served for reclining during the course of the meal, as was the practice in those days, with the couches they sat on made of silver, and the ones they reclined on made of gold. According to the fashion of the time, one sat on relatively simpler couches and reclined on more costly ones.

In any case, in order to protect the privacy of those who were resting, a canopy of valuable fabrics – white and blue fine cotton was set up between the couches to serve as a separation between the beds.

During the meal, the atmosphere was enhanced by a grand symphony orchestra comprised of the finest musicians in the vast empire.[66] This orchestra is not specifically mentioned in the *megillah* because it did not contain any new innovation unknown at other feasts, although the royal orchestra was something out of the ordinary.

Apart from the splendor that pervaded the feast, Achashverosh would announce from time to time special perks to increase his guests' ecstasy. For example, at one point he proclaimed a special tax exemption for all the businessmen of the city, an announcement that spurred a roaring round of applause and endeared the king to his subjects – just as he had intended.

---

[65] Yosef Lekach

[66] Yosef Lekach. On the other hand, the Minchas Erev writes that there were no musical instruments at the feast since music is not enjoyed equally by all ears; every person likes a different type of music. Since it was not possible to play for each person separately the melodies that he liked, Achashverosh preferred to omit musical instruments from the feast altogether, so as not to disturb anyone with music that was not to his taste.

One thing we must know,[67] though, is that the *megillah* did not paint this picture of lavish splendor for nothing. The words were meant to teach us something important about the great reward that awaits *tzaddikim* in the World to Come.

As we have learned (Avos 4:17), "One moment of pleasure in the World to Come is better than all of life in this world." Therefore, if so much pomp and grandeur existed here, in this world, at the feast of such a *rasha*, how much more, we can conclude, will be the rewards and the pleasure of *tzaddikim* in the World to Come!

Achashverosh's Secret Plot

After this lengthy description, we might find ourselves deceived, perceiving Achashverosh as a generous soul.

But, as we said at the outset, behind the screen of Achashverosh's generosity was a satanic scheme; his entire purpose was to destroy the Jewish people and lead them into a situation where their God would neither save them in their time of trouble nor ever bring the redemption that Achashverosh dreaded.[68]

In the Midrash[69] we find a terrifying description of the heavenly events that took place behind the scenes at the time

---

[67] Perush HaGra

[68] Therefore, we can understand the opinion cited earlier, according to which it was specifically the Jewish residents of Shushan who were invited to the second feast, since they were the ones the king wished to draw into sin. According to the other opinion, which maintains that all the residents of Shushan – Jews and non-Jews – were invited to the party, we have to say that Achashverosh concealed his satanic scheme by inviting all the Shushanites to the feast so as not to rouse the Jews' suspicion and lead them to understand that there were malicious intentions behind his gracious invitation.

[69] Esther Rabbah 7:13

of the feast, which set into motion the decree of Haman years later.

Indeed, it was actually Haman who told Achashverosh, "The God of the Jews despises immorality. Therefore, if you want to finish them off,[70] make them a party and command them to eat and drink. In the course of the feast, you will surely be able to get them to transgress the most serious sins in their Torah!"

Mordechai Hatzaddik and his disciples were not fooled by Achashverosh's declared intentions. Mordechai Hatzaddik and the *gedolei hador* and *talmidei chachomim* clearly saw the looming danger. They understood the motive behind King Achashverosh's invitation. They tried to warn the Jews and convince them not to attend the events, but to no avail.

The Jews would not listen. They thought they were smarter, more enlightened, more progressive, and that they could participate in the royal festivities without slipping into sin. But they ended up falling right into the trap the king had set for them.

The Jews probably argued with Mordechai Hatzaddik, telling him, "What do you want, Mordechai? Aren't you yourself the *kashrus mashgiach* at the king's feast? Didn't you hear the king announce that the party would be 'without force' and that the meal would be on the highest level of *kashrus*? That being the case, why should we abstain from a little fun and entertainment? Why should we refuse the king's invitation, which might mortally offend his honor and sabotage our diplomatic relations with the royal house?"

---

[70] As we mentioned earlier, Achashverosh hated the Jewish people no less than Haman did.

What followed was just as expected. The king succeeded in causing the Jews to sin, providing ample material to prosecute the Jews before their Creator and leading to a decree of destruction.[71]

---

[71] We should emphasize here that the Gemara (Megillah 12a) and several places in Chazal explain that the decree of destruction was not decreed just as a result of the Jews' participation in the feast of Achashverosh.

QUEEN VASHTI

"Queen Vashti, too, made a feast for the women,
in the royal house of King Achashverosh. On the
seventh day, when the king's heart was merry
with wine, he told Mehuman, Biz'sa, Charvona,
Bigsa, Avagsa, Zesar and Karkas, the seven
chamberlains who attended King Achashverosh,
to bring Queen Vashti before the king wearing
her royal crown, so as to display her beauty to the
people and the officers, since she was beautiful to
look at. But Queen Vashti refused to come at the
order of the king conveyed by the chamberlains,
and the king became extremely angry and his
rage burned within him." (1:9-12)

Now a new character joins the narrative – Queen Vashti.

Vashti was of very honorable lineage, much more esteemed than the lineage of Achashverosh. The daughter of Belshatzar, the king of Bavel, Vashti was a descendant of Nevuchadnetzar. Achashverosh, in contrast, was no more than the keeper of the royal stables for the king of Bavel, before he appropriated the kingship of Paras.

When the king decided to hold a feast in his palace for all the residents of the capital city, Vashti resolved that she would not sit idly by;[1] instead, she announced that she would preside over a corresponding party for all the women of the capital.[2]

---

[1] The Vilna Gaon points out that Vashti's feast was absolutely extraneous. The king himself could claim that his party was necessary for diplomatic reasons; he needed

On the surface, it appeared that Achashverosh and Vashti made sure the guidelines of *tznius*, modesty, were observed at the festivities. Rather than simply putting up *mechitzos*, dividers, between the men and women, they were seated in absolutely separate locations! The men dined outside, in the courtyard of the garden, while the women were seated indoors, as befits a woman's dignity.[3]

It is easy to understand, then, why the Jews saw nothing wrong with the feast of Achashverosh, which appeared to be arranged according to the strictest moral demands. The Jews did not know at the outset that though the women's feast was conducted indoors, the hall was situated alongside and in full view of the courtyard of the royal garden, such that the men could gaze easily at the women inside and be lured into sin.[4]

to find favor in the eyes of the ministers of the distant provinces and strengthen his foreign relations so that they would not rebel against him. Queen Vashti, however, had no such excuse; she did not need to strengthen the foundation of her rule. But the queen did not look for excuses or explanations. She simply wanted to make a feast. What she did not know was that her urge was prompted by a heavenly force, so as to bring about her downfall.

On the other hand, the Radal maintains that the feast of Achashverosh was held in honor of his coronation (as we mentioned above). According to this version, Vashti's party was for just as good a reason as the feast of Achashverosh. The Radal goes on to say that since the women's feast was intended as a celebration of Vashti's coronation as queen, the king sent for her to be brought before him to show off her fine points so that everyone would see how eminently suitable she was to be his queen. However, in Vashti's response to the king, she stressed that she was always a queen in her own right, due to her illustrious lineage. These words were what really incensed the king and intensified his disgrace when the queen refused to appear before him.

The Ralbag takes an entirely different angle and explains that King Achashverosh was the one who ordered that a feast be held by Vashti, in order to enable the women as well to take an honorable part in the gala events.

[2] According to other opinions in the commentaries (Malbim and others), Vashti invited only the wives of the dignitaries to her party, not all the women of Shushan.

[3] Radal

[4] Megillah 12a

A Feast for the Women

In contrast to the feast of Achashverosh, Vashti's feast was especially geared for the women and their interests.[5]

While men derive great pleasure from sumptuous food and fine wines, women are interested in pretty décor and design. Therefore, Vashti held her party in picturesque rooms decorated with uniquely beautiful adornments, the work of the finest artists in the entire world.[6]

The feast took place in the personal chamber of the king, a room which was absolutely off limits to anyone but the king himself, under ordinary circumstances. By situating the feast in this particular room, Vashti wished to emphasize her strong position and lofty status in the palace.[7] In fact, this idea actually entered her mind as a result of Divine intervention, so as to raise her up to the highest possible peak – and from there to cast her down to the lowest nadir in the utmost disgrace.

The delicacies that were served to the women at Vashti's party were totally different from those served to the men at the feast of Achashverosh.[8] While the men were given meat and wine, the royal chefs prepared for the women a variety of sweets and other delicate foods, appealing to female tastes.

In addition, Vashti was aware that the women of Shushan were naturally curious about what went on in other people's houses, and especially in the palace of the king. She showed them where the king eats, where he sits and sleeps. She

---

[5] Ibn Yichyeh explains that the queen held the party in the royal residence and not in her own since the king's quarters were more beautiful than hers.
[6] Esther Rabbah 3:10
[7] Perush HaGra
[8] Esther Rabbah 3:10

described the daily schedule of Achashverosh in great detail, chatting freely about his favorite pastimes. This glimpse into the personal life of the royal family was the most wonderful attraction possible.

Vashti also spared no opportunity to display her equality to the king. [9] Vashti, too, displayed the treasures of the king before the ladies,[10] and even went so far as to sacrilegiously adorn herself in the garments of the *kohen gadol*.[11]

---

[9] Esther Rabbah 3:9

[10] The Midrash (Esther Rabbah 3:9) explains that Vashti too presented six treasure rooms to her guests every day, just as the king did. From this we can conclude that she too held two separate parties. The first one was for the wives of the dignitaries, for 180 days, during which she displayed the 1080 treasure rooms of the king – treasures which actually belonged originally to her grandfather, the wicked Nevuchadnetzar. Only afterwards did she hold another party, seven days long, for the women of Shushan.

However, from the words of the commentaries, it sounds as if Vashti held only one feast, which was geared for all the women of Shushan, not for the wives of the dignitaries of Paras and Madai. According to this approach, we have to assume that Vashti did not show the women all the king's treasures, but rather a small sampling.

Similarly, it could be that these commentaries understand that the words of Chazal mentioned earlier, which maintain that Vashti's feast was distinguished by different attractions from those offered to the men at the feast of Achashverosh, disagree with the view of the other Midrash stating that Vashti showed the women the treasures, since it could be that the treasures of the king – or at least a good part of them – did not interest the women in the least.

On the other hand, the Etz Yosef (Esther Rabbah 3:9) explains that Queen Vashti displayed *her own* treasures to the women. From this we can infer that she had treasures that *were* of interest to women, but which may not have been as numerous as those of King Achashverosh; hence, seven days were sufficient in order to display the whole lot.

[11] See Etz Yosef on Esther Rabbah 3:9, where he explains that half of the garments of the *kohen gadol* were in Achashverosh's hands, while the other half was in Vashti's possession. Alternately, we can understand that the division was not in number of garments, but rather in time – some of the time they were by the king, and some of the time by the queen. This is a more reasonable assumption, since the garments of the *kohen gadol* are only of value when they are a complete set of eight items.

And so, the women celebrated along with Vashti while the men reveled at their feast – until the seventh day, when Vashti was hurled down from the highest of heights to the deepest of depths, to her death.

On the Seventh Day

The seventh day of the feast[12] fell on the holy day of Shabbos.[13] On this day,[14] the Jews among the guests were seated around elegantly set tables in the courtyard of the king, conducting a Shabbos meal with all its details and stringencies.

At the same time, the non-Jewish guests reveled in frivolous, vulgar talk.[15] Indeed, in this spirit, a discussion arose among the guests regarding the external virtues of women of different nationalities.[16]

Some of the guests insisted that the women of Madai were the prettiest, while others stood up for the Parsi women, maintaining that they were more attractive. When echoes of this argument reached the ears of King Achashverosh, he rushed to express his opinion. "Neither the Parsi women nor those of Madai are the prettiest. My wife, who is from Bavel, is the most beautiful of all!" the king insisted, and even offered to prove his words. "I am willing to summon Queen Vashti here

---

[12] Megillah 12b; Esther Rabbah 3:12

[13] We cited above the words of the Y'aros D'vash (2:2), according to which it was not an ordinary Shabbos, but rather Yom Kippur, which came out on Shabbos.

[14] Esther Rabbah 3:13

[15] See Anaf Yosef on Esther Rabbah 3:11, where he explains that on Shabbos the gentiles are under the influence of the zodiac of *Shabtai*, Saturn, and this naturally imposes on them a spirit of sadness. Therefore, on this day, the king needed wine in order to cheer his heart and dissipate his troubled mood. While he was in this state of drunkenness, the entire episode described in the *megillah* came about.

[16] Megillah 12b

at this very moment, wearing only a golden crown upon her head, and then you will all see that there is no one like her in the entire world!" His suggestion was enthusiastically accepted by the depraved gentiles.

Under ordinary circumstances, when in full possession of his faculties, the king would never have suggested such a lowly idea. He was degrading himself, exactly as he was degrading his queen![17] However, since the king's heart was "merry with

---

[17] The Malbim asserts that Achashverosh actually was completely lucid when he ordered Vashti brought before him. He explains that there are two kinds of royal rule: total rule – when the king conquers a nation and dominates it by brutal strength, and non-total rule – when the king is chosen by the people. Five differences exist between these two types of rule: a) The absolute monarch can do whatever he wants with the people, while the non-absolute monarch can only use them for the service of the state; b) The absolute monarch has full possession of the royal treasures, while the non-absolute monarch has no such right; c) The absolute monarch does not have to take counsel before acting, while the other needs to discuss matters with his advisors; d) The absolute monarch can change the laws as he pleases, while the elected king has to follow the national rules; e) The absolute monarch can live wherever he chooses, while the non-absolute one must set up his throne in the place of his predecessors.

The Malbim goes on to explain that Achashverosh originally became king in the merit of his wife Vashti who was of royal lineage, a daughter of Belshatzar the king of Bavel, and a granddaughter of the mighty Nevuchadnetzar. However, as time went by, Achashverosh sought to make himself an absolute monarch by dint of his own power. For that purpose, he moved the seat of his empire to Shushan, the new capital, to show that he was not obligated to remain in the place of the kings who preceded him. (In doing so, he also made the arrogant statement that he did not see it as enough of an honor to sit on the throne of his predecessors.)

This is also the reason behind his public display of the royal treasures at the feast – to make it perfectly clear that these treasures belonged to him personally, not to the national coffers, and that he may do with them as he pleases. If not, how could he boast about treasures that were not his own? In this way, Achashverosh sought to prove that he is not subject to the second principle mentioned, that the royal treasures are only considered the possession of an absolute monarch who gained his position by force.

The king held his party for all the people of Shushan, even though entry to the king's courtyard is permitted only for honorable officers, in order to make it clear that he regarded all of his subjects as equals; no one citizen had a higher status than any other since they were all his humble servants – an approach that contradicts the

wine," he did not invest too much thought into what he was saying. Thus, the chamberlains were summoned to bring Vashti before him wearing her golden crown and holding two golden goblets in her hands.[18]

The strange demand of the king regarding the queen's appearance at his feast was preceded by seven days of fasting and intense prayer on the part of Mordechai Hatzaddik and the members of the Sanhedrin. They stood in fervent prayer, immersed in fasting for the duration of the party in order to annul the decree that hung over the Jews because of their participation in the feast.

On the seventh day, the prayers of Mordechai and the Sanhedrin were accepted. Thus, the seeds of the Jews' eventual deliverance were planted, in the guise of the king's strange command which would lead to Esther's coronation as queen.

Vashti deserved the fate that was about to befall her. She was far from innocent. In fact, Vashti, too, hated the Jews.

As an example of her cruelty, Queen Vashti had a practice of making Jewish girls work for her on Shabbos, while inappropriately dressed,[19] forcing them to beat flax and wool – a degrading task. Therefore, the queen met her death under

---

first principle stating that the people are not considered the slaves of a non-absolute monarch.

The same reason compelled Achashverosh to bring Vashti before him adorned in her crown. He wanted to prove that he did not gain the kingship in her merit, but quite the opposite; she was the queen in his merit. Therefore, he ordered that Vashti's feast take place in his own royal quarters, as if to imply that the queen has no palace of her own and all that is hers belongs to the king. Vashti understood the intentions of the king, and therefore she refused to come before him as requested. In doing so, she sabotaged his entire plan – a fact which infuriated him intensely.

[18] Targum Sheini

[19] Megillah 12b

similar circumstances, when the king demanded that she degrade herself by appearing before him on Shabbos, clad only in the royal crown.

Queen Vashti Refused

Vashti did not immediately incite the king's anger and refuse his express command. At first, she tried to explain to him the foolishness of his command, but the king was in no shape to understand anything at that moment.

To begin with, Vashti sent a message to Achashverosh:[20]

"My master the king, think what will happen when I come and stand before you.

"Two possibilities exist: The kings and officers sitting around you will be impressed by my appearance and will agree that there is no one like me in the entire world. If that happens, they may become so jealous of you that they will murder you in order to take me for themselves!

"On the other hand, there is always the second possibility. Perhaps I will not find favor in their eyes and they will not be impressed by my beauty. In that case, your honor will be irreparably damaged! That being the case, my master the king, what exactly do you stand to gain by the fulfillment of your command? You can only lose!"

But, as we said, Achashverosh was not convinced.

Vashti then sent another message to the king:

---

[20] Esther Rabbah 3:14

"My master the king, do you consider me less than my father considered those who were sentenced to death? Even those sentenced to die are allowed to meet their deaths in fitting, modest attire, while you, Achashverosh, do not care a whit for my honor! How can it be?" Vashti wondered.

But, once again, Achashverosh was not moved. He stood firmly by his demand that the queen appear before him as ordered. This led the queen to insolently send the king a searing message that incited his fury.

She transmitted the following words through the chamberlains who came to bring her to the king:[21]

"My master the king, you are insane. Your officers and nobles are equally insane, as are the servants who serve before you. How do you dare make such an audacious request of me – to appear in such an inappropriate manner before your guests? Perhaps you do not remember, perhaps you would like to forget, but not too long ago you were no more than the stable-keeper for my father, the king of Bavel! If my father were alive, you could never have dreamed of marrying me; you wouldn't even have been worthy to run before his chariot![22]

"And besides," the queen went on in her message to the king, "you would do well to learn a thing or two from your father-in-law, my father Belshatzar. My father could drink wine enough for a thousand men, and he held his drink so well that it would not affect his clarity of thought or the propriety

---

[21] Megillah 12b; Targum Sheini

[22] Yalkut 1048. The Yalkut explains that the marriage of Achashverosh to Vashti only became possible after her father Belshatzar was killed and she was left alone and forlorn. In the storm of the battle in which her father met his death, Daryavesh found her and married her off to his son, Achashverosh.

of his conduct one bit! As for you, look what happened to you after drinking just a drop!"

It is easy to imagine how the king felt when the chamberlains returned and delivered the queen's words to him. His entire intention had been to boast and increase his honor by showing off the queen's beauty. Now, not only did he fail to reap the great honor he had hoped for, but his pride was shattered as well. If the queen, the king's wife, was not willing to carry out his will, what would the citizens of his empire say?

Besides, Achashverosh could not even reveal to his guests the reason the queen gave to explain her refusal,[23] since his past occupation was not particularly flattering. All he could do was uncomfortably mumble that the queen was not willing to come.

Nevertheless, the king's reaction that followed still seems a bit exaggerated. After all, it is not logical that a person should order his wife killed, especially when he knows that there is no one as good and beautiful as she is. More than that, Chazal teach us that the king's fury was so strong that he did not completely calm down from it for many years until Haman was hanged on the tree that he erected for Mordechai![24]

---

[23] The reason the king became angry is clear, yet in the words of the *posuk* we find an additional stress, *"v'chamaso ba'arah vo,"* his rage burned *within* him. This emphasis implies an internal conflagration in the heart of the king. The Gaon explains that the nature of this conflagration refers to the degrading words sent to him by the queen through the chamberlains, in which she mentions his previous position as her father's stable-keeper and adds insult to injury by scorning his poor drinking habits.

The king's fury regarding these degrading words burned *within him*, without his being able to give them external expression, since the king naturally did not want to reveal these highly uncomplimentary words to the honored officers and other guests.

[24] Only then does the *megillah* make a point that *"chamas hamelech shochacha,"* the king's anger subsided (7:10), while after the execution of Vashti, the *posuk* only

Why, then, was the king so inordinately incensed?

The king's fury was unnatural.[25] Hashem sent the angels appointed over anger to rouse intense fury in the king's heart. Therefore, we can look at the king's anger as a whipping stick in Hashem's Hand, created for the purpose of punishing Vashti for her abuse of the Jewish girls, and implemented in order to set the stage for the deliverance of the Jewish people several years down the line, through Queen Esther, Vashti's replacement!

Why Did Vashti Refuse?

The truth is that Vashti had no problem appearing before the king and the guests in an immodest fashion. The only reason Vashti was so adamant in her refusal to follow the king's order was because when the emissaries came to summon her she had something to conceal.

Some say[26] she had a sudden eruption of *tzora'as* – a skin ailment that made her look hideous and made her ashamed to appear before the king and his officers. Others maintain that the angel Gavriel was sent from heaven to affix a tail behind her!

Needless to say, it wouldn't be honorable for her to appear before the king and his guests with a tail or an embarrassing skin disease, but she couldn't shame herself by announcing that she wasn't coming because of them, either. Her only choice was

---

writes "*k'shoch chamas hamelech*," using the prefix "*K*," implying that "the king's anger *as if* subsided," but did not truly subside.
[25] Esther Rabbah 3:15
[26] Megillah 12b

to refuse the king's express command for reasons of "modesty" or "discomfort."

Two other approaches to explain the queen's refusal to appear before the king and his guests are found in the words of our later Rabbis.

The Radal[27] maintains that had King Achashverosh appealed to Vashti in a respectful manner and asked her to come honor him at his feast with her presence, she would have willingly agreed. The king, however, had *demanded* that the queen appear, even conveying his command through the chamberlains, as if sending them to haul her in against her will.[28]

The Rishon Letzion, on the other hand, explains that the queen was displeased with the king's motivations for summoning her. Had he asked her to come for his honor, she would have done so willingly and happily. But since the king sent the chamberlains to tell her that he wanted everyone to see her, she felt that it was beneath her dignity to be seen by the common people and refused his command.

---

[27] Cited also by Yosef Lekach and others.

[28] The commentary Minchas Erev adds also that the king should have allowed the queen to appear with her maidservants or chambermaids, as was the general practice. However, he did not do so, but rather ordered that she appear before him with *his chamberlains*. This demand also roused the queen's opposition and led her to refuse to come. The Ralbag, on the other hand, explains that the queen was not satisfied with the chamberlains, who were not esteemed enough escorts for her taste, and that is why she refused to join them.

VASHTI'S FATE

*"Then the king spoke to the wise ones who knew
the times – since that was the king's practice, to
[confer with] those who knew law and judgment,
the ones closest to him: Karsh'na, Shesar, Admasa,
Tarshish, Meres, Marsena, Memuchan, the seven
officers of Paras and Madai who would see the
king regularly and were of foremost rank in the
kingdom, as to what should be legally done to
Queen Vashti for not having carried out the order
of the king as conveyed by the chamberlains. And
Memuchan said before the king and the officers,
'Queen Vashti did not commit a wrong against
the king alone, but rather against all the officers
and all the people in all the provinces of King
Achashverosh. For word of the queen's deed will
reach all the women, causing them to hold their
own husbands in contempt, since they will say,
"King Achashverosh himself ordered that Queen
Vashti be brought before him and she did not
come!" On this day, the noblewomen of Paras and
Madai who hear of the queen's deed will mention
it to all the king's officers, and there will be much
contempt and wrath. If it pleases the king, let a
royal edict go out before him, and let it be written
irrevocably in the statutes of Paras and Madai
that Vashti shall never again appear before King
Achashverosh, and that the king shall confer her*

> *royal position upon another who is better than*
> *she. Then, when the king's statement which he*
> *shall enact shall be heard throughout the kingdom*
> *in all its vastness, all the women will show*
> *respect to their husbands, great and small alike.'*
> *This proposal pleased the king and the officers,*
> *and the king did as Memuchan suggested. He sent*
> *letters to all the provinces of the empire, to each*
> *province in its own script and to every nation in*
> *its own language, stating that every man should*
> *rule in his own home and speak the language of*
> *his own people." (1:13-22)*

Achashverosh was sullen, dejected, and boiling with anger. The disgrace he had just suffered at the hands of Queen Vashti stung terribly, and he craved instant revenge.

Achashverosh chose to bring the matter before the *"chochmei ha'itim,"*[1] literally, the wise ones who knew the times. These were Jewish sages of the tribe of Yissochor,[2] called *"chochmei*

---

[1] The Malbim explains that the king actually wished to exonerate Vashti from guilt. It was clear to him that if her judgment would be brought before the *yod'ai ha'itim*, the judges responsible for judging anyone who offended the honor of the king, she would surely be sentenced to death, since she offended the king's honor and caused him great disgrace in such a public forum. Therefore, the king asserted that the *yod'ai ha'itim* were not authorized to rule in this matter, and consulted the *yod'ai das v'din*, those who knew law and judgment.

The king founded his argument on the claim that the law requiring the judgment of someone who offended the royal honor to be brought before the *yod'ai ha'itim* was not valid in this case, since it was not a commoner who insulted the king, but rather his wife, the queen. Therefore, the matter must be addressed as a clash between spouses, which is brought before *yod'ai das v'din*.

[2] Esther Rabbah 4:1; Megillah 12b – although the Gemara does not mention that these sages were necessarily from the tribe of Yissochor.

ha'itim" due to their expertise in determining leap years and setting the length of the months.[3]

"What should I do with Queen Vashti, who disobeyed my command and refused to appear at the feast as I ordered her?"[4] the king asked the Yissochorites. The sages didn't know how to reply.

---

[3] See Ibn Ezra on this *posuk.* He explains that the *chochmei ha'itim* were those sages who were erudite in the history of the royal dynasty. Accordingly, the king sought the counsel of these sages in order to verify if an incident similar to what happened to him with Queen Vashti had ever occurred before. If so, that incident could be seen as a precedent, and the punishment allotted to the queen would be in keeping with the earlier ruling. When the *chochmei ha'itim* responded that such an incident never took place before in royal history, Achashverosh was left with no alternative but to "create the precedent" himself. Therefore, he assembled his close advisors and asked their opinion.

In contrast, the Perush HaGra explains that the *chochmei ha'itim* were wise men who knew how to take into account the circumstances of the incident, including the particular place and time at which it took place, before composing their decision. King Achashverosh, according to the Gra, really wanted to clear Vashti of guilt; he knew that he would not find another queen like her anywhere in the world. On the other hand, he could not simply excuse her without judgment. Doing so would be a blatant disparagement of his honor and would set the stage for a possible rebellion.

Therefore, the king brought Vashti's case before the *yod'ai ha'itim,* hoping to find a loophole or some defense that would allow her to be exonerated. Only when a defense of this kind could not be found was the king forced to turn to the counsel of the *yod'ai das v'din,* at which Memuchan made the suggestion that led to Vashti's death.

According to another explanation cited in the commentaries (Yosef Lekach, Rishon Letzion and others), the king hoped to exonerate the queen on the basis of astrological factors. It was common practice in that time to take into consideration the zodiac sign under which the crime was committed. Sometimes the astrologers would assert that the misdeed was not done out of the offender's free will, but rather under the irresistible influence of the stars at that moment. Only after the *yod'ai ha'itim* clarified the fact that the wrong was not done under astrological compulsion but rather out of the queen's free will did the king have no choice but to present her case to the *yod'ai das v'din,* as we explained above.

[4] It should be stressed that the king did not lodge any complaints regarding the disgrace to which the queen subjected him, since he was under the impression that this aspect was not witnessed by the esteemed officers and remained between him and the queen. Therefore, he mentioned only the wrong she committed by refusing

The Tzaddik *is Delivered from Catastrophe*

"What a calamity! What on earth should we do now?" they agonized. "If we advise the king to kill his wife Vashti we are bound to pay for it tomorrow, when the king sobers up and looks for his queen, only to discover that he had her executed by our suggestion! On the other hand, if we advise him to forgo his honor and forgive the queen who disobeyed him, it will appear that we are disparaging the honor of the king. Who knows what the king's reaction will be to that! So what should we say?"

Finally, they found an honorable way out. "We are terribly sorry, Your Majesty, but it would be unfair on our part to answer your question," they said.

Achashverosh demanded to know why.

The sages from Yissochor explained, "When we lived tranquilly in our own land, we were capable of passing judgment on capital crimes. And if we were uncertain regarding one issue or another, we had the *urim v'tumim* (the oracle of the *kohen gadol*) to which we could ask all our questions. Now, however, since the *Bais Hamikdash* was destroyed and we were exiled from our land, we are deprived of the ability to seek counsel, and at the same time, we lack the necessary peace of mind to consider all sides with the requisite clarity. Therefore, under these circumstances it would be absolutely irresponsible on our part to rule on serious, life and death issues!"

---

to carry out his request, without demanding that she receive punishment for the personal affront she gave the king. Quoting the queen's degrading words publicly, he understood, would just serve as a repeat of the disgrace, and understandably, he had no interest in repeating that.

Faced with such an argument, there was little Achashverosh could say in reply. What fault could he find in the righteous stand of the Jewish sages who could not bring themselves to offer him unjust advice? He accepted their words, asking only for their recommendation as to which judges *would* be qualified to judge Vashti's case thoroughly and accurately.

"If you want our advice, Your Majesty," the sages replied, "we think you would be best off consulting with the wise men of Ammon and Moav who did not have to cope with the tribulations of exile as we did. Their minds are as calm and composed as preserved wine. Our prophet Yirmiyahu already noted this virtue when he prophesied,[5] 'Moav has been tranquil from his youth, settled on his lees, not having been emptied from vessel to vessel, nor having gone into exile; therefore his taste remains in him and his fragrance is not changed.'"

Again, Achashverosh accepted their advice, but asked how he could find the wise men of Ammon and Moav in order to bring Vashti before them in judgment.

The sages did not have a clear answer. "Ever since Sancheriv came and turned the world upside down, exiling nations from their land and mixing them with other peoples, it is hard to clearly distinguish the members of one nation from another. However, it is conceivable that among your own counselors there might be someone related to the Ammonites or Moavites," the sages of Yissochor advised. "Therefore, the best thing would be to ask the counsel of your own wise men who *might* be descendants of Moav, rather than seeking advice from us, who surely are not Moavites!"

---

[5] Yirmiyahu 48:11

The king acted precisely according to their instructions.[6] He gathered together the *yod'ai das v'din*[7] – the officers of high rank who were closest to him. These seven officers were from six different countries: Karsh'na (from Tarshish), Shesar (from Hodu), Admasa (from Edom), Tarshish (from Mitzrayim), Meres and Marsena (from the far-flung country of Meres), and Memuchan (from Yerushalayim).

This was a clear case of, "The *tzaddik* is delivered from calamity and the *rasha* comes in his place."[8] The sages of Yissochor managed to evade the dangerous assignment, while the wicked advisors were forced to pronounce the queen's judgment.

For a Holy Nation – No Legalities Necessary

Chazal[9] note that when it came to Queen Vashti's judgment, who had clearly wronged him, Achashverosh spared no effort in seeking out the best judges available so that a true, fair judgment would emerge. In addition, it was evident that he hoped the queen would not be killed.

But just a few years later, when the wicked Haman came to his palace and asked him to murder *an entire nation, young and old, women and children, all in one day*, the king gave his approval on the spot! He did not seek out a fair and true judgment. With hardly a moment's hesitation he cooperated

---

[6] Etz Yosef

[7] The Malbim explains that the king, who sought to clear the queen of guilt, brought her case before the *yod'ai das v'din* who would take into consideration the *das* – the religious side of the issue – according to which Vashti was actually permitted to refuse his unseemly command.

[8] Mishlei 11:8

[9] Esther Rabbah 4:5

in decreeing the mass murder of a holy nation, innocent of any wrongdoing! This contradiction is a clear indication of the hatred that burned in his heart against the Jews.

The Boor Jumps to the Fore

And so, Vashti's case was brought before the high ranking officers of the king.[10]

---

[10] It was already explained above in the name of the Malbim that the king's true objective was to gain total control over the empire and become an absolute monarch, not dependent on the will of the people. For that reason, he wanted to make it clear to all that Vashti was a queen in his merit – and not the opposite. When Vashti foiled his plans, he was furious, but he still wanted to clear her of guilt. However, Haman told him in no uncertain terms that he could not do so, since Vashti had committed a wrong not against the king alone, but against all of the officers. The women who did not know why the king summoned Vashti will assume that she simply refused to appear for no particular reason, and as a result, will follow her example and hold their husbands in contempt too. The noblewomen who were present at the party, on the other hand, knew that the king was trying to take full control of the kingdom and present matters as if Vashti was a queen only in his merit. Since they understood that a substantial reason prevented the queen from coming at the king's summons, they would not be led to hold their husbands in contempt. However, they might reveal the king's foiled plans to the officers, and that could prevent the king from taking full control of the kingdom at a later stage, since the officers will be alert to any signs of such a scheme.

Therefore, Haman told the king to immediately order Vashti's execution, without seeking any counsel. In this way, he would show that he did not have to meet the fourth condition mentioned earlier, according to which a non-absolute monarch must adhere to the laws of the state, nor the third condition, which required the non-absolute king to take counsel at every step. Thus, he would make it perfectly clear that he was an absolute ruler, summarily correcting the impression that he was king only in Vashti's merit. Haman also recommended enacting a law stating that every man should rule in his own home – thus removing the contempt the women of Paras and Madai might harbor towards their husbands. Furthermore, Haman advised the king to pass a law prohibiting the queen from coming before the king, in order to create the impression that the queen had relented and wished to correct her deeds and come before the king, but he rejected her and did not allow her into his presence.

Similarly, the Malbim explains that the king ordered missives sent to each nation in its own language, even though until that time it was common practice to send all the king's letters in the Parsi language. This was because he wished to make it clear to all that his empire was not founded on the rule of Madai and Paras in particular,

Among the high ranking advisors of the king was Memuchan, whose identity is a matter of debate among the Sages. Some maintain that he was Daniel Hatzaddik[11] and that the deliverance of the Jews came about through him. He was the one who advised the king to oust Vashti from her position and send her to her death – advice that eventually led to the appointment of Esther. According to these opinions, Daniel is known by the name Memuchan due to his being *muchan*, prepared, that Vashti should be killed through him.

On the other hand, others maintain that this Memuchan was none other than the wicked Haman,[12] called Memuchan due to his being *muchan*, ready and set up for punishment. This Memuchan acted like a boor and jumped to the fore,[13] announcing that he had advice for the king.

Haman opened his words with a dramatic description of the terrible wrong committed by the wayward queen. "You must understand, Your Majesty," said Memuchan, "that Vashti did not commit a private offense against the king alone.[14] It is a

---

but rather on his being a king in his own right. That being the case, there was no difference between the various provinces; they should all be treated equally, and the letters should be sent to each in its own national language.

[11] Midrash Ponim Acheirim 52, 81

[12] Megillah 12b

[13] Esther Rabbah 4:6

[14] With this statement, Haman wished to hint to the king that he could not pardon the queen and forgo her punishment, since her wrongdoing did not relate to him alone, but rather to all the officers (Megillas S'sorim). Similarly, Haman sought to prevent the king from pleading on Vashti's behalf before the royal court, by getting him to understand that in doing so he would be disparaging the honor of his officers who were offended by the queen's refusal to follow her husband's orders (Minchas Erev). Ibn Yichyeh, on the other hand, explains that Haman understood that the king himself was interested in having Vashti sentenced to death, but was fearful of the officers' reaction. Therefore, Haman prefaced his words with this introduction in order to convince the officers to support the execution of the queen due to the benefit they would derive from such a step.

wrongdoing of weighty public ramifications. From now on, all the women of the empire will allow themselves to degrade their husbands, saying, 'Even Vashti, the wife of the king, publicly disgraced her spouse[15] and nothing happened to her!'

"And besides," Haman emphasized, "Your Majesty must understand that if you allow Vashti to go unpunished, the women in your domain will conclude that the queen is of a higher status than the king! This conclusion may even lead women to take control of the government in the various provinces. Who knows, from this day on we may not hear anymore about princes and noblemen – only princesses and noblewomen![16]

"If you don't want matters to deteriorate to such a serious state," Haman concluded, "you must punish Vashti severely, a punishment that will make it clear beyond any shadow of a doubt what the fate of a woman who does not obey her

---

In addition, Haman wanted to argue that the king could determine the queen's verdict himself, since it was not a personal ruling relating to him but rather a ruling affecting all the officers (Yosef Lekach). This opinion does not agree with the approach of the Gra in his commentary (see below), according to which a special ruling was necessary in order to enable the king to judge Vashti. Even after this ruling was enacted though, it would still be inappropriate for the king to sentence someone to death for having offended his personal honor. However, once the matter is seen as affecting others, there would be nothing wrong with the king passing judgment.

[15] The Gra emphasizes in his commentary that Haman wished to indicate to the king that even the degrading words transmitted to him by the queen had already leaked out. "The same way that the information reached me," Haman explained in a sinister, poisonous tone, "it is bound to reach all the officers, when their wives, who were present when Vashti delivered her message through the chamberlains, will tell them all that took place in the royal house at Vashti's feast. Therefore, Your Majesty, you have to take into account your honor that is being trampled, rather than focusing only on the fact that your order was disobeyed!" Haman insisted.

[16] Megillas S'sorim

husband is – the death sentence![17] Simultaneously, you must pronounce a new edict that the husband is the sole ruler of his household. Even the language spoken in the house should be determined by the mother tongue of the husband, without giving any weight to the language of the wife!" he added.

Haman was dealing with this issue personally, experiencing problems in his domestic harmony. His wife was wealthier than he was, and for this reason, considered herself superior to him and refused to speak in his language. "I have to resolve the problem once and for all! I must break that woman's pride and force her to speak in my mother tongue!" Memuchan said to himself. That was one of the underlying motivations for his counsel to King Achashverosh.

In addition, there are three[18] other reasons why Haman was interested in Vashti's death.

---

[17] The language of the Targum implies that Haman did not advise the king outright to *kill* Vashti, but only to decree that she may not come before the king ever again. Then, when she would inevitably ignore the ruling and come before him at some point, she would be killed. Ibn Yichyeh maintains that Haman indeed advised only that the queen not be allowed to come to him and that her position should be given to another, but on a practical level, it was not possible to oust her from her position since she was of royal lineage. The only way to abrogate her position as queen was to execute her.

Another approach found in the commentaries (Perush HaGra, Megillas S'sorim and others) states that officially Haman did not suggest that Vashti be killed; he only advised that she be prohibited from coming before the king ever again. He knew that once she would lose her status as queen, there would be nothing preventing them from executing her, in keeping with the accepted practice regarding any commoner who rebels against the king or disobeys a royal order.

In contrast, in the Midrashim of Chazal we find explicit quotes according to which Haman spoke openly and specifically with the king about how to kill Vashti, urging him to decapitate her at the guillotine, and even offering to do so himself, as we shall explain.

[18] Esther Rabbah 4:6

Some of the Rabbis explain that Vashti used to degrade Memuchan and slap him on the face with her shoe. Therefore, he wanted revenge. Others connect Memuchan's hatred of Vashti to the fact that she intentionally excluded his wife Zeresh from the invitees to her feast.

On the other hand, a third opinion maintains that Memuchan did not have anything against Vashti personally; rather, he had a grown daughter whom he wanted to marry off to the king. Therefore, he wanted to clear the way for his daughter to become queen, or, more importantly, for him to become the king's father-in-law.[19]

Obviously, Haman knew that it would not be so simple to convince the king to agree to kill his queen. Therefore, he used all his power of persuasion.[20] "Surely the king will argue that the queen's wrongdoing is not so terrible and that it is not proper to kill Vashti, a descendant of kings, for such a trivial sin!" Haman said. "However, Your Majesty must know that what she did was actually a terrible crime that can potentially cause such serious damage that only death would be enough of a punishment!

"Your Majesty," Haman went on, taking the opposite approach to cement his argument, "you might say that if the crime is so severe, even the perpetuator's death will not suffice to undo the damage caused. After all, if the women of the

---

[19] Interestingly, we do not hear anything further about this daughter of Haman with regard to suggesting her as a match for King Achashverosh. The Targum explains (at the beginning of *perek* 5) that this daughter did get to the harem together with the other candidates, but there she suffered a terrible case of stomach cramps. Without going into the gory details, we will suffice by saying that in the end, the daughter of Haman found herself unceremoniously tossed out of the harem.

[20] Esther Rabbah 4:8; see also Etz Yosef and Matnos Kehuna.

kingdom learn from her to hold their husbands in contempt, you might say, the punishment given to the queen will not deter them from following in her footsteps. Every woman understands that her husband is not a king and does not have the power to execute his wife just because she belittled him!

"Nevertheless, I must counter that argument and point out," the villain went on, "that there is no reason to harbor this concern! True, the women will know that they won't be killed if they scorn their husbands, but they will be deeply impressed by the severity with which the king relates to a woman not properly respecting her husband. This impression will be enough to prevent them from following the example of the wayward queen!" Haman finished with a flourish, leaving the king amply convinced of the necessity for such severe punitive measures.

The King's Authority

Sending the queen to her death was still not simple. Two major problems stood in King Achashverosh's way.

According to the constitution of Paras and Madai, the king was only authorized to rule in cases not regarding himself. The law concerned itself with the fact that the king was liable to be biased in personal matters. Instead, he had to present the case before the *yod'ai das v'din* so that they could rule fairly without bias.

Since the queen had wronged the king, he was forbidden to hand down a verdict on her case. He had to pass on judgment of the case to the *yod'ai das v'din*, which entailed the risk that the judges would exonerate the queen due to her position and lineage.

What did Haman do? He proposed that the officers amend the law. According to his suggestion, the king's powers would be broadened so that he would be able to judge even matters that affected him personally. "Would anybody dare suggest that our exalted king might distort the judgment for personal considerations?" Haman asked the officers, who naturally answered in the negative.

Actually, by agreeing to amend the law, the officers acted against their own interests. First of all, they were limiting the extent of their own influence. Secondly, from now on, the king would be able to pass judgment on them as well, if they would inadvertently offend his honor! From a logical standpoint, it was inconceivable that the officers should adopt Haman's suggestion. But Hashem arranged it that they would agree in order to start the process that would eventually lead to the Jewish people's deliverance.

Just a few years later, the king found Haman sprawled on Esther's couch and heard from Charvona that Haman had prepared a tree upon which to hang Mordechai who had helped the king. Achashverosh then ordered Haman hanged on the spot. This command would have been devoid of any power had Haman not passed the amendment empowering the king to judge even in matters that were directly related to him!

Clearly, the decision the advisors came to was the result of Divine intervention, preparing the means for the deliverance of the Jews and the downfall of their mortal enemy. Divine Providence set matters up such that Haman *himself* initiated the process that would enable the king to send him to his death a few years down the line!

After Haman's suggestion was accepted and inscribed in the law books of Paras and Madai, the king was now authorized to sentence Queen Vashti to death. But another problem stood between Haman and the execution of Vashti, a problem that stemmed not from legalities, but rather from King Achashverosh's character.

The king was actually quite a coward. Haman was well aware that Achashverosh was afraid that Vashti's relatives would avenge her death. Therefore, Haman announced that the moment the king would utter the decree of death, Haman would personally take upon himself the responsibility to carry out the sentence.[21] In this way, all complaints about the punishment would be directed towards the officer who carried out the execution and not to the king.[22]

Relieved, Achashverosh gave Memuchan permission to carry out Vashti's verdict,[23] and also sent out the letters in which he stated that from that point on, by royal order, all the

---

[21] Esther Rabbah 4:9

[22] At the same time, Haman made sure to "cover" himself in the event that the sentence might not be carried out in the end and Vashti would return to her original status and seek revenge against those who were behind the attempt to have her killed. Therefore, he saw to it that the king would be the one who would actually utter the ruling regarding Vashti's punishment, and he was also careful not to expressly state that Vashti should be killed; he sufficed with saying that she should be deposed from her position – which would automatically make her subject to death, as we explained in an earlier footnote. He also made sure that the verdict passed by the king would be recorded in the law books of Paras and Madai so that Achashverosh would not be able to deny what he said (Minchas Erev).

[23] According to some opinions, the king himself carried out the verdict on Vashti, serving as the hangman in order to publicly display the strength of his resolution (Etz Yosef Esther Rabbah 4:11).

women of the empire were required to obey their husbands and speak in their husbands' mother tongue.

The decision was accepted by the officers, but the *chachomim*, the sages, took no part in it. The *chachomim*, the *yod'ai das v'din*, understood that Vashti was not deserving of death and that it was only Memuchan's sinister advice that led to her demise.[24]

Were it Not for the First Letters

These royal letters may appear insignificant as far as the Jewish people were concerned, related only to the internal matters of the empire. However, this assumption is an error. The Gemara[25] points out that were it not for those first letters, not a trace would have remained of the Jewish people! These letters gave widespread publicity throughout the empire of King Achashverosh's foolishness. Had they not been written, when the second letters arrived calling for the decimation of the Jewish people, the people in all the provinces would have rushed to immediately implement those instructions, without waiting for the stipulated date, the thirteenth of Adar, almost a year later. Then, even before the next letters overriding the decree would have arrived, Haman's plot to destroy the Jewish people would have already been carried out!

But, in sending out the first letters, Achashverosh demonstrated to everyone that his words should not be taken too seriously. After all, what kind of king makes a special decree requiring women to obey their husbands? Every rational

---

[24] Minchas Erev
[25] Megillah 12b

person knows that even the simplest of men is a king in his own home![26]

Consequently, when the nations in all the provinces received the second set of letters in which Haman ordered in the king's name to exterminate the Jews, they did not take his instructions seriously. Instead, they waited to see how things would develop, knowing they should not rely too heavily on the letters stamped with the king's signet.

Here again, we find that Memuchan – actually, Haman – *himself* set up an escape hatch for the Jewish people that would save them from the decimation he himself would decree upon them.

Why Was Vashti Killed?

Why did Vashti deserve to be sent to her death?

On the simplest level, as was explained above, Vashti was far from righteous. In fact, she was a real shrew who abused Jewish girls. But this still does not constitute grounds for being subject to death. After all, Vashti was not the only villainous woman in Shushan, and King Achashverosh was certainly no *tzaddik* himself.

---

[26] In Etz Yosef (Esther Rabbah 4:12); the opposite logic is cited: He states that the ruling of the king that every woman must speak in her husband's tongue is *defiant* of logic. Under natural circumstances, the woman, who is ensconced in her home and does not mingle with others, would find it difficult to learn her husband's language, while the husband, who goes about the streets and marketplaces making contact with all kinds of people, would not find it so hard to learn his wife's language. Therefore, the common practice all over the world is that the husband learns to speak his wife's mother tongue! But Achashverosh, acting on Haman's advice, decreed that from that day on the custom would be reversed, and the women would be the ones to learn their husbands' languages. This illogical demand revealed to all how much they could rely on the king's judgment.

Chazal bring several answers to our question. In the Gemara[27] as well as the Midrash[28] we find a description of the words of the *malachei hashores*, the ministering angels, who came to the defense of the Jewish people when Vashti refused to appear before the king. They asked that Vashti be killed and Esther brought in to take her place to bring salvation to Hashem's nation.

The defense of the angels asked Hashem to focus on the merit of the *korbonos*, the offerings, that the Jewish people served Hashem with when the *Bais Hamikdash* was standing. The words of the *malochim* are hinted at in the names of the seven chamberlains who stood in the presence of the king. Each of these names is interpreted as an allusion to one of the seven arguments the *malochim* presented to Hashem:

Karsh'na refers to the *karim*, the unblemished, young lambs that the Jewish people brought as offerings;

Shesar alludes to the two *torim*, turtledoves, that they brought up on the altar;

Admasa recalls the *mizbeiach ha'adoma*, the ground-filled altar in the *Bais Hamikdash*;

Tarshish refers to the *bigdei kehuna* (Tarshish being reminiscent of *shesh*, fine linen), the garments the priests wore;

Meres alludes to the blood of the *korbonos* that the Jews *mir'su*, mixed constantly;

---

[27] Megillah 12b
[28] Esther Rabbah 4:2

Marsena refers to their mixing of the *menachos*, the meal offerings;

Finally, **Memuchan** alludes to the *shulchan*, the holy table in the Temple.

"Who is like Your nation of Israel," the *malochim* pleaded, "who offered all these *korbonos* before You! Now, when they are in dire straits, surely it is just that You should arrange for their deliverance!"

Indeed, the Midrash relates that the defense presented by the *malochim* roused Hashem's mercy, and He promised that He would save them from the destruction that was decreed upon them following their participation in the feast of Achashverosh.

There were reasons why Vashti deserved to be punished, besides for the benefit of the Jews. One opinion[29] maintains that Vashti was responsible for King Achashverosh's refusal to allow the Jewish people to return to their land and build the *Bais Hamikdash*.[30] She ardently asserted that it was not fitting for her husband, King Achashverosh, to build the edifice that her grandfather, the wicked Nevuchadnetzar, had worked so hard to destroy. Therefore, Vashti was liable to death.

---

[29] Esther Rabbah 5:2

[30] This opinion could be seen as being in agreement with the words of the Gemara and the Midrash, according to which the *malochim* defended the Jews and asked Hashem to kill Vashti and bring Esther in her place, all in the merit of the *korbonos* that they used to offer Him. Perhaps, since Vashti was the one to suspend the work of the reconstruction of the sanctuary where these *korbonos* were brought, it was only fitting that she be killed for the benefit of the people of Israel who were so meticulous in bringing the *korbonos* each day without fail.

The second opinion[31] explains that Vashti was not killed as a result of her own sins, but rather for the sins of her father, King Belshatzar, who dared to use the vessels of the *Bais Hamikdash*. As a result of this dire transgression, Belshatzar himself was executed the very same day,[32] but the sin was so profound that it caused a death sentence to be decreed on his daughter,[33] Queen Vashti, as well.[34]

A New Perspective to Understanding the Events[35]

By seeing what Achashverosh was liable to do to his wife of illustrious lineage in the heat of anger, we can understand how dangerous it was for Esther to later appear before the king without being summoned.

There was nothing to stop Achashverosh from executing the queen of anonymous origins. The only thing that prevented him from doing so was the kindness of Hashem!

Furthermore, the commentaries[36] explain, even when Achashverosh ordered Vashti killed, it was not because he

---

[31] Esther Rabbah 2:12

[32] Daniel 5:30

[33] Keep in mind that Vashti continued the "tradition" of her forefathers; she too held a party in which the vessels of the *Bais Hamikdash* were used, and she too had the audacity to don the garments of the *kohen gadol*, as we mentioned earlier. Therefore, it was highly appropriate that Vashti should be struck by the sin of her forbears in whose path she followed.

[34] The Gemara explains that because of Achashverosh's use of the vessels of the *Bais Hamikdash*, the Satan "danced" at his feast and caused Vashti's death. According to the Gemara, there would be room to say that punishment was decreed on *Achashverosh*, that his queen should be killed at the feast as a result of *his* use of the holy vessels. At the same time, it was decreed on Vashti herself to be killed at that same feast because of her *father's* use of the vessels of the *Bais Hamikdash* at his own party, a sin that she embraced after him, as we stated in the previous footnote.

[35] Esther Rabbah, Introduction:9

[36] Anaf Yosef; Esther Rabbah, Introduction:9

thought she deserved to die, but because of the king's love for Haman and the tremendous trust he had in him!

Once again we can see the extent of Hashem's kindness. Just a few years later, after Haman had risen in stature to the greatest of heights, Hashem put it into the king's heart to kill his beloved Haman when he discovered that he wished to harm his queen, Esther! In contrast to his previous actions, this makes no sense! We see very clearly that each and every step in the process of the Jews' deliverance was intentionally and thoughtfully arranged by Divine Providence out of Hashem's fervent love for His nation.

ACHASHVEROSH SEEKS A WIFE

"After these things, when the wrath of King
Achashverosh subsided, he remembered Vashti
and what she had done and what had been
decreed upon her. Then the king's pages said, 'Let
beautiful young maidens be sought for the king,
and let the king appoint clerks in all the provinces
of his empire to gather all the beautiful young
maidens to Shushan the capital, to the harem,
into the hand of Hegai, the king's chamberlain,
custodian of the women, and let their cosmetics be
given to them. And the girl who shall find favor
in the king's eyes shall rule instead of Vashti.' The
idea pleased the king and so he did." (2:1-4)

What She Had Done and What Had Been Decreed Upon Her

The morning after Vashti's execution, the king arose, sobered up from his drunken state of the previous night, and looked about for Vashti.

"Where's Vashti?" he shouted, demanding an immediate answer from his servants. Left with no alternative, they had to tell him the painful truth as it was. As delicately as they could, they tried to remind him of the previous night's events, but the king really did not remember what had taken place.[1] As

---

[1] The Targum Yonasan implies that the king actually did recall the previous night's events, but he thought he had only decreed that the queen may not appear before

we said, in his besotted state he was not aware of what he was doing.

"How could I possibly have done such a despicable deed?" the king wondered, aghast, and his servants dutifully filled him in on the details.

When the king's heart was merry with wine, they told him, he had ordered Vashti brought before him inappropriately clothed, and the queen had refused to obey the explicit order. They tried to rouse the king's memory of his terrible wrath, and reminded him of the discussion that took place between the king and his officers. They even revealed to him that Memuchan was the one who had advised him to kill Vashti, and that his suggestion was accepted and immediately carried out.

When Achashverosh heard the servants' report, his wrath was rekindled, only this time his anger was not directed at the late queen, but rather at those officers who had advised him to have her executed. He summoned these officers, and when they came he told them, "I want you to know that I am furious with you! You fools! You should have understood last night that my anger at the queen was only a result of my drunken state! You should have considered the fact that when I would sober up, I would miss the queen very much! You should have calmed my fury and encouraged me to put off her judgment until morning!

---

him again. This approach of the Targum agrees with the opinion cited in the footnote in the previous chapter which explained that Memuchan's advice was to forbid the queen to come before the king, and in this way to bring about her death, since inevitably she would inadvertently violate the order. Similarly, the words of the Targum match the opinion that Haman did not counsel the king outright to kill Vashti, but rather to depose her from her position, at which point she would in any case be killed, since she would be subject to capital punishment as a commoner who rebelled against the king.

"But what did you do instead? Just the opposite! Instead of alleviating my anger, you fanned the fires, incited me against my queen and led me to declare such a horrible verdict and personally cause her death!

"Now, I'll have you know, I put the responsibility for Queen Vashti's death on your heads! I will seek my vengeance from every one of you! The seven of you who counseled me to kill Vashti shall all be executed; the sentence you passed on the queen shall be done to you!" the king concluded,[2] and his order was carried out on the spot.[3] It now became clear how right the *chachomim* of the tribe of Yissochor were in evading the queen's judgment.

We mentioned earlier that according to the Gemara, Memuchan, one of the officers with whom the king consulted, was none other than the wicked Haman. Since we know for a fact that Haman was not killed with his colleagues, we have to assume that he found some way to escape the terrible sentence that was carried out on his contemporaries.

Even according to the other opinions, that Memuchan was Daniel, we still have to assume that he was not killed along with the other advisors since we find no mention of Daniel's death under such circumstances.

---

[2] The Midrash Ponim Acheirim explains that these advisors were the same ones who counseled King Achashverosh not to rebuild the *Bais Hamikdash* (or to suspend its construction) and that is why death was decreed on them.

[3] Actually, from the Targum Sheini, it sounds as if the king did not *kill* the advisors, but rather ordered that they should not appear before him again. In fact, the Midrash Ponim Acheirim cites two opinions – either that he killed them or that he banished them from his presence. On the other hand, Ibn Yichyeh maintains that these advisors continued to stand before the king, but they did not dare to ever again give him advice after seeing what happened as a result of their last counsel.

In any case, it turns out that the very officer who actually proffered the advice that led to Vashti's death was the only one who was not killed as a result of his counsel. The other advisors, who apparently remained silent when they understood that the king was leaning towards accepting the advice, were killed.

Let the King Appoint Clerks

After executing the officers who counseled him to kill his queen, the king was free to plan out his next steps.

Achashverosh understood that he had made a mistake when he decreed the death sentence on Vashti for such a minor infraction. It could be that he even justified her refusal in his heart, and understood that it was unfair on his part to even make such a shameful demand.

Nevertheless, the king knew that the past could not be undone. Since he could not bring Vashti back to life, he had no choice but to try and rehabilitate his life by remarrying.

The king, who was accustomed to Vashti's rare and extraordinary beauty, could not imagine marrying a woman whose appearance was not on par with that of his first queen. Where would he find a queen like Vashti? The king himself could think of no solution to his problem.

The servants suggested that the king gather the beautiful women from all the provinces of the empire[4] to his palace.

---

[4] The commentary Yosef Lekach explains the matter a bit differently. It is not logical to say that Achashverosh brought all the beautiful girls from the entire kingdom, because the entire city of Shushan would not be able to hold such a large number of girls. Apparently, the Yosef Lekach maintains, the job of the appointed clerks was to choose the one most attractive girl in each province and bring her before the

Then, the king could pick out as his queen the most beautiful girl of all, whoever pleased him.

The king agreed to their suggestion. That very day, he appointed a clerk in every province who would be responsible to gather together all the beautiful girls in that province.

The king assembled all the girls who were gathered to the capital city of Shushan to the custody of Hegai, the chamberlain of the women. His job was to provide them with everything necessary to enable them to achieve the finest aesthetic state possible.

According to the servants' suggestion, the king was to gather all the *maidens* in his vast empire; the harem where they stayed should have been called the "house of maidens." Yet we find the harem was called the "house of women." Why was that?

The answer is that Achashverosh did not suffice with instructing the clerks to gather all the beautiful young maidens; he allowed himself the liberty of taking the *married women* who found favor in his eyes as well.

---

king. Then, from among the 127 girls brought before him, the king would be able to select the most beautiful of all as his next queen.

The Yosef Lekach also emphasizes a point, mentioned as well in the Perush HaGra, that the servants intentionally ignored the need to find a wife of fine lineage. On the contrary, they figured, a simple girl who is not of royal stock will not dare to disobey the king as Vashti did; therefore, the best thing would be to choose such a girl.

For the same reason, they also advised the king to appoint Hegai, the king's chamberlain, as custodian of the maidens until they would come before the king, so that the girl who would be chosen would not feel superior to the king's chamberlains and disobey their orders as Vashti did. Their final recommendation was not to appoint a new *queen*, but rather to choose a girl "instead of Vashti," i.e., a woman who would bear the title, "Vashti's replacement."

However, Divine Providence had matters evolve differently, as we shall point out in footnotes in the continued development of the story.

We can see from this the extent of Achashverosh's wickedness. He stopped short at nothing, not even the most lowly of deeds, in order to satiate his desires.[5]

At this juncture, the king committed a serious error.[6] Had he sent emissaries to all the provinces to search for *one woman* who would please him, logically, the public response would have been much higher!

But Achashverosh did not do so. He did not rely on his messengers to pick out his queen for him, but wanted to get a personal impression of each and every woman. For that purpose, he decided to gather all the girls to his palace to check each one separately, and only afterwards to choose from among them the most fitting candidate.

This plan might have allowed the Persian king to choose the woman who was most to his liking, without relying on his clerks to decide what his preferences were. However, this approach proved itself to be a mistake, since it caused many parents to conceal their daughters.

"If the king was really seeking a woman to take as his wife, we would surely be glad to offer our daughters," most of the parents said to themselves. "But the king wants to take them for a trial period, and that is a different matter entirely. We have no interest in sending our daughters to the capital city of Shushan for a long stretch of time, handing them over to the king for a trial, and then discovering at the end that they were not chosen to marry him!" Consequently, they hid their daughters from the clerks.

---

[5] Esther Rabbah 6:11, see also Anaf Yosef Esther Rabbah 4:15.
[6] Megillah 12b

For this reason, the king could not suffice with sending emissaries to go from land to land to find the choicest girl. He needed *p'kidim,* clerks who were like *m'fakdim,* commanding officers, i.e., people of authority who could exercise their powers and force the parents to hand over their daughters.

For the same reason, the king needed special clerks in each and every province, since the appropriate women first had to be located before they could be sent to Shushan.

However, all we have said related only to the *parents.*[7] They weren't interested in handing over their daughters to the king's clerks. The women themselves were rather enthusiastic. Their childish imaginations were sparked by the hope that they might be the ones chosen to marry the king and be received with royal honor in his splendorous palace.

Therefore, there were many women who assembled in the "house of women" of their own free will, where they did whatever they could to beautify and adorn themselves so as to please the king.

We can assume that the women who were taken to Shushan against their parents' desires also did whatever possible to be chosen by the king, dreaming of marrying the most exalted personage in the entire kingdom, an honor that came hand in hand with a life of wealth and unimaginable pleasures.

But there was one woman who thought differently, one woman who truly and sincerely *did not want to marry the king!*

---

[7] Apparently, that is how we can reconcile the words of Chazal in the Gemara (12b) which states that everyone who had a daughter concealed her from Achashverosh with the words of Chazal in the Yalkut (1051) which implies that the girls themselves tried to find favor in the king's eyes.

It was not that she was afraid of the "trial," nor that she feared she would not be selected; on the contrary, she did not want to become the wife of this gentile! Needless to say, this was Esther, the daughter of Avichayil!

MORDECHAI AND ESTHER

"There was a Jewish man in Shushan the capital,
and his name was Mordechai, the son of Ya'ir, the
son of Shim'i, the son of Kish, a Binyaminite, who
had been exiled from Yerushalayim along with
the exiles who were exiled together with Y'chonia
the king of Yehuda, whom Nevuchadnetzar
the king of Bavel had sent into exile. He reared
Hadassah, that is, Esther, his cousin's daughter,
since she had neither father nor mother. The
girl was beautiful in form and in appearance,
and, upon the death of her father and mother,
Mordechai took her as a daughter. It came to pass,
when the king's word and decree were heard,
and when many girls were brought together in
Shushan the capital to the charge of Hegai, that
Esther was taken to the palace, to the charge
of Hegai, custodian of the women. The girl
pleased him and she obtained his kindness. He
rushed to prepare her cosmetics and to give her
the portion that was hers as well as the seven
special maidservants that were allotted to serve
her from the palace, and he transferred her and
her maidservants to the best part of the harem.
Esther did not tell of her nation or family lineage,
because Mordechai had commanded her not to
tell. Every day, Mordechai used to walk about
in front of the courtyard of the harem, to gain

*knowledge of Esther's well-being and what was
to become of her." (2:5-11)*

The first person we encounter in this chapter is Mordechai Hatzaddik, the head of the Sanhedrin, the *gadol hador* who lived in Shushan.[1]

The name "Mordechai" was given to him because he was compared to *mord'chai*, i.e., *mor d'ror*, a type of fragrant spice. The essence of the *tzaddik*, just like the fragrant spice, permeates his entire surroundings, sweetening and rejuvenating the members of his nation. On the other hand, just as the flavor of the *mor d'ror* is bitter, so was the *tzaddik* bitter for his enemy, Haman the Agagite, who ended up destroyed.

Mordechai Hatzaddik's towering level is discussed in the Midrash,[2] where Chazal teach us that Mordechai in his generation was equivalent to Moshe Rabenu in his generation!

Just as Moshe stood at the breach and saved his people with his prayers, so did Mordechai. Just as Moshe Rabbbenu brought down the Torah from the upper heavens and taught it to the Jewish nation, so did Mordechai Hatzaddik teach Hashem's Torah to the Jewish people.

Indeed, when we read the Targum's description of the character of Mordechai Hatzaddik, we find an emphasis placed on his dedication to his Jewish brethren, a characteristic of a true leader. As the Targum[3] writes, "A pious person, a grateful

---

[1] Esther Rabbah 6:3
[2] Esther Rabbah 6:2
[3] According to the description of Yayin Hatov.

person, one who prayed to his God on his people's behalf, was in Shushan the capital, and his name was Mordechai!"

As we explained, Mordechai had been living for some time in Shushan. Achashverosh moved there, ostensibly because of his throne – but the true cause was to bring the arena of events closer to Mordechai Hatzaddik.[4]

Although Mordechai presently resided in Shushan, originally Mordechai was from the holy city of Yerushalayim. When Y'chonia went into exile, in the first stage of the Bavel exile, Mordechai went into exile with him, but later returned to Yerushalayim.

However, the tranquil life of the *tzaddik* back in Yerushalayim did not last long. Soon enough he was exiled once again, returned, and then was exiled a third time, until finally, left with no choice, he settled in Shushan. Actually, it is as if Mordechai went into exile again and again of his own volition, since by coming back to Eretz Yisroel due to his ardent love for the land, he subjected himself to the trying experience of exile over and over again.[5]

Another opinion brought in Chazal[6] maintains that Mordechai only went into exile twice: He accompanied Y'chonia into exile of his own free will, and then returned to Yerushalayim, from where he was later exiled by Nevuchadnetzar with the final group of exiles. According to this opinion as well, we see his deep love for Eretz Yisroel and Yerushalayim, since he came back after having left to the diaspora and did not

---

[4] Perush HaGra
[5] Perush HaGra
[6] Yalkut Esther 1053

settle in a foreign land until he was exiled by force and could not return.

A third view in Chazal states that Mordechai went into exile to Bavel and set up house in Shushan of his own free will, in order to care for his cousin Esther who had been orphaned of both parents and left alone and forlorn.[7] "I am better off being in exile, as long as I can take care of Esther and guide her in the straight and proper path!" Mordechai said to himself.[8]

From Yehuda or Binyamin?

The *megillah* relates Mordechai Hatzaddik's lineage, specifying that he was "the son of Ya'ir, the son of Shim'i, the son of Kish, a Binyaminite."[9]

Mordechai Hatzaddik was a descendant of Shim'i,[10] who lived in the time of King Dovid. He had cursed the king roundly, and as a result was liable to the death penalty. However, Dovid,

---

[7] According to the first two approaches as well, it may be that Mordechai ended up settling in Shushan and quitting his efforts to return to Eretz Yisroel because of the responsibility that had fallen on his shoulders – caring for his orphaned cousin, Esther.

[8] Targum Sheini

[9] Even though Mordechai was a descendant of King Shaul, Shaul's name is not mentioned specifically, since it would have been no honor for him to be mentioned in a *megillah* describing the catastrophe that almost befell the Jewish people as a result of his failure to kill Agag, the king of Amalek, as he was commanded. Indeed, the reason matters evolved so that the deliverance of the Jews came about through Mordechai Hatzaddik in particular was because he was a descendant of Shaul. Since King Shaul had played a role in facilitating the birth of Haman, Mordechai was given the opportunity to correct his great-grandfather's transgression through his deeds (Megillas S'sorim).

[10] The Yalkut also mentions (1053) that because Shim'i's wife saved Tzadok and Evyosor from the hands of Avshalom who sought to kill them, her reward was that two *tzaddikim* who would save the Jewish people should descend from her – Mordechai and Esther.

with his Divine inspiration, foresaw the *tzaddik* who was destined to emerge from Shim'i's descendants, i.e., Mordechai Hatzaddik, and therefore he instructed his supporters not to kill him.

In Dovid's testament before his death, he commanded his son Shlomo to harass Shim'i and drive him to his grave, but he emphasized that this retribution should be administered in Shim'i's old age, when he would have completed his role of fathering the chain of generations leading to Mordechai Hatzaddik. Hence, in a sense, Dovid was responsible for the birth of Mordechai.

Against these facts, we can address the apparent conflict that Chazal say seems to exist in the listing of Mordechai Hatzaddik's lineage. On the one hand, the *megillah* calls him an *ish Yehudi*, which literally means a man from the tribe of Yehuda, while the same *posuk* explicitly states that he was a member of the tribe of Binyamin.

The Gemara answers this seeming contradiction by clarifying that, without a doubt, Mordechai Hatzaddik was a member of the tribe of Binyamin. However, he is called an *ish Yehudi* nonetheless because King Dovid of the tribe of Yehuda prophetically foresaw his birth and therefore prevented the death of his forbear Shim'i.[11]

Several other explanations for why Mordechai was called an *ish Yehudi* are offered by the Gemara and Midrashim.[12] Some of them explain that while Mordechai's father was a Binyaminite, his mother came from the tribe of Yehuda. Others claim that

---

[11] Megillah 12b
[12] Megillah 12b - 13a

the title *Yehudi* was given to Mordechai when he joined the kings of Yehuda in their exile, though he was definitely from the tribe of Binyamin.

Yet others maintain that the term *Yehudi* is a general title that does not indicate any particular connection to the tribe of Yehuda. According to that opinion, anyone who rejects idolatry and proclaims the oneness of Hashem is worthy of being crowned with the title *Yehudi*. Mordechai Hatzaddik stood out in his rejection of idolatry when he adamantly refused to bow down to Haman because that *rasha* had inscribed an idol on his chest, and so certainly deserved to be adorned by the honorable appellation *Yehudi*.[13]

An additional view cited in the Midrash concurs that the title *Yehudi* was granted to Mordechai because of his deeds, but explains that he was awarded the name because he was considered equivalent to Avraham *"ha'ivri"* – literally, " who was on one side," since he also stood alone in battle for the sanctification of Hashem's Name. Further, just as Avraham sanctified the Creator's Name in the world, so did Mordechai Hatzaddik. We find later that, due to his influence on the events of the time, "many of the people of the land professed themselves to be Jews." In recognition of that sanctification of Hashem, Mordechai earned the title *Yehudi*.[14]

In the Yalkut,[15] on the other hand, we read that Yehuda was the one who endangered his life in Mitzrayim in order to save his brother Binyamin. In that merit, the *tzaddik* who was

---

[13] Esther Rabbah 6:2
[14] Esther Rabbah ibid
[15] 1053

destined to arise from Binyamin's offspring was called on his name.

Hadassah – That Is, Esther

Esther, as we said, was an orphan and Mordechai's cousin. Her father passed away even before she was born, and her mother passed on immediately after Esther's birth.[16]

After her parents' death, Mordechai, Esther's cousin, took her in as his daughter.[17] Chazal add that he also took her as a wife – "*l'bayis*," as his home.[18] Esther was modest and chaste; Chazal tell us that she did not leave Mordechai's house nor see other men for *seventy five years*!

Esther was also referred to as Hadassah. Chazal differ regarding which of Esther's names was the original one.[19] Some maintain that her given name was Esther and that the title Hadassah is an allusion to her righteousness, since *tzaddikim* are called *haddasim*, myrtles.[20] In addition, she was as beautiful as a myrtle, which is neither too long nor too short.

---

[16] Esther Rabbah 6:5; Megillah 13a

[17] The Perush HaGra explains that three reasons led Mordechai to adopt Esther and all three are hinted to in the *posuk*: a) "Esther, his cousin's daughter" – due to their family ties; b)"Upon the death of her father and mother" – because of the necessity involved; c) "The girl was beautiful " – i.e., in her deeds; therefore Mordechai understood that she was destined for great things and needed to be given an appropriate upbringing.

[18] Megillah 13a. Ibn Yichyeh adds that Mordechai took Esther as a wife since she was an orphan and nobody would want to marry her.

[19] Megillah 13a

[20] The Gemara cites a source in the *posuk* proving that *tzaddikim* are called *haddasim*. The Midrash Ponim Acheirim adds that just as the myrtle never dries up, neither in winter nor summer, so the *tzaddikim* do not wither, neither in this world nor the next.

On the other hand, others claim that she was originally called Hadassah, while the name Esther was awarded to her at a later stage, either because she *histeera,* concealed her words and refused to reveal to the king her name and family origin, or because she was as beautiful as the moon, which is called "*istahar.*"[21]

We have pointed out Queen Esther's external beauty, and we shall encounter many passages in the *megillah* that deal with her charm. However, we should be aware that an opinion in the Gemara[22] maintains that Esther the *tzaddekes* was graced with neither external charm nor beauty.

According to this view, Esther was not particularly becoming, perhaps even the opposite. Chazal tell us that Esther was "*y'rakrokes,*" of greenish pallor. Her charm was not the result of her external beauty, but rather the "thread of kindness" that permeated her countenance. In other words, it was a charm granted to her from Heaven, unrelated to any natural cause.[23]

When we think about it, Esther was actually seventy five years old when she came before the king, or, some say, eighty

---

[21] The Yalkut (1053) explains that the title "Esther" was given to the *tzaddekes* by the gentiles after she was brought to King Achashverosh.

[22] Megillah 13a

[23] The fact that Esther was "*y'rakrokes*" is mentioned, as we said, in the Gemara. However, some commentaries explain that the words of the *megillah* stating explicitly that Esther was beautiful in form and appearance can still be understood literally. The Gra, for example, explains that originally Esther really was beautiful in form and appearance, whereas her greenish pallor only set in when she was taken to King Achashverosh. In her anguish at being taken to this *rasha,* her beauty dimmed.

The Megillas S'sorim suggests a similar explanation. He claims that even after Esther came before the king she maintained her full charm and majestic beauty, but *in the king's eyes* she appeared greenish, so that she would not be forced to be together with him. Indeed, the Megillas S'sorim explains that taken by Esther's charm, Achashverosh married her, but at no point did he actively defile her.

years old.[24] Even the most moderate estimates place her age at forty.[25] That being the case, how did an elderly woman of seventy five or eighty compare favorably to the most ravishing girls gathered from all corners of the vast empire of King Achashverosh? The only explanation is that a "thread of kindness" illuminated Esther's countenance and gave her a special charm that enchanted those who saw her.[26]

Before continuing our narrative, we need to pause and consider an important point that Chazal relate to a number of times in the Midrash – the fact that Esther was an orphan. A girl growing up without parents, with only her cousin to care for her, might feel lost and insignificant.

But when we follow Esther's life, we can't help but notice how the opposite is true. The deliverance of the entire Jewish nation was in her merit! Haman's downfall, too, was brought about through her actions![27] Until the end of time, she will

---

[24] Bereishis Rabbah 39:13

[25] Yalkut 1053

[26] Indeed, for this reason, the Midrash asks (Esther Rabbah 1:8) by what merit Esther came to rule over 127 provinces and to save the people of Israel, since it was clearly not natural that the elderly Esther should be chosen from among all the girls assembled in Shushan. Rather, the Midrash responds, Esther received this honor in the merit of her ancestor Sarah Imeinu, who lived 127 years, and, after already showing the wear of old age, was rejuvenated and bore a child at the age of one hundred. Esther too, like her great-grandmother Sarah, was rejuvenated after showing signs of old age, and succeeded in charming King Achashverosh (Etz Yosef ibid).

[27] In fact, the Y'aros D'vash explains that Haman's downfall came about through Esther specifically *because* she was an orphan! What is the connection? Haman's merit stemmed from the merit of the *kibbud av va'em*, honor for parents, exhibited by his forbear, Esav the *rasha*. In order to counteract this merit, it was necessary to put forward a person whose perfection in carrying out the *mitzvah* of *kibbud av va'em* exceeded that which Esav displayed.

Now, the statement of Chazal (Kiddushin 31b) is well known, "Fortunate is he who never laid eyes on them (his parents)." This cryptic statement comes to teach us that it is almost impossible for a person to fulfill the *mitzvah* of *kibbud av va'em*

be remembered and the story of her experiences read in every Jewish community year after year! She reached the apex of success!

This shows us clearly that environmental factors do not determine any individual person's success. Even if someone begins his life from a miserable starting point, lacking the most basic of necessities – e.g., parents, siblings, financial means, and so on – it is not impossible for him to reach the peak of success and the ultimate happiness!

Esther Was Taken

Now getting back to our story.... The emissaries were sent, the clerks appointed in each of the king's provinces, and the women summoned to come before the king and try to find favor in his eyes. But while the women competed amongst themselves who would please the king more, Esther remained totally uninvolved in what was going on around her.

On the contrary, the yearning in every other woman's heart, to gain a life of wealth and comfort in the company of the king, represented the most horrible of threats for Esther the *tzaddekes*, the wife of Mordechai, the *gadol hador*!

---

to perfection; therefore, in a way, a person who never merited to see his parents is better off, since by wishing to fulfill this *mitzvah* and anguishing over his inability to do so, it is considered as if he fulfilled the *mitzvah* perfectly (Berachos 6a), a level which is almost impossible for someone whose parents are alive to achieve.

For Esther, who never saw her parents, yet felt sorry every day that she did not have the opportunity to do the *mitzvah* of *kibbud av va'em*, it was indeed considered as if she had carried out the *mitzvah* in all its minute details and to its fullest perfection! Consequently, the merit of Queen Esther's *kibbud av va'em* was suitable to stand up against the power Haman wielded in the merit of his ancestor Esav. Therefore, Esther the orphan was specifically chosen to be the agent to bring about Haman's downfall and save the Jewish nation (see Esther Rabbah 6:7).

But as much as Esther dreaded the thought of being taken to the king's palace and tried to avoid meeting up with the emissaries, the king's emissaries sought after her. Word of the uniquely charming woman[28] had reached them, but, after searching high and low, they still had not found her.

The reason was simple: Mordechai had concealed her from the emissaries, and, in doing so, had put himself in terrible danger! After all, living in the capital city Shushan, he would not be able to claim that he didn't know the king was looking for a wife. In addition, he was not a native Shushanite, but rather had come to Shushan in exile with Y'chonia. It's well known that the punishment for a foreigner who violates the law is more severe than that of a citizen who commits the same infraction.[29] Fearlessly, he tried to save Esther from the disgrace of being taken to the king.

The emissaries returned to King Achashverosh and told him the truth. "We found many maidens for you, all beautiful, but the most beautiful one of all who enchants all who see her has eluded us! Apparently, she is hiding from us!" the envoys reported. The king promptly issued an order of execution on any girl who hides from the king's emissaries.

At this point, Mordechai Hatzaddik decided that he must not endanger his cousin's life and took Esther out of hiding.[30]

---

[28] Since we explained that the clerks were assigned to search for maidens alone, we have to assume that they did not know Esther was married to Mordechai.

[29] Malbim. He also points out that since Esther had neither father nor mother, and it was known that Mordechai was her adopted guardian and she would do nothing without his explicit instructions, he would have no excuse if he would be charged with concealing her.

[30] To a certain extent, our impression of Mordechai tends to be that of a "fanatic." He forbade the Jews to participate in the feast of Achashverosh, he refused to bow

Esther was soon found by the emissaries[31] and brought to the king *against her will.*[32]

Even after Esther was found by the king's emissaries, she did not go along with them of her own free will. She dug her heels in the ground until she was finally dragged away forcibly. The commentaries find a hint to this in the words, "Esther was taken," which imply that Esther did not go voluntarily. Esther was not led astray by the false glitter of the royal palace. She was unimpressed by the wealth and honor, status or power. She knew where true happiness lay – in the home of her cousin, Mordechai Hatzaddik.

The entire process, from the beginning of the search until Esther actually appeared before the king, presented in the *megillah* in just a few *pesukim*, actually took *four full years.* The

---

down to Haman, and so on. Of course his stand was always justified, but nonetheless it may seem to us that he took an irrational, extremist approach, without taking mitigating circumstances into consideration.

But this *posuk* dissipates that impression and demonstrates the balanced judgment of a true *gadol*. We see that the level-headed judgment of Mordechai led him to decide that, under the present circumstances, it would not be right to endanger his cousin, Esther. The same Mordechai who risked his own life when he deemed it necessary and refused to bow down to Haman, determined that in this case the proper thing to do would be to avoid danger and take Esther out of hiding. From here we can infer that all along, Mordechai's supposed "fanaticism" actually stemmed from carefully considered, pure *halachic* considerations alone.

[31] The commentary of Rabbenu Yisach Nachmiash explains that Esther was not taken by the emissaries directly from Mordechai's house, since then they would certainly have known her family origin. Rather, she left the house and was captured on the street. At the same time, see later on, where we will explain that the connection between Esther and Mordechai may have been known to the king, however, Mordechai fervently insisted that, despite their connection, he himself did not know anything about the adopted girl who had grown up in his house.

[32] Perush HaGra and others. The Gra also emphasizes that every stage Esther experienced on her way to the king entailed force and compulsion. She was forced to go from Mordechai's house to the harem, forced to go from the harem to the palace, and even forced to go to the king's sleeping quarters.

search for a queen began in the third year of Achashverosh's reign, right after the party that concluded with the tragic death of Vashti, while it was only in the seventh year of the king's reign that Esther came before the king.

Esther in the Harem

Esther spent three out of those four years "underground," hiding in her cousin Mordechai's house.[33] The last of these years was spent in the harem along with the other women, under the patronage of Hegai, the king's chamberlain and custodian of the women.

Esther's charm, which left its mark on all who saw her, naturally exerted an influence on Hegai as well. He rushed to prepare her cosmetics and also provided her with seven girls from the staff of the king's maidservants to serve her and carry out all her requests.

The truth is, the moment Hegai first saw Esther, he understood that the future queen stood before him and therefore granted her the conditions befitting a queen right from the start. That is why he granted her seven maidservants, as was customary to provide for the queen, and also gave preferential treatment to her girls in the harem, as was fitting for maidservants of the future queen![34]

---

[33] Perush HaGra

[34] Earlier, we cited the words of the Yosef Lekach, who explained that the king's pages suggested he limit the powers of the queen so that an incident like Vashti's refusal to appear before the king should not repeat itself. According to this opinion, the pages intentionally wished to put the girls up in the harem under the supervision of Hegai, the chamberlain of the king, so that they would get used to subordinating themselves to the king's officers. Now we see how matters evolved – by Divine Providence – directly counter to the royal pages' plan. Not only was Esther not subordinate to Hegai, but he related to her like a queen in every way, from the moment she set foot on the threshold of the harem.

Miraculously, without Hegai knowing a thing about Esther's family ties or nationality, he picked out for her seven *Jewish* maids! Similarly, Hegai ordered for Esther all the necessary *halachic* provisions, such as kosher food, which was no simple matter to acquire in the king's palace![35]

Esther derived a special benefit from these seven maidservants, certainly different from what Hegai had intended. She had no need for pampering, but she *did* have an urgent need to keep track of the days of the week so she would know when it was Shabbos. Therefore, Esther appointed each of her maidservants to be responsible for a particular day. In this way, she could easily know that on the day one particular maidservant served her, it was Shabbos![36]

---

[35] Megillas S'sorim. In the Gemara (13a) there is a discussion among Chazal as to how Esther was nourished during her stay in the harem. Some maintain that Hegai arranged kosher food for her, others state that she was forced to eat ham, but was not punished for it since she was compelled to do so, while yet others claim that she lived on seeds for the entire duration.

The Megillas S'sorim explains that all three opinions actually agree that Esther did not actively defile herself with non-kosher food. They differ only on which special miracle was done to make that possible.

The first opinion, which we cited in the regular text, states that an outright miracle took place; Hegai arranged for kosher food for Esther, even though he knew nothing of her background.

The second opinion maintains that she was served non-kosher foods but that the *tzaddekes* most certainly did not partake of them. Rather, a spirit in Esther's image came in her place and ate the non-kosher food instead of her. (The Megillas S'sorim brings a similar explanation in the name of the Zohar regarding Esther's relations with the wicked Achashverosh. The Zohar insists that Esther never had relations with Achashverosh; instead, a spirit in her image was with him. We can safely assume, states the Megillas S'sorim, that the same way Esther was spared from having to be with the *rasha*, even by compulsion, she also was spared from having to defile herself with non-kosher food, even by compulsion.)

In the case of the third opinion, which says that Esther was nourished from seeds for the duration of her stay in the harem, we see the great miracle in that her beauty was not marred nor her body weakened, even though a diet based on seeds alone would not naturally be enough to provide adequate nourishment for an adult.

[36] The Y'aros D'vash (Part 2, derush 2) explains that Esther surely must have known when Shabbos came out, but she had to conceal the fact that she was keeping

Esther did not make any effort to please those around her. Even when she was in the harem, far from the influence of her cousin Mordechai and subject to heavy pressures and destructive influences, Esther did not change even one bit. Esther genuinely feared Hashem and meticulously obeyed the instructions that Mordechai had transmitted to her before she was separated from him.

Mordechai had advised his cousin how she should conduct herself in the palace. However, in contrast to the other parents who counseled their daughters how best to curry the king's favor, Mordechai guided his cousin as to what she could do so as *not* to find favor in the king's eyes.

For example, the foremost, unequivocal instruction that Mordechai gave to his cousin Esther was that under no circumstances should she reveal her background! She was not to tell anyone her nation or family origin, nor should she discuss her lineage from King Shaul and the fact that she was actually a descendant of royalty. She was told to act as if she was a homeless girl, an orphan child who never knew her parents.

The reason for this was simple. Mordechai Hatzaddik figured that if the king would hear of Esther's royal lineage, he would certainly want her as a wife, and that is exactly what Mordechai did *not* want! That is why he instructed her to

---

Shabbos so that the secret of her origin should not be revealed. In order to cover up the sensitive information, Esther utilized her seven maidservants. Since she appointed a different maidservant for each day of the week, none of the maidservants knew what went on the other days. This way, Esther could avoid forbidden acts on Shabbos, while the maidservant serving on that day assumed that this was how she conducted herself every day. Meanwhile, all the other maidservants, who knew that the queen does "work" on their day, did not have any idea that on Shabbos she conducted herself otherwise.

present herself as an orphan waif who does not even know her family roots, in the hope that this would lead the king to summarily reject her.[37] But his strategy did not help,[38] as we shall see later on.[39]

Furthermore, Chazal teach us that there was an additional reason why Mordechai instructed Esther not to reveal her nation and family origin.[40] Mordechai said to himself, "Just a few years ago we saw how the king executed his wife for a minor infraction. If a similar fate would be decreed on my cousin, there would be no way to help her. But, at the very least, we have to prevent the endangerment of the Jewish people. If the king would be aware of Esther's nation and get angry at her, he might release his fury on the entire Jewish people, putting them in tremendous peril!"

---

[37] Ibn Ezra, on the other hand, explains that Mordechai actually *wanted* the king to take Esther as his wife once he saw that she was taken to him, and after he saw prophetically that she was destined to save the Jewish people. That being the case, he was concerned that if the king were to know that she hailed from the exiled Jewish nation, he would be repelled and reject her.

[38] This was the result of Hashem's kindness to His nation, as He wished to arrange for them a savior who would be the agent to deliver them from their mortal enemy.

[39] It should be emphasized that even after the king chose Esther, and it became clear beyond a shadow of a doubt that her mysterious background did not bother him in the least, the *tzaddekes* still did not alter her conduct; she continued to conceal her nation and her family lineage. At that point, she was not motivated by Mordechai's command, since the order was no longer extant once the reason for it ceased to exist. Now, the only rationale for her continued concealment was her inherent modesty and the power of silence that she inherited from Rachel Imeinu, her great-grandmother – and Chazal in the Midrash praise her for this (Etz Yosef, Esther Rabbah 6:12). We might add, however, that Esther did not know the precise reason for Mordechai's instruction; therefore she could not independently decide that the command was no longer in effect.

[40] In the Yalkut (1053) we find a further explanation – that Mordechai wished to avoid the limelight; therefore he asked Esther not to reveal the relationship between them.

In addition, there are other explanations for Mordechai's orders:[41]

Some maintain that Mordechai was afraid the king or his envoys would make trouble for Esther's family when they realized that these relatives had concealed her for three full years despite the explicit warning not to dare evade the royal emissaries.[42]

---

[41] An additional reason is cited by the Minchas Erev, who explains that Mordechai was concerned that a decree might be proposed in the future against the Jewish people. He wished to take advantage of Esther's position in the palace, ex post facto, in order to abolish such a decree. Therefore, he was afraid that if Esther's national origin and family lineage were to become known, then any decree against the Jews would be phrased such that the queen's family would be excluded from it, and then she would no longer have a valid objection to the execution of the decree.

Therefore, Mordechai told Esther to keep her origin a secret, so that any decree that would be proposed would include her and her close family as well, and then, when she would come to the king and assert that an edict was decreed against her and her nation, he would be shocked and immediately nullify the decision.

That is in fact exactly what happened just a few years later. The far-reaching vision of the *gadol hador* proved itself! When Esther came before King Achashverosh and told him that a decree of decimation had been issued against her and her family, he was absolutely shocked and immediately acted to nullify the decree. However, had she come before him pleading for her nation, without the decree having a personal connection to the queen herself, her pleas may well have fallen on deaf ears.

Ibn Yichyeh makes a similar point, but he explains that Mordechai wanted to ensure that Esther would be able to plead on behalf of her nation, and if the king were to know that she was a member of the Jewish nation, he would not accept what she had to say, since he would insist that she had a personal bias in the matter.

The Ibn Ezra writes that Mordechai wanted to enable Esther to secretly keep the *mitzvos*. Therefore, he advised her not to reveal her background, since if they would know she was Jewish, they would keep a close eye on her and she would not be able to act freely.

[42] Perush HaGra. Even after it became absolutely clear to Esther that nobody remembered her evasion of the royal emissaries and after she was beloved by all the people in the palace, she did not veer from Mordechai's instructions. This was due to her great righteousness, which led her to decide not to veer from her cousin Mordechai's command even once the reason for it was a thing of the past.

[43] Rishon Letzion

Others claim[43] that the reason was a lot simpler. Mordechai wanted to keep track of his cousin's situation. He realized that if everyone knew that he was her cousin, the royal servants and officers would avoid speaking about her in his presence. He preferred to conceal this information, and in this way retain an important conduit of information.[44]

Esther indeed obeyed the instruction uncompromisingly. No matter what pressure was placed on her, she adamantly refused to reveal her nation and her family origin. She stubbornly kept her silence like her great-grandmother Rachel, who remained silent when her father Lavan gave her sister to Yaakov as a wife in her stead!

Mordechai Used to Walk About

Mordechai continued to worry about Esther even after she was taken to the king's palace. He expressed this concern by walking about near the courtyard of the harem every single day, without fail, to gain knowledge about his cousin's well-being.[45]

There were several reasons for these visits:[46]

First of all, Mordechai wanted to be sure that they were not putting Esther under a spell and forcibly extracting from her

---

[44] This conduit was especially vital in light of the fact that Esther was in danger of having witchcraft employed upon her. Esther's physical state could be determined by simple observation. But the only way Mordechai could acquire information regarding any witchcraft that might have been exercised upon her was by hearsay. Therefore, it was extremely important for Mordechai to retain the guise of neutrality that would enable him to overhear such information (ibid).

[45] Ibn Yichyeh concludes from here that Mordechai was allowed to walk about the harem courtyard because he retained a position of some kind in the palace, a position that he held before Esther arrived there.

[46] Esther Rabbah 6:8

the information that she refused to hand over about her nation and family. In addition, they might have used such witchcraft to force Esther to convert, and Mordechai wished to prevent that at any price.

Second of all, Mordechai figured that Esther was likely to encounter *halachic* questions. "To whom will she present her questions there, ensconced among those gentiles in the palace?" Mordechai pondered. Therefore, he made sure to make himself available to her, so as to respond to her *halachic* queries.

Thirdly, since Mordechai was constantly plagued by the concern that at some point the king might lose his temper and order Esther killed, he kept tabs of her situation every day. After all, Achashverosh became infuriated at Queen Vashti after she refused to obey his unreasonable command. There was every reason to expect that the king would become enraged at Esther, who adamantly refused, without offering any reason, to cede to his perfectly reasonable request to reveal her family origin.

Aside from that, Mordechai was afraid that the king might remember that Esther had concealed herself from his emissaries, and that, even when discovered, she had to be brought against her will. As we know, Achashverosh did not exactly have a soft spot in his heart for women who did not come at his bidding.[47]

The fourth reason for Mordechai's visits concerned why Queen Esther was sent to the palace. Mordechai was one of two

---

[47] Perush HaGra. He adds there that Mordechai was also concerned for Esther's health, since her misery at having been brought to the king was so great that it would not have been unusual for her to take ill due to her anguish.

tzaddikim who were given a hint from Heaven that deliverance was to come.[48] Mordechai understood that if Esther was taken to the palace, there was to be a decree of some kind on the Jewish people from the royal palace, and that Esther's role would be to undo that decree! Therefore, Mordechai visited Esther day after day, in order to find out what would happen to her in the end, and to observe the Hand of Divine Providence that would surely become evident!

---

[48] Esther Rabbah 6:6

ESTHER IS BROUGHT TO THE KING

"When the turn came for each girl to come to King Achashverosh, after having been given twelve months [preparation] in the manner prescribed for women, (since with that the prescribed length of their cosmetics was completed – six months in myrrh oil and six months in perfumes and feminine cosmetics) when the girl would then come to the king, she would be given anything she asked for to accompany her from the harem to the king's palace. In the evening she would come and the next morning she would return to the second harem, to the hand of Shash'gez, the king's chamberlain, custodian of the concubines. She would not come again to the king unless he desired her and she was summoned by name. When the turn of Esther – the daughter of Avichayil, the cousin of Mordechai who had taken her as a daughter – arrived to come to the king, she did not request anything beyond what Hegai, the king's chamberlain, custodian of the women, advised. And yet Esther found favor in the eyes of all who saw her. Esther was taken to King Achashverosh, into his royal palace, in the tenth month, which is the month of Teves, in the seventh year of his reign. The king loved Esther more than all the women, and she won his grace and favor more than all the other maidens. He set

the royal crown on her head and made her queen
instead of Vashti. Then the king made a great feast
for all his officers and servants, the feast of Esther,
and he remitted taxes for the provinces and gave
gifts in royal fashion. And when maidens were
gathered a second time, and Mordechai sat at
the king's gate, Esther still told nothing of her
family origin and her nation, as Mordechai
had commanded her, for Esther continued to do
whatever Mordechai said, just as she had when
he raised her." (2:12-20)

And so time passed and Esther – against her will – was busily involved preparing for her appearance before the king. The process each girl had to undergo before she was permitted to come to the king for the first time was long and wearisome. Every woman had to undergo a beauty regimen, using the best cosmetic accessories that existed in those days.

For six months – yes, six full months – she anointed her flesh daily with myrrh oil, special olive oil made from olives that had not reached a third of their full ripening, since this oil possessed qualities that helped soften the skin.

After that, for another six months, the woman had to anoint herself each day with perfumes and feminine cosmetics. Only then, after twelve months of preparations, was she ready to come before the king.[1]

---

[1] Rabbi Yitzchok Cohen, as cited by the Minchas Erev, adds another reason for the twelve months of preparations. He explains that the king wished to check out each girl's health condition during the course of the year. As we know, some girls are sensitive to cold weather, while others suffer from the heat. The king wanted a girl who was hale and hearty all seasons of the year.

It should be emphasized that every woman received an equal portion of these cosmetics from the royal treasury. The king wished to compare each woman to the others, so controlled conditions were necessary to make sure he was getting the right picture. If each woman was to do her preparations at home, there would always be the possibility that one girl's beauty supplies were of higher quality than those of her friend, and this fact would lead her to appear more beautiful than her competitor, when, in fact, that was not the case.[2]

When the joyous day finally came, the day appointed for the woman to come to the king, she was allowed to request anything she wanted as an accompaniment on her way to Achashverosh's palace – drummers and dancers, a fancy chariot, or even jugglers to enhance her way.

Furthermore, each girl proceeded from the harem to the royal palace via the streets and marketplaces. As she walked, she was allowed to ask for anything her heart desired from the items displayed in the various shops.[3] Any wish the girl expressed on her way to the king was granted. In this way he ensured that she would arrive at the king relaxed and content.[4]

The "beauty regimen" that each girl underwent during those twelve months was geared towards that same purpose, in Rabbi Yitzchak Cohen's opinion. Myrrh oil has a quality of warming the body, while perfumes and feminine cosmetics relieve the heat and its related symptoms. The king wanted to check if this would be enough to protect the girl's health throughout the year, and that is just what he did during the months that the girls were in the custody of Hegai in the harem.

[2] Perush HaGra. The Gaon clarifies that this detail was included in the advice of the king's pages when they suggested, "Let the king appoint clerks… to gather all the beautiful young maidens… *and let their cosmetics be given to them.*"

[3] Yosef Lekach

[4] Yosef Lekach explains further that King Achashverosh understood that it was not right to act as he did – forcing all the girls to come before him. It was especially lowly in light of the fact - which we will later stress - that the girls who were

And so, each woman would be brought to the king, spend some time in his company, and then return to the harem of the concubines where she would remain in a rather unpleasant situation. She could not marry another man, since it would be considered an offense to the king that a woman who had been with him should marry an ordinary fellow, yet only one of the many competitors was to be chosen for the honor of marrying the king![5]

Consequently, all those women who came to the king and were rejected were doomed to a life of spinsterhood! They remained living in the harem, not far from the royal palace, but aside from the comforts that were afforded them there, they had nothing![6]

The extent of Achashverosh's cruelty becomes clear. He was ready to condemn the many, many women who had passed

---

brought to Shushan and came before the king were not allowed to marry anyone else afterwards, as that would be an affront to the honor of the king. Therefore, the king came up with an idea: He allowed each girl to ask for whatever her heart desired, and in this way he "paid her off," so to speak, for the years of loneliness that were decreed upon her. This was enough to allay his mind and ease his conscience. For this reason, Esther did not ask for anything when she came before the king; she wanted to keep her visit to the palace in the category of absolute compulsion, without the slightest aspect of willingness on her part.

[5] The Minchas Erev explains that in order that the women and girls should not hesitate to come before the king due to their concern that only one would be chosen and the rest rejected, the king promised to take every one of the girls as a wife, even though only one of them would be crowned queen instead of Vashti.

[6] The Midrash points out that the reason these girls deserved this terrible fate of forced spinsterhood was because they used to degrade the Jewish girls in their generation whose appearance had been marred by the tribulations of exile. Therefore, tit for tat, Hashem arranged that all the non-Jewish maidens should be gathered together to the royal palace to compete in winning King Achashverosh's heart, and from among all of them, Esther, the Jewish girl, would be chosen, while the non-Jewish girls would be rejected and lose the option of marrying another man ever again (Esther Rabbah 5:3; Etz Yosef ibid).

before him during the tiresome years of his search to a life of misery, permanently denying them the possibility of marrying a man with whom they could find peace and happiness – just in order to enable him, the king, to choose the finest girl in the world.

Esther is Taken to the King's Palace

As we said, Esther did not ask for a thing on her way to the palace. She had no interest in the trivialities that the other women desired and did not feel any need for accompaniment. She had no interest in pleasing the king.

Esther understood that it was undignified to make the kinds of requests that her fellow candidates presented. In her typical modesty and captivating simplicity, she left the decision of how she should be brought to the king and who should accompany her in the hands of Hegai.

But although Esther didn't care who would accompany her to the palace, the servants whose job it was to accompany each girl on her way to the king fought amongst themselves who would be the lucky one to escort Esther to the palace.

The argument did not remain a mere verbal debate; it actually developed into a public auction. Each of the servants bid the price he was willing to pay for the honor of bringing Esther to the king, and at the end, the servant who bid the highest price won the opportunity.[7]

---

[7] Esther Rabbah 6:10. Chazal derive this from the words, "*Esther was taken* to King Achashverosh, into his royal palace." These words indicate the significance that was attached to the actual *taking* of Esther to the king. However, as we cited in an earlier footnote, the Gra explains in his commentary that these same words emphasize a different point – the need to take Esther *against her will* to the royal palace.

Finally, Esther arrived before the king. The timing at which the encounter between Esther and King Achashverosh took place was not by chance. It was in the month of Teves, the month when wintry weather rages outside and every person likes to sit ensconced in his cozy home with his wife.[8] Achashverosh was no exception, and this subconscious yearning added to Esther's charm.

In addition, a special miracle was done for Esther. During the time she spent with Achashverosh, the king felt that he was missing nothing in his wife.[9]

While external beauty is perceived differently by different people, each with their own taste, Esther's *chen,* her inner charm, was universal. The "thread of kindness" she was granted by Heaven affected everyone she met. Even if a thousand people were to line up before her, she would find favor in the eyes of every one.[10]

Therefore, when Esther was compared to the girls of Paras and Madai, the comparison inevitably came out in her favor. There was not a single girl whose virtues overshadowed the special charm that was granted to Esther, that "thread of kindness." In addition, whoever came into Esther's presence got the feeling that they were of the same nationality and immediately felt comfortable with her.

Esther's good deeds and righteousness made her find favor in the heavens,[11] while her charm made her find favor below.

---

[8] Megillah 13a
[9] Ibid
[10] Esther Rabbah 6:9
[11] Esther Rabbah ibid

The king, too, was enchanted by her *chen* and rushed to choose her as queen,[12] setting the crown on her head on the spot.[13]

Not only did the king choose Esther, but immediately after he met with her the memory of Vashti was erased from his heart. All his feelings of longing for the late queen that used to come over him from time to time disappeared. That very day, he ordered the picture of Vashti that hung over his bed taken down, and a picture of Esther, the new queen, hung there instead.

Esther Still Told Nothing

One detail alone clouded the king's happiness. Despite his many attempts of persuasion, under no circumstances was Esther willing to reveal her family background![14] "I'm an orphan, I have neither father nor mother, and that's that! I have nothing to add!" Esther insisted.

---

[12] The Malbim explains that at the same opportunity, the king announced that he forgave Esther for concealing herself from him during the first years of the search.

[13] The Yosef Lekach writes that when the king saw Esther, he did two things. First of all, he set the crown on her head, granting her the status of queen. Then he went a step further and chose her as queen *in place of Vashti*, and in this way crowned her as queen of all his provinces. By doing so, the king wished to equalize Esther's status to that of Vashti, who was inherently a descendant of royalty, and also ruled over the king's provinces by virtue of her being married to him.

Furthermore, we find here a deviation from the plan of the pages described in an earlier footnote. While the pages advised the king not to appoint his next wife as queen, but rather just as a "fill-in" for Vashti, in practice, the king rushed to set the royal crown on Esther's head and endow her with full royalty – with all the honor and powers that the position of queen carries with it.

[14] From the words of the *megillah* and Chazal, it is hard to conclude definitively if the king knew that Mordechai was Esther's adoptive father. This fact did not help him verify her origin since Mordechai claimed that he knew nothing of her lineage and past. Proofs can be brought in both directions, and it seems that the commentaries differ on this question, as can be seen in the course of the following chapters (see also Yosef Lekach 2:19).

Furthermore, when the king kept badgering her, Esther even took a risk and snapped back at him,[15] "Excuse me, but before I tell you who I am, perhaps you should tell me who *you* are?" When Achashverosh replied that he was a king, the son of a king, Esther countered by saying that she too was a queen, the daughter of queens.

But Achashverosh did not believe her. He figured that Esther must come from a lowly nation or a disreputable family, and surmised that this was the reason she was ashamed to reveal her background. Therefore, he promised that no matter what information she would give him, she would remain queen. But Esther could not be persuaded to talk.

Achashverosh decided to try different approaches to encourage her to reveal her secret.

At first, he held a grand feast in honor of Esther, in the hope that during the banquet Esther would open up and reveal her great secret.[16] But the feast came and went, and Esther remained silent.

Next, he announced a remittance of taxes, this too in honor of Esther, in the hope that the great honor he bestowed on her would persuade Esther to change her approach towards him and answer his question. But once again, his efforts bore no fruit.[17]

---

[15] Yalkut; Ponim Acheirim

[16] Megillah 13a

[17] The Yosef Lekach explains that the king abolished the taxation of all the nations except for the Jewish nation, because of his hatred for the Jews. In actuality, the king's decision to remit the taxes from the citizens of all the provinces, a decision brought about by Divine Providence of course, proved to be a great favor for the Jews. When Haman sought to destroy the Jewish people, he had to offer the king payment in place of the taxes he would lose as a result of decimating the Jews.

Even when the king doled out valuable gifts to his people,[18] informing them that the gifts were in honor of the new queen,[19] Esther did not relent. "I'm not saying a word!" she announced.

When the king realized that he would not get anything out of Esther by taking the positive approach, he decided to try the opposite tack.

The king could not bring himself to actually harm Esther. After all, he wanted to win her heart and earn her trust. He consulted with Mordechai Hatzaddik,[20] who came up with an excellent idea by which he could threaten Esther on the one hand, yet, at the same time, not damage the delicate bond between them.

"We can assume," Mordechai explained, "that even if Esther is not willing to give in to your requests to reveal her background

---

On the other hand, when Mordechai came and asked him to sign a similar order in regard to the gentiles of the provinces who were poised to kill the Jews, he did not have to pay a thing, since the king had already canceled the taxes from all the citizens of the other nations at an earlier stage!

Indeed, it was for this reason that it entered the king's mind not to cancel the Jews taxes, since this remittance simply was not necessary; it would have brought benefit to no one but the wicked Haman, who would not have had to offer the king anything in return for the murder of the Jewish people.

On the other hand, after the miracle of Purim, when the Jews overpowered their enemies and finished killing those who sought to kill them, the king restored the taxes, as the last *pesukim* of the *megillah* explicitly state, "King Achashverosh placed a tax on the land and on the islands of the sea."

[18] The Targum Sheini explains that through these gifts, the king wished to benefit the members of Esther's nation, and since she fervently insisted that she was an orphan and did not know her family, he gave out gifts to all the different nations. Perhaps the king did not exactly believe Esther, but thought that if he would grant gifts to the members of all the nations, the new queen's nation and family among them, it would give her pleasure, and as a result she would cede to his request and reveal the secret of her origin.

[19] Ibn Yichyeh maintains that the gifts were meant to conciliate the nations for the death of Vashti, their natural queen, and on Esther's taking her place.

[20] The Gemara (13a) cites that the king consulted with Mordechai on this topic. The Targum Sheini, on the other hand, maintains that he consulted with his officers.

willingly, if you threaten her with taking another wife, she will not be able to tolerate the possibility of being replaced by another woman and she will thus reveal her secret to find favor in your eyes! She will be very jealous of the prospect of your taking a second wife, especially if she is to take her place."

In fact, Mordechai knew that Esther was sincerely not interested in being married to the king! Mordechai realized that he could only gain from Achashverosh following his plan. At best, King Achashverosh would find himself another girl and Queen Esther would be saved from the king's clutches.

Besides, Mordechai figured that by advising the king how to uncover Esther's hidden background, he would actually be helping to keep her true identity concealed. The king would never suspect that she was the cousin of Mordechai after he tried to help reveal her lineage.

Mordechai's suggestion was enthusiastically accepted by the king, who decided to immediately renew the parade of girls coming before him. Once again, he gathered women,[21] assuming that Esther would infer that her place in the king's court was not assured. "Once Esther understands where the wind is blowing, she will surely open up and give the necessary information!" thought Achashverosh, basing himself on the insight into human nature Mordechai had shared with him.

Achashverosh couldn't possibly imagine that Esther honestly did not want to marry him. He would never have believed that

---

[21] In contrast, the Perush HaGra explains that the second gathering of women was not for the purpose of choosing a queen; on the contrary, it was in order to send home those who had not yet had a chance to come before the king.

when Esther heard about the second round-up of girls, she was thrilled!

Indeed, the advice did not prove itself effective. Esther was unmoved by the gathering of the girls. Unconcerned about her status in the palace, she remained unwilling to deliver any details about her background, no matter what!

Esther, the cousin of the *gadol hador* and head of the Sanhedrin, was undoubtedly a familiar figure in the Jewish community. We can assume that most of the Jews in Shushan had heard of her and were aware that she had been taken to the palace and chosen as queen. The fact that the king had held a feast and given out gifts in order to persuade Esther to reveal her background was also common knowledge, as was the fact that knowing Esther's origin was very important to the king.

That being the case, what could be simpler than for one of the Jews in Shushan to approach the king, tell him who Esther was and from which nation she hails, and thus earn the king's homage as well as a generous prize! The king had invested so much money in the banquet and the gifts, all in order to uncover the secret of Esther's background; he certainly would not have skimped in rewarding the one who would hand over this information voluntarily!

Here we see the towering qualities of the Jews in that generation. Not a single one of them opened his mouth to reveal anything to the king! Not one Jew gave in to the temptation to betray his sister who was concealing the secret of her origin for reasons known only to her! "Who is like Your nation, Israel!"[22]

---

[22] Perush HaRambam on Esther

Whatever Mordechai Said - Esther Did

While Esther was not concerned by the renewed line-up of girls, Mordechai was actually extremely perturbed by it.[23] Perhaps, he fretted, this turn of events indicates that some calamity has befallen the queen, Esther.

Therefore, when Mordechai heard that girls were once again being gathered to the harem, he sat himself down at the gate of the king in order to verify that his Esther was all right.

Soon enough, his worries were allayed. He found out that the king's command to gather the girls was not the result of Esther being harmed in some way, but because she remained adamant in her silence – a refusal that was rooted in the instruction he had given her. "Ah, Esther remains whole both in body and in spirit!" Mordechai was relieved to know.

Indeed, Esther was whole in spirit. Uncompromisingly faithful to her religion, her spiritual level did not suffer even the slightest nick from the time she entered the royal palace. She was Esther – firm in her righteousness from beginning to end.[24]

Even after she was wed to the king, she continued to meticulously observe every one of the *halachos*, from *hilchos kashrus* to the complicated *halachos* of Shabbos. She was

---

[23] Midrash Ponim Acheirim. It should be emphasized that the words of this Midrash do not concur with the view of the Gemara stating that Mordechai was the one to give the king the idea of rousing Esther's jealousy by creating the impression that he was searching for another queen. However, this Midrash does agree with the words of the Targum which state that the suggestion was given to the king by the royal officers and advisors.

[24] Indeed, as we mentioned, the Zohar explains that Esther had no actual contact with Achashverosh; a spirit in her image was actually married to him.

even stringent in those *halachos* that were not *d'oraysa*, Torah ordained, but rather *d'rabbanan*, rabbinically ordained, such as refraining from eating *bishulei akum*, food cooked by non-Jews, or drinking *yayin nesech*, wine handled by them.[25]

We can imagine that it was no simple task to keep these *halachos* in the royal palace, especially regarding *bishulei akum* and *yayin nesech*. Esther was forced to abstain completely from food cooked in the palace and from drinking wine. But the stalwart training she received in her youth in the home of her cousin, the *gadol hador*, left its mark. She withstood the challenge heroically and remained loyal to her God and to His Torah and *mitzvos*.

Furthermore, even during those days when Esther was married to King Achashverosh, she did not neglect her husband, Mordechai the *tzaddik*. She did not consider it below her dignity to return to the dilapidated Jewish quarter after growing accustomed to a life of luxury in the royal palace. On the contrary, at every possible moment Esther would slip away from the palace and go directly to Mordechai.[26]

If we wish to find a true model of someone who stood up strongly to a spiritual challenge, with head held high and with true Jewish pride – we could find no better example than Queen Esther!

---

[25] Targum
[26] Megillah 13b

BIGSAN AND TERESH

> *"Those days, while Mordechai was sitting at the gate of the king, Bigsan and Teresh, two chamberlains of the king who served among the guardians of the threshold, became angry and plotted to assassinate King Achashverosh. The matter became known to Mordechai, and he told Queen Esther, and Esther informed the king in Mordechai's name. The matter was investigated and confirmed, and the two were hung on a gallows. The incident was recorded in the book of chronicles before the king." (2:21-23)*

At this point a significant episode took place at the gate of the palace. Bigsan and Teresh, two chamberlains who served as guardians of the threshold, hatched a secret plot to assassinate King Achashverosh.

Two different opinions appear in Chazal regarding the motives that led Bigsan and Teresh to want to kill the king. According to the first view, they were envious of Mordechai.

One of the first acts that Esther carried out when awarded her powers as queen was to allocate generous funding to the Sanhedrin, headed by Mordechai Hatzaddik. She allotted a prime piece of real estate for the erection of a building for the Sanhedrin, in no less desirable a spot than at the gate of the king's palace.[1]

---

[1] Targum

Due to his position as leader of the Sanhedrin, Mordechai spent most hours of the day at the gate of the king. From that spot, he also maintained his daily contact with Queen Esther. Bigsan and Teresh inferred from this that the new queen was planning to displace them from their post and to install Mordechai in their place. In order to foil this imaginary "plot," they contrived a scheme of their own – a plot to assassinate the king.[2]

The second opinion, on the other hand, maintains that the plot of Bigsan and Teresh was directly connected to Queen Esther. Ever since Esther had arrived at the palace, they claimed, festivities went on in the palace day and night,[3] a fact that led the king to require their services around the clock. Therefore, they wished to kill the king and, according to one opinion, Esther as well, simply in order to rid themselves of this "nuisance."[4]

[2] The Yalkut (1053) explains that Bigsan and Teresh were in fact dismissed from their posts by the king, and Mordechai appointed to sit in their stead at the king's gate, after Esther suggested that the king follow the example of his royal predecessors who installed a righteous Jew at their gates. For example, Nevuchadnetzar put Daniel at the king's gate. In keeping with this opinion, the Etz Yosef explains that Bigsan and Teresh sought to assassinate the king in his private sleeping quarters, so that it would be clear to all that Mordechai had failed at his responsibility to guard the king, a task which they performed successfully for so many years.
This view agrees with the second one that we will cite later on regarding the method by which the assassination was meant to take place, which maintains that Bigsan and Teresh wished to poison Esther and to kill the king in his bedroom. Since Esther was the direct cause of their dismissal, it is logical to assume that they wished to take revenge against her personally, while they wanted to kill the king in a manner that would accentuate Mordechai's negligence in guarding his life. This would better be accomplished by simple murder, rather than by poisoning – a method that Mordechai would not have been expected to prevent in the purview of his role as the new guardian of the threshold.
[3] Megillah 13b
[4] Ibn Yichyeh adds that Mordechai occupied an official post in the palace; therefore, he had the opportunity to walk about in the area of the harem and check on Esther's well-being. In the course of these visits to the harem, the officers came to recognize

Chazal also explicitly discuss the method by which the assassination was to be carried out. Bigsan and Teresh planned to drop fatal venom into the king's golden goblet[5] and kill him by poisoning.[6] Another view states that Bigsan and Teresh also wanted to kill Queen Esther, and the fatal poison was actually earmarked for her, while they planned to finish off the king by stabbing him in his bedroom.[7]

A third opinion[8] discusses that they intended to slip a venomous snake into the king's barrel of drinking water. Yet a fourth view maintains[9] that Bigsan and Teresh were not so clever; they simply wished to poison the king.

In any case, the actual assassination was supposed to be carried out by one of the two – either Bigsan or Teresh – while the other would stand in for him and make sure that his friend's absence would not be noticed.[10]

But Bigsan and Teresh neglected to take one tiny detail into account: the fact that the dialogue between them took place in a public area, at the gate of the king. They spoke in Tarsis,

---

his wisdom, and eventually they assigned him an honorable position in the palace. That is what roused the anger of Bigsan and Teresh, who felt that they, having served the king for so many years, were worthy of serving in this elevated position, not Mordechai, a relative newcomer. The Yosef Lekach writes that the wrath of Bigsan and Teresh was roused by the license that was given to Mordechai to *sit* at the gate of the king, while they, by dint of their positions as guardians of the threshold, were forced to *stand*.

[5] Targum Sheini

[6] Even though Bigsan and Teresh were guardians of the threshold, they would also serve in assorted other roles when necessary. Among other positions, they occasionally served as the royal wine butlers. Their plan was to utilize such an opportunity to carry out their devious plot (Ibn Yichyeh).

[7] Targum

[8] Midrash Ponim Acheirim

[9] Ibid

[10] Megillah ibid

a language virtually unknown to anyone else in Shushan. At that particular moment the one person who was fluent in this language "happened" to be sitting right nearby. Mordechai, as a member of the Sanhedrin, was fluent in seventy languages, including Tarsis. Therefore, the scheme was laid out before Mordechai in all its detail.

There is another view[11] that maintains that the information reached Mordechai in an entirely different manner – through *ru'ach hakodesh*, the prophetic Holy Spirit.[12]

In any case, the moment Mordechai became aware of the scheme, he rushed to update Esther. Esther, on her part, hurried to bring the disconcerting information to the king, who investigated the matter in a very simple way. He checked out Bigsan and Teresh's shift schedule, and found that, indeed, a change had been introduced into the regular schedule.[13] This fact fell right into line with the information provided by Mordechai, confirming the suspicions[14] and serving as adequate basis to have Bigsan and Teresh hanged to death at once.

---

[11] The Ralbag cites an additional opinion, according to which Mordechai learned of Bigsan and Teresh's plot by the process of deduction. He heard that they were angry at the king and that they were trying to get hold of fatal poison, and he deduced that they must be trying to poison the king.

[12] Midrash Ponim Acheirim

[13] According to the Yosef Lekach, Mordechai's words were verified by a search through Bigsan and Teresh's possessions, which led to the discovery of the fatal poison.

[14] There is an opinion in Chazal that Bigsan and Teresh found out that word of their plot had reached the king, and they therefore delayed the execution of their plan, but Hashem created another snake in the jug so that the words of the *tzaddik* should not be disproved (Yalkut, Midrash Ponim Acheirim). In fact, according to this view, Esther delivered the information to the king in Mordechai's name, not only because of the importance of "giving credit where credit is due," but also because she was concerned that some hitch might arise in Bigsan and Teresh's plot, and then her words would not stand the test of proof. "If the information is conveyed to the king

Of course, Esther did not forget to point out to the king the source of the information that saved his life. She told him specifically that Mordechai was the one who had heard the dialogue between the two chamberlains and had rushed to report it.

Indeed, Mordechai was written down in the king's book of chronicles, which the king frequently perused. This was the only reward he granted to the person who saved his life.

Surely, if someone would save us from mortal danger, we would feel morally indebted to him for the rest of our lives. But King Achashverosh sufficed with marking the incident down in his records,[15] and with that the matter was sealed.

In fact, the commentaries explain,[16] matters were Divinely engineered such that Achashverosh would refrain from granting any reward to Mordechai, because Mordechai was destined to receive his true compensation at a different time, when Haman the Agagite sought to kill him and destroy his nation.

Incited Servants against their Master

Divine Providence directed every detail of the events that were taking place. Not only did Hashem summon Mordechai

---

in the name of Mordechai Hatzaddik," Esther thought to herself, "Hashem will undoubtedly see to it that his words are proven true!" And, as we see, her approach showed itself to be correct.

[15] Divine Providence manipulated matters so that the incident would be recorded in the book of chronicles before the king, i.e., the book that remained at all times in the king's possession, with no possibility of any of its contents being erased (Malbim). However, the Malbim's words require clarification, since, as we will explain at a later point, according to the words of Chazal there were those who tried to rub out the words that were recorded in Mordechai's merit, but an angel was Divinely dispatched to rewrite the lines that were erased.

in time to hear Bigsan and Teresh's plans, but *all* events, without exception, are intentionally planned, directed by Divine Providence!

Chazal teach us[17] that not only was Mordechai's presence at the king's gate and his overhearing the dialogue of the chamberlains part of Hashem's plan, but the very plot to kill the king was an integral part of the Creator's rescue plan![18]

Since Hashem wanted to save the Jewish people using Mordechai's name that was recorded in the book of chronicles, He roused the anger of Bigsan and Teresh against King Achashverosh and planted in their minds the idea of assassinating the king.

In conclusion, we will cite the words of the Midrash,[19] which derives a *kal v'chomer*, an inference from minor to major, from the king's book of chronicles to Hashem's book of chronicles.

Such blessing sprouted from that meager recording in King Achashverosh's book of chronicles!

The prophet Malachi[20] said, "Then those who fear Hashem spoke one to the other, and Hashem harkened and heard, and a book of chronicles was written before Him for those who fear Hashem and revere His Name!" The prophet revealed to us

---

[16] Malbim

[17] Esther Rabbah 6:13; Megillah 13b

[18] The matter takes on an even greater light according to the view that the plot became known to Mordechai through *ru'ach hakodesh*. It turns out, then, that Hashem roused the anger of Bigsan and Teresh against their master, planting in their minds the idea to assassinate him. Then, afterwards, He revealed the plan to Mordechai so that he could foil it and, in this way, earn the king's esteem. Remarkable!

[19] Esther Rabbah 6:14

[20] Malachi 3:16

that every good deed performed in this world is duly recorded in the book of chronicles that lies before the King of all kings!

Now, if the benefit that resulted from a few scant words recorded in the king's book of chronicles was so vast, how much more so is an act recorded in Hashem's eternal record books destined to bring immeasurable blessing!

Why did Mordechai Save Achashverosh?

Another point demands explanation.

Mordechai discovered the plot of Bigsan and Teresh and the information was passed on to King Achashverosh. But why in fact did Mordechai decide to deliver the information to King Achashverosh? Why did Mordechai Hatzaddik care if the assassination scheme against the wicked king would be carried out as planned?[21]

To this question as well, Chazal offer a number of answers:[22]

The first explanation is that Mordechai wanted Achashverosh to remain alive. Since he had once given his permission to rebuild the *Bais Hamikdash*, even though that license was later retracted, there was still room for hope that he would revert to his original decision.[23]

---

[21] According to the views cited above, in which Mordechai was appointed to the post of guardian of the threshold in place of Bigsan and Teresh, the Yalkut explains that Mordechai wished to prevent anyone from claiming that just when the king began to be guarded by a Jew, he met his death – a claim that could cause severe repercussions to the Jewish nation.

[22] Yalkut Esther 1053

[23] The words of the Yalkut fall in line with the opinion maintaining that Achashverosh is identical with Koresh. In addition, it could be that at the beginning

The second explanation is that Mordechai had certain connections in the royal palace; he served as the wine butler at the feast of Achashverosh and the king consulted him on various subjects.[24] Mordechai sought to preserve these connections for the benefit of his people, and therefore he had a distinct interest in saving King Achashverosh.

In addition, Mordechai wished to preempt a possible claim that the entire time the king was married to the gentile Vashti he was safe and protected from harm, and that only when he married a Jewess – Queen Esther[25] – did he meet his death![26]

We should also emphasize here Queen Esther's outstanding righteousness. As we have stressed, Esther had no interest in life in the company of King Achashverosh. Now, when a plot was being hatched to kill the king, it would appear that she had come across the chance she was waiting for! All she had to do was conceal the information and within a short time her troubles would be over!

---

of his reign, Achashverosh granted his permission to rebuild the *Bais Hamikdash*, but that shortly afterwards the letter of indictment reached him and he quickly retracted his permission. See above, at the beginning of the chapter "In the Days of Achashverosh," for more details.

[24] See Megillah 13, where the Gemara explains that the king consulted him on how to extract from Esther information about her background.

[25] Even though at this point the queen's origin was unknown, Mordechai apparently was concerned that the information might emerge at a later stage.

[26] In the Midrash Rabbah (Bereishis Rabbah 39:12) we find two additional answers to this question. The first is that Mordechai learned from the deeds of his forefathers, who did what they could to benefit the ruling king, e.g., Yaakov, who blessed Pharaoh, and Daniel, who interpreted Nevuchadnetzar's dreams. The second answer cited is that Mordechai found a basis in the Torah for his conduct when he interpreted the *posuk*, "The nations of the earth shall be blessed in you," (Bereishis 12:3) as an order to the people of Israel to act on behalf of the nations of the world and come to their aid in their times of trouble.

But Esther did not do so. Whatever Mordechai said, Esther did, without taking any other considerations into account![27]

---

[27] Tangentially, this incident affords us a window through which to observe the Providence of Hashem. Earlier, we cited opinions according to which Bigsan and Teresh removed the poisonous snake from the jug of the king's drinking water. At this point, there was no threat to his life. Now, let us imagine what would have happened had Esther decided to "be smart" and refrain from telling the king about Bigsan and Teresh's scheme. The king would not have been killed, she would not have been rescued from his clutches, and the special merit that was set aside for Mordechai in regard to King Achashverosh, a merit that eventually served as the means to bring about the deliverance of the Jews, would never have come about at all! Esther might have ceded all this – without gaining a thing. This teaches us that by heeding the words of the *gedolim*, we can only benefit!

HAMAN'S RISE TO GREATNESS

*"After these things, King Achashverosh promoted
Haman ben Hamedasa the Agagite, and raised
his status, and elevated his seat above all the other
officers who were with him. All the servants
of the king at the king's gate would bow down
and prostrate themselves to Haman, since this
is what the king commanded concerning him.
But Mordechai would neither bow nor prostrate
himself. The king's servants at the king's gate said
to Mordechai, 'Why are you disobeying the king's
command?' And when they said this to him day
after day and he refused to listen to them, they
reported to Haman, to see if Mordechai's words
would prevail, for he had told them that he was
a Jew. When Haman saw that Mordechai would
not bow or prostrate himself to him, he became
full of rage. It was contemptible to him to strike
at Mordechai alone, for they revealed to him
Mordechai's nation. So Haman sought to destroy
all the Jews – the people of Mordechai – in
Achashverosh's entire empire." (3:1-6)*

As a result of the Jews' participation in the feast of
Achashverosh,[1] a Divine decree of destruction was pronounced
against the nation of Israel. Now, five years after Esther's arrival

---

[1] See above in the footnote where we explained that the decree of decimation was
issued not only as a result of the Jews' participation in the feast of Achashverosh, but
also for their prostration to the idol in the time of Nevuchadnetzar.

at the royal palace and nine years after the infamous feast, the beginning of that decree was set into motion.

However, even when Hashem sees fit to strike the Jewish nation, He does so only to rouse them to repentance and always prepares the means of salvation before the punishment. Only after Hashem initiated the episode with Bigsan and Teresh did he allow Haman the Agagite to rise against the Jews.

The circumstances that led to Haman's birth are recorded in the *Navi*. When King Shaul was anointed as king, the prophet Shmuel was sent to deliver Hashem's instruction to him to fight Amalek to the bitter end, slaying the entire nation by sword, men, women, children and infants. Even the livestock were not to be left alive (Shmuel I:15).

Loyal to Hashem's word, Shaul obediently went out to war and destroyed the entire Amalekite people. Only in one small point did he veer from the explicit orders he had received: He left Agag, the king of Amalek, alive, as well as a number of animals that he planned to offer as sacrifices to Hashem.

As a result of this "tiny change" that Shaul made in executing Hashem's command, he lost his kingship to Dovid. But that was not the only outcome of this deed. Agag was allowed to remain alive for just one more night; by the next day, Shmuel had already smitten him by the sword. Yet, as a result of that one extraneous night, a son was born to King Agag, the one surviving branch of the seed of Amalek.

Among the descendants of that son born to Agag was Haman the Amalekite. Thus, the decree that threatened to wipe out the entire Chosen Nation can actually be attributed to the error King Shaul committed by leaving Agag alive. Had he followed his instructions exactly and not left even that one single remnant of Amalek, Haman Harasha would not have come into this world, and the terrible decree would have been prevented.

But Shaul did not kill Agag, and the Amalekite king did sire a son, and Haman Harasha is counted among his offspring.

The King Promoted Haman

The chain of events that led to the decree against the Jews begins with the tremendous honor that the king awarded Haman Harasha, promoting and aggrandizing him above all the officers who were with him, and even going so far as ordering the people[2] to prostrate themselves before Haman Harasha every time they would encounter him.

King Achashverosh, we ought to stress, had no particular interest in Haman's welfare;[3] he was interested only in his own

---

[2] The commentary Yosef Lekach writes that in fact, the king's order regarding the obligation to bow before Haman was not directed towards all the citizens of the empire, but only to the *king's servants* who were *at the king's gate*, i.e., only those who met both of these conditions. He infers this from the wording of the *posuk*, "All the *servants of the king at the king's gate* would bow down and prostrate themselves to Haman, since *this* is what the king commanded concerning him." *This* is what the king commanded, that the *servants of the king* who were *at the king's gate* should prostrate themselves before Haman.

However, the Malbim understands the *posuk* differently. The command was not addressed *only* to the servants at the king's gate, but *even* to the servants at the king's gate, since were we not to explicitly relate to them, there might be room to err and say that in the king's court, nobody should be shown honor other than the king himself.

[3] This is how the Midrash (Esther Rabbah 7:5) explains it. However, in the Perush HaGra and other commentaries another reason is cited, stating that the king elevated Haman after he gave the advice that lead to Vashti's death. As a result of this advice, the king was awarded broad powers to pass judgment on his own,

personal benefit. Seeing that Haman was extremely wealthy, as the treasures of the kings of Yehuda had fallen into his hands, the king decided that a close association with Haman might bring him benefit one day. That is why Achashverosh became so friendly with Haman and elevated his position – to find favor in his eyes as an investment for the future.[4]

In any case, the order was given, and all the people, including the king's servants and attendants, obeyed the command religiously. Each time Haman would pass by in the street, everyone would prostrate himself down to the ground. Even the Jews were forced to obey the decree, because of the mortal danger that was involved in resisting.[5]

---

even in cases that were directly related to him. Once this suggestion was accepted, the king gained a status that exceeded anything his predecessors had enjoyed, and in recognition of the benefit the king derived from this counsel, he promoted the counselor – Haman.

The Malbim suggests another angle. He maintains that the king "forgot" – or wanted to forget – that Mordechai was the one who revealed to Esther the plot that was being hatched by Bigsan and Teresh. He was under the impression that Esther had delivered the information to him on her own. Therefore, the king felt indebted to Haman, since it was as a result of his advice – the advice of Memuchan, who is identical to Haman – that matters evolved such that Vashti was killed and Esther came into her position. Furthermore, the Malbim explains that Haman might even have taken advantage of the king's shaky, short-lived memory and convinced him that it was *Haman* who revealed to Esther the plot and asked her to inform the king.

Ibn Yichyeh adds another point. He says that the king at first was enraged at Haman for causing Vashti's execution and summarily dismissed him (and indeed, the Targum seems to imply that the officers did not appear before him again, and not that he killed them, as we explained earlier). However, now that it became clear to the king that, as mentioned, Vashti's death was really for the best since it led to his life being saved by Esther the king felt grateful to Haman and promoted him above all the other officers who were with him.

[4] Esther Rabbah 7:5

[5] It should be pointed out that bowing to Haman himself would not have been considered idolatry, since it would be perceived as a gesture of respect, not equivalent to bowing to a deity as a form of worship. True, in Aggadas Esther we find one view stating that the king's command was to bow down to Haman in a manner of

But Haman was not satisfied with that. The tremendous honor he garnered was not enough for him. Haman, in his great wickedness, wanted to intentionally cause the Jewish nation to sin, so he had the image of a false god embroidered onto his garment.[6] "When the Jews prostrate themselves before me," Haman sneered to himself, "they will automatically be prostrating themselves to an idol, without even realizing it! This sin will surely incite the wrath of their God Who will be quick to punish them!"

Some say Haman went a step further; he actually declared himself a deity,[7] announcing that prostration before him is required in deference to his divinity. This statement rendered prostration before Haman a serious violation of the prohibition against idolatry. According to this view, Haman indeed caused the Jews to transgress a terrible sin, one of the three sins for which the principle of *yehareg v'al ya'avor* applies, i.e., that we are required to sacrifice our lives rather than violate them.

And so, Haman paraded about the streets and marketplaces, glowing with happiness and basking in pleasure at the sight of the hordes bowing down to him.

But one important thing escaped Haman's attention, a point that would certainly have clouded his happiness had he been

---

worship. However, in all the other Midrashim of Chazal, there is no indication of this direction, with the possible exception of the Etz Yosef on Esther Rabbah, which mentions that the king interpreted Haman's wealth as a sign of his good fortune; therefore, he commanded everyone to bow down to him as a form of worshipping the "god of wealth," so to speak. According to the Etz Yosef, we could perhaps say that the king's command constituted prostration before Haman specifically as a manner of worship.

[6] Esther Rabbah 7:5

[7] The Ralbag explains that *this* is what the king commanded – to make Haman a deity.

aware of it. He did not know, however, that Hashem elevated him to the highest heights only to make his downfall all the more drastic.[8]

Haman's situation is compared to that of a royal servant who cursed the king's son. The king said to himself, "If I kill the servant now, it will not effectively compensate for my son's offended honor. Everyone will say, 'What's the big deal? Who cares if the king killed a simple servant for offending his son's honor?'"

Therefore, the king decided that he would first promote the servant and appoint him to a ministerial post in the royal government. Next, he would pronounce him governor of one of the districts in his empire. Only then, once he had reached the apex, would the king hurl him down and have him executed! "This way, everyone will appreciate the severity of the servant's deed and also give homage to my son. It will be clear to all that even an honored minister will not escape punishment if he offends the prince's honor!" the king concluded.

This, Chazal teach us, was Hashem's objective when He elevated Haman to greatness. "If everyone will see that even such an honored minister as Haman will not elude punishment if he starts up with My children, the glory of My children will spread throughout the entire world!" With that goal, Hashem instilled in King Achashverosh's heart the desire to promote Haman the Agagite to greatness.

Indeed, this was the answer Hashem gave to the *midas hadin,* the angel of justice, when the angel came before Him to denounce Haman Harasha. "How can You allow Achashverosh

---

[8] Esther Rabbah 7:3

to aggrandize Haman, the *rasha* who came from Yerushalayim for the express purpose of sabotaging the renewed construction of the *Bais Hamikdash*?"[9] the *midas hadin* contended.

"Don't worry!" Hashem assured him. "I'm just letting Haman boast a bit, and then I will punish him for all the evil he himself and all his ancestors did to the Jewish nation!"[10]

Mordechai Would Neither Bow nor Prostrate Himself

At this stage, Haman felt rather good. He was pleased with his new position and delighted at the sight of everyone bowing before him. Only one thing cast a shadow on his happiness. There was one man in Shushan the capital who openly regarded Haman with contempt, one man who absolutely refused to bow to him, one man who would pass by him intentionally with his head proudly raised high. That person was none other than Mordechai.

---

[9] At the beginning of the chapter "In the Days of Achashverosh," we elaborated on the king's refusal to renew the construction of the *Bais Hamikdash*. In the same chapter, we cited the words of Chazal stating that Vashti was the one who prevented him from granting his sanction to the renewed construction. Now we find that Haman took part in that scheme as well; he too did whatever he could to block the work on the sanctuary. For that purpose, he traveled a great distance from Yerushalayim to Shushan and incited the king against the continued construction. Indeed, Chazal say that the letter of indictment that was sent to King Achashverosh, the missive mentioned in the book of Ezra (4:6), was actually dispatched by Haman Harasha and his ten sons.

[10] It comes out, then, that right from the start Haman deserved punishment because of the role he played in halting the construction of the *Bais Hamikdash*. The question arises – if Haman was deserving of death in any case, why didn't Hashem bring about his downfall before he had a chance to cause harm to the Jews and frighten them with his decree? The commentaries discuss this point (Anaf Yosef Esther Rabbah 6:2, in the name of the Ohr Chodosh) and explain that if Haman would have been killed before he instigated the decree, it never would have become known that he died for his sin! Therefore, Hashem arranged matters so that it would be clear to all that Haman's downfall came about as a result of his efforts to harm the Jewish people, Hashem's children.

Not only did Mordechai intentionally not bow down to Haman; he also made sure that no false impression would be created that he did so.[11] If Haman would happen to pass alongside Mordechai at a time when he was bent over or leaning on his side, the *tzaddik* was careful to immediately rise to his full height, in order to make it perfectly clear that *he does not prostrate himself to Haman*!

Furthermore, when Mordechai would notice a group of people prostrating themselves to the ground before Haman, he would rush over to where they were gathered and intentionally pass through the crowd standing erect, in order to emphasize for all to see that he intentionally refrains from prostrating himself before this *rasha*.

Haman Harasha, who noticed that Mordechai was not prostrating himself, understood that it would be beneath his dignity to make a commotion about it. Instead, he sidled up to Mordechai and passed right by him, so that it was absolutely clear the *tzaddik* saw him. "Surely Mordechai would not ignore me outright! He probably intends to claim that he did not notice me!" thought Haman to himself. But even when Haman positioned himself directly in front of Mordechai, the *tzaddik* would neither bow nor prostrate himself.[12]

Next, Haman decided to forgo his honor a bit. He went over to Mordechai, and, standing alongside him, addressed him as if he was responding to a greeting from Mordechai. "*Aleichem sholom*, peace be with you," Haman announced. But Mordechai immediately acted to correct any wrong impression that may

---

[11] Rishon Letzion
[12] Yalkut Esther 1054

have been created. "There is no peace for *resha'im!*" he stated clearly to Haman, then turned his back and walked away.

Mordechai did not only suffice with not bowing to Haman and refusing to greet him or return his greeting. Mordechai went even further. He degraded and disgraced Haman, reminding him at every opportunity that in fact, he – Haman – was Mordechai's servant. "Surely it would not be in place for a master to prostrate himself to his servant!" Mordechai asserted, displaying the document of sale signed in Haman's handwriting.[13]

How did it come about that Haman sold himself to Mordechai? The story goes back to a time in the distant past, when the two were alone in the desert, on their way back from a royal battle to which they had been sent together as generals. While Mordechai planned out his journey home intelligently, rationing his bread so he would have food available when he needed it, Haman Harasha conducted himself otherwise. Taking the attitude of "eat, drink and be merry for tomorrow you may die," he ate and drank whatever he wanted. And so, at a certain point, the provisions of Haman Harasha and his entourage were consumed to the last drop, while Mordechai still had a great deal of bread in his possession.

"Give me some of your bread!" Haman pleaded with Mordechai, but Mordechai was not quick to grant his request. "I will gladly split my bread with you," he said to the *rasha*, "but on one condition. If you want bread to eat, you will have to compensate me appropriately!"

"What do you want?" Haman asked suspiciously.

---

[13] Aggadas Esther

Without hesitation, Mordechai answered, "I want you as my servant! If you sign right now a bill of sale, stating that you sold yourself to me as a slave in exchange for a loaf of bread that I gave you in the desert, then I will give you a loaf to satiate your hunger right now." Starving, Haman agreed to Mordechai's condition.

Mordechai obviously did not travel through the desert with a supply of parchment scrolls in his kitbag. Instead, he wrote the document on the one item in his possession suitable for this purpose – the shoe on his foot. Mordechai pulled off the shoe, wrote on it the bill of sale, had Haman sign the statement, and put the shoe back on.

Now, years later, when Haman suddenly rose to a high rank and demanded that Mordechai bow down to him, all the latter needed to do was hold up his shoe to remind Haman which of the two ought to bow to the other.

As can be expected, Haman did not derive much pleasure at the sight of the document signed in his handwriting, which Mordechai made sure to wave in his face at every opportunity. Haman was ready to do anything, literally anything, in order to rid himself of any memory of that embarrassing episode. But Mordechai would not leave him alone. At every opportunity he would again display the document for all to see, to Haman Harasha's shame and fury.

Though it may seem that Mordechai would calmly and unconcernedly tease Haman and harass him day after day, Mordechai knew quite well that if Haman wanted to, he could ask the king to have him killed, as indeed occurred at the end.

Nevertheless, Mordechai did not back down; he absolutely and unequivocally refused to prostrate himself to Haman. "I do not bow to flesh and blood. I subordinate myself to no one other than the God of heaven and earth!" Mordechai proclaimed as a proud Jew, in the full knowledge that he was endangering his life.

In fact, Chazal explain[14] that the *nisoyon*, spiritual challenge, that Mordechai was faced with when he had to choose between bowing to Haman and risking his life corresponded to the terrible *nisoyon* faced by Yosef Hatzaddik in Mitzrayim, when the wife of Potiphar tried to incite him to sin! That is how weighty Mordechai Hatzaddik's challenge was, but he stood up to it courageously, steadfast in his decision and in his faith.[15]

But while we know that Mordechai stuck to his position religiously, his attitude towards Haman was not appreciated among his own people.

"Don't you understand the situation, Mordechai Hatzaddik?" the Jews desperately tried to persuade him. "Don't you see that you are likely to bring a calamity upon all of us if you incite the *rasha*'s anger? Can't you see how powerful he is now?" they argued.

But Mordechai wouldn't budge.[16] "You are right. The danger is great. But what is the alternative? To bow to Haman

---

[14] Esther Rabbah 7:7

[15] Just as Mordechai's *nisoyon* equaled that of Yosef's, so did his reward correspond to Yosef's reward. Both of them merited a high position in the royal court and the active rule over their land, with the king alone exceeding them in authority. Yosef was appointed second in command to the king, and Mordechai was handed the king's signet ring so that he could write whatever he saw fit and seal it in the king's name.

[16] Aggadas Esther

who declared himself a deity?! To bow to the idol engraved on his garments? Heaven forbid! I will not do so, no matter how great the risk!" Mordechai made his stand absolutely clear to his concerned fellow Jews.

Mordechai the Binyaminite Does not Bow to Esav

We can imagine what a storm Mordechai's conduct raised in the royal court. The servants, attendants, and officers were all talking about the old Jewish rabbi who was not afraid to belittle the honor of Haman and who absolutely refused to prostrate himself before him.

The subject was definitely the hot topic in all of Shushan, and the fact that everyone was busy talking about it certainly did not enhance Haman's honor. After all, when someone dares to openly show his contempt for the most esteemed minister, it says something about the extent of that minister's power.

One day, a few of the king's servants even went over to Mordechai and decided to ask him point blank if he was disobeying the king's order. "You understand, Mordechai, we too are not happy to have to kneel down before this Haman character. We are doing it only because the king explicitly ordered us to do so. Why do you think you have to be different from the rest of us and refrain from bowing to Haman?" the servants asked Mordechai,[17] the envy obvious in their words.[18]

---

[17] We cited earlier the opinion of the Yosef Lekach, which states that the command to bow to Haman was directed only towards those who met two conditions: One, that they were *servants of the king*, and two, that they sat *at the gate of the king*. Now, let us address the chain of events as it would be explained according to this opinion. Mordechai, as we know, was an officer of the king and also sat at the king's gate. Therefore, ostensibly, he should be included in the decree. But Mordechai argued

Mordechai was quick to answer and present his clearly thought out philosophy. "Haman, with all his glory and rank, is no more than flesh and blood, born of woman, dust of the earth, and destined to become eaten by worms! Do you really think that such a creature has a right to feel arrogant? Well, I believe he does not. I see no reason to bow to Haman, and I personally do not bow down to anyone but the God of heaven and earth!

"And in particular," Mordechai added, "since Haman presents himself as a deity, there is all the more reason why I cannot prostrate myself to him, due to the laws of our holy Torah that prohibit us from bowing before any idol or molten image!"[19]

---

that since he was a Jew, he was not considered a "servant of the king," since the Torah has already told us, "The people of Israel are servants to Me," (Vayikra 25:55) they are *My* servants, and not servants of other servants!

The servants of the king were up in arms at that response, since they perceived it as an offense to their honor, as if Mordechai considered himself greater than them. Therefore, in their envy, they rushed to report Mordechai's argument to Haman, in order to test out if his argument would stand up to Haman's wrath. That is what they meant when they said, "For he had told them *that he was a Jew*," and a Jew cannot be a servant.

[18] Ibn Yichyeh

[19] The Megillas S'sorim explains that Mordechai responded to the king's servants as follows: "The king certainly never intended that *he* should bow down to Haman since he was a Jew, and such prostration is prohibited to the Jews, and the king certainly respects the Jewish religion as an extremely honorable religion." The servants presented Mordechai's argument to Haman, in order to see if he would get an explicit order from the king relating specifically to the Jewish nation, but this argument infuriated the *rasha*. Therefore, he sought to destroy all the Jews in all the provinces of the king, so as to make it perfectly clear what the king's opinion was regarding the Jews and their religion.

In contrast, the Rishon Letzion on Megillas Esther writes that Mordechai explained to the king's servants that he cannot bow to Haman because of the image of an idol that was engraved on his garments. Bowing to such an idol contradicted the principles of the Jewish religion. In order to verify the truth of Mordechai's words, the servants of the king asked Haman to remove the idol from his clothing and then

"Excuse us, Mordechai," the servants answered him, "even your ancestors prostrated themselves to the ancestors of this Haman! What makes you any better than your forefathers?" they challenged.

Mordechai responded with a question of his own. "My forefathers? Bowed down to Haman's ancestors? It cannot be... perhaps you could explain to me what exactly you are talking about?" Mordechai asked.

The servants were quick to explain, "Your grandfather Yaakov prostrated himself before his brother Esav when he met him on his way to the land of Canaan.[20] This Haman is a descendant of Esav, so it is only fitting that you should do as your forefather did and prostrate yourself before Haman, as the king commanded!"

---

check to see if Mordechai would really bow to Haman. As a result of this "test," it became clear to Haman that "Mordechai would not bow or prostrate himself to *him*," i.e., he was not willing to bow down to Haman at all, unrelated to the presence of an idolatrous image on his garment.

The Malbim makes a similar point, but according to him, the king's servants understood that the only prostration that would be considered bowing to the idol or to the divinity of Haman was that which would take place upon seeing him from afar. Such prostration is devoid of any aspect of honor, since Haman would not see him bowing at all. On the other hand, when Haman came close, the king's servants understood that prostration before him would be for the sake of honoring him alone, and such prostration would not be prohibited. Therefore, they asked Haman to go close to Mordechai and see if he would prostrate himself before him. But Mordechai would not prostrate himself, since he refused to bow before any man. As we shall explain, he argued that he was from the tribe of Binyamin, who never bowed to anyone. In any case, the Malbim explains that even after Haman realized that Mordechai's refusal to bow to him was unconnected to his religion, he still sought to destroy all members of the Jewish religion, because their beliefs had served as Mordechai's "excuse" in explaining to the king's servants his refusal to bow.

[20] Bereishis 33

But here, Mordechai took the opportunity to point out the servants' mistake.[21] "When my grandfather Yaakov prostrated himself to Esav, my ancestor Binyamin had not yet been born. My grandfather Binyamin only came into the world at a later point, and he never bowed down to any mortal man![22] I too shall follow in his footsteps and will not bow down to any flesh and blood, no matter what!" After hearing his position, the servants rushed over to Haman to share Mordechai's words.

It Was Contemptible to Him

As expected, the *rasha* boiled with rage.[23] He wanted to get his revenge from Mordechai, but understood that taking private revenge would degrade him.

"If I want to really avenge myself on Mordechai," Haman said to himself, "I have to strike at him, at his friends the *talmidei chachomim*, and at the entire Jewish nation![24] Only then will my vengeance be complete!"

---

[21] Esther Rabbah 7:8; according to the Midrash, Mordechai said it to Haman himself.

[22] The king's pages reasoned that since "the fetus is considered a part of his mother," and when Yaakov met up with Esav Rochel was already in the midst of her final pregnancy with Binyamin, therefore, when Rochel prostrated herself to Esav, it would be considered as if Binyamin did so as well (Anaf Yosef).

[23] The Minchas Erev explains that Haman's fury burned within him in particular after he *saw* personally that Mordechai would not bow and prostrate himself to him. The report of the king's servants did not anger him as much, since, as we know, hearing is not like seeing firsthand.

The Yosef Lekach, on the other hand, explains that Haman became angry only when he saw Mordechai, because beforehand, he did not know that Mordechai was not bowing to him. When the servants of the king spoke to him, they did not report Mordechai's conduct explicitly; they spoke in vague terms and recommended that he take note of Mordechai's behavior when he sees him.

[24] Megillah 13b

Besides, Haman wanted to close another account he had with the Jews. Haman also wanted to take revenge on behalf of his grandfather Esav from Yaakov, Mordechai's ancestor, for having deceitfully taken his blessings as well as his birthright.[25]

---

[25] Targum

THE LOT IS CAST

"In the first month, the month of Nisan, in the twelfth year of King Achashverosh's reign, a lot was cast before Haman, from day to day and from month to month, [coming to] the twelfth month – the month of Adar." (3:7)

Once Haman decided to destroy the Jewish people, he set out to put his plan into action. The first issue he had to deal with was choosing which would be the most auspicious day to bring the Jews to their downfall. Therefore, he decided to cast lots in order to determine the answer to this question.[1]

In the beginning,[2] Haman figured he would choose the day of the week to implement his plan based on the *mazal* of the day.[3] If one day of the week would prove auspicious for

---

[1] Haman cast the lot before he came to the king, since it would not be fitting to come before the king with a suggestion that was not workable (Ralbag).

[2] There is some discussion regarding the date on which Haman cast the lot. The commentaries seem to indicate that it took place on the thirteenth day of Nisan, and on that same day, the decree was made and the letters sent out. However, the Midrash (Esther Rabbah 6:13) explains that the king pushed Haman off at first, and was not persuaded until Haman came to nudge him again and again. According to this opinion, it would seem that the matter did not evolve in one day, leading us to assume that the lots were cast some time before the decree was issued.

[3] The Perush HaGra explains that Haman did not seek a day when the *mazal* of the Jews was low, since he knew that the Jews were above *mazal*, as Hashem told Avraham when he claimed that his astrology showed he was not destined to bear a son (Shabbos 156a). Therefore, Haman only sought a day when *his own mazal* was at its peak, with the assumption that on such a day, his *mazal* would empower him to succeed in his plan to destroy the Jewish people. The commentary of Yosef Lekach, on the other hand, maintains otherwise. He says that Haman figured the *mazal* of the Jews was indeed at a nadir at that point; after all, they had been exiled from their land and their sanctuary burned to the ground. Nevertheless, he did not rely

destroying the Jews according to the lottery, he thought, the date would not be significant.[4]

Therefore, Haman called Shamshi the scribe[5] and instructed him to cast lots for each day, to determine if he would be successful at destroying the Jewish people on that day.[6]

---

on the fact that the Jews were at an unlucky point, but rather sought a day when his *mazal* would be good, since on such a day all the circumstances would work to his advantage – both the Jews' bad fortune, and his own good fortune.

[4] Chazal explain the lot in this way both in the Targum Sheini and the Midrash. The Perush HaGra adds that according to the simple meaning of the verses, Haman first cast a lot *"from day to day,"* i.e., to determine on which day of the month he could succeed to destroy the Jews. After the lot fell on the thirteenth day of the month, he cast another lot *"from month to month,"* in order to determine in which month his *mazal* would be the strongest to carry out his dastardly plan.

The Malbim adds a proof that Haman started out by casting a lot for the day. We see, he explains, that since Hashem wanted to save His children and give them a chance to repent, He caused the lot to fall each time on the latest possible date. Haman began the lot of the days on the day of the month that was closest to him at that particular time. Since the lot was cast on the thirteenth of Nisan, he began the lots from the fourteenth, and when he came to the end of the month, he started again from the first, until the lot fell on the last possible day – the thirteenth. The same was true by the months; the lot fell on the month that was furthest from him – the month of Adar. The Malbim emphasizes that had the lot of the months been cast before the lot of the days, it would have fallen on the twenty ninth of Adar, since first the month of Adar would have been chosen, and then the last day of the month – the twenty ninth.

In contrast, the Yosef Lekach maintains that there was just one lot cast. Haman regarded the day on which he cast the lot – the thirteenth of the month – as the ideal day of the month. It was left for him only to cast lots as to which month would be most auspicious for destroying the Jews on its thirteenth day.

[5] Targum Sheini

[6] Had Haman drawn lots in the usual way, picking out one of seven slips of paper on which the names of the days of the week were inscribed, the lot would necessarily have fallen on one of the days; no other possibility existed. Therefore, we have to say that he did not draw lots from *among the days*, but rather cast lots on each day with two possible outcomes – *"will succeed"* or *"will not succeed."* The same was evidently done in regard to the months.

However, the Anaf Yosef (Esther Rabbah 7:13) explains the lottery system in an entirely different fashion. He understands that Haman held two lotteries: the first was the lot of the days, in which he chose one of the 354 days of the year. By simple arithmetic, he could then determine to which calendar date this number corresponds. For example, day ten falls out on the tenth of Nisan, ten days from

But to Haman's great surprise, the lot did not point to any day of the week. Each day had its own merit which entitled the Jewish people to be spared.[7]

A Lot from Day to Day

Shamshi attempted to cast the lot on the first day of the week, as per Haman's instructions. But when the heavenly minister appointed over the first day of the week heard about it, he appeared before the Creator and said to Him:

"Master of the Universe, the heavens and earth were created on the first day of Creation. It says about them,[8] 'If not for My covenant day and night, I would not have set up the ordinances of heaven and earth.' This refers to the covenant with the Jewish people of *bris milah* and the Torah. Therefore, if You wish to destroy the Jewish people, You will first have to uproot the heavens and the earth!

"And besides," the minister of the first day of the week went on to argue, "You have already said,[9] 'If the heavens above shall be measured, and the foundations of the earth probed, I too shall reject the seed of Israel for all they have done, so states

---

the beginning of the year, and so on. The second lottery was for the months, and in that one, Haman chose one of the months by lots. In order for the lot to take effect, Haman had to arrive at a situation in which the day that came out in the lot of days fell out in the same month that was drawn in the lot of months. Indeed, the thirteenth of Adar emerged from the lot of days, and the month of Adar in the lot of months.

[7] We did not exhaust all of the many opinions on the matter of the lots, since "the ink will be used up before we complete the task...." We brought a few examples in each area, just as an idea of how broad the topic really is. In the entire subject of the lots, we merged the opinions of the Midrashim (Esther Rabbah 7:12 and the Yalkut) and the various Targumim.

[8] Yirmiyahu 33:25

[9] Yirmiyahu 31:36

Hashem.' Just as it is not feasible to measure the height of the heavens or the depth of the earth, so shall You never reject the seed of Israel!" His argument was accepted, and the lot did not fall on the first day.

Haman tried his luck on the second day of the week. The heavenly minister of the second day pleaded, "Master of the Universe, on the second day of Creation You made a separation between the upper waters and the lower ones, just as You separated the Jews and the nations, as You wrote in Your Torah,[10] 'I have separated you from the nations to be Mine.' Therefore, if You wish to destroy the Jewish nation that You separated for Yourself, You first ought to undo the first separation – the separation between the upper waters and the lower ones!"

His argument too was accepted, and the lot did not fall on the second day of the week.

The scene repeated itself when Haman attempted to cast the lot on the third day of the week. Standing before Hashem, the minister cited the merit of the Jewish people who set aside *terumos* and *ma'asros*, priestly offerings and tithes, from the various growing things created on the third day of Creation. He cited as well the praise they sing before their Creator with the fruit of the trees created on that day, with the four species of *lulav* and *esrog* on the festival of Sukkos.

"Furthermore," the minister of the third day said,[11] "on the third day of Creation the waters spread out upon the earth were

---

[10] Vayikra 20:26
[11] The Targum Sheini also points out that on the third day, the Garden of Eden was created, and therefore, the minister argued, it would not be appropriate to destroy the Jewish people on the very day when the reward for *tzaddikim* in the World to Come was prepared.

gathered into one place. For the people of Israel You veered from the natural course of the world and split the waters! If the merit of the Jewish people – which is greater than that of the seas and rivers, which were split before them – does not stand in their stead, how can we possibly continue to exist?" And so the lot did not fall on the third day either.

Next came the turn of the minister of the fourth day. He too had a foolproof argument to offer: "Master of the Universe, the luminaries were created on me, and the entire purpose of their creation was to serve the Jewish people! And besides, the people of Israel are compared to the stars! If You decimate the Jews, by what merit will the luminaries continue to exist?" His argument was accepted and the lot did not fall on the fourth day of the week.

The minister of the fifth day drew on the merit of the *korbonos*, the burnt offerings. "Master of the Universe, the birds the Jews use as *korbonos* were created on the fifth day. If the Jewish people will be destroyed, who will offer *korbonos*?" The lot did not fall on the fifth day either.[12]

Needless to say, when Haman attempted to cast the lot on the sixth day of the week, the minister of this day as well rushed to the fore, saying, "Master of the Universe, on the sixth day You created *adam*, man. You called Your children '*adam*,' but the nations of the world do not deserve this title! Therefore, if You wish to destroy the Jewish nation, You will first have to wipe out all of mankind from the face of the earth!" The

---

[12] The Targum mentions that the merit of the fifth day was that on this day the *livyoson* and the *shor habar* were created, from which Hashem will prepare a meal for the *tzaddikim* at the end of days. Here too, the minister of the day asserted, if the Jewish people will be destroyed, these creations will have been proven extraneous.

argument of the minister of the sixth day was accepted as well; the lot did not fall on his day.

Now all that was left for Haman was to try and cast the lot on the last day of the week – Shabbos. "The holy day of Shabbos serves as a covenant between You and the Jewish nation for all generations!" the minister of Shabbos cried to Hashem. "If You wish to destroy them, You will have to first destroy the Shabbos day!" The lot did not fall on Shabbos either.

At this point, Haman understood that if he insisted on hinging his decision on a day of the week, he would never be able to destroy the Jewish people. None of the days would allow him to use its *mazal* in order to wipe out the Jews!

The Lot from Month to Month

Once Haman understood this, he decided to hinge his *mazal* on the months of the year[13] instead of the days of the week. He began to cast lots on each month, attempting to locate the month in which his *mazal* would enable him to destroy the nation of Mordechai.

But in the lottery of the months as well, Haman did not meet with much success.[14] Most of the months drew out a

---

[13] The Anaf Yosef (Esther Rabbah 7:13) follows this opinion, explaining that Haman first tried to hinge his *mazal* on the days of the week, and then, when he saw that on each day a merit was found for the Jews to save them from this decree and push aside the day's *mazal*, he decided to try hinging the decree on the months. But in each of the months as well, a merit was found for the Jews – except for the month of Adar, when no merit could be found.

[14] The Aggadas Esther explains that Haman specifically searched for a month in which *no miracles had ever been done for the Jews*, and he found that – aside from the month of Adar - they had merited miracles every month of the year. For details of the miracles done every month, refer to the above source. We did not bring the entire discussion here, since we have already devoted much space to the subject.

merit for the Jewish people and made it clear that due to this merit, their *mazal* would not work for Haman if he sought to destroy the Jews.

The month of Nisan mentioned the merit of the festival of Pesach, during which the Jewish people demonstrated their faith in the Creator when they prepared the sheep idolized by the Egyptians for sacrifice and circumcised their flesh before they left Mitzrayim. They were not concerned with the danger it entailed!

The month of Iyar cited the merit of Pesach Sheini, which proves the love of the Jews for their Creator's commandments. They came of their own accord to seek counsel on how to avoid missing out on the opportunity to offer the *korbon* Pesach even though they were ritually unclean, and they were then given the *mitzvah* of Pesach Sheini. In addition, there was the merit of the *man,* the heavenly food that began to fall in the month of Iyar for the Jewish people in the wilderness.

The month of Sivan roused the merit of the Torah that was given during this month, while the months of Tamuz and Av argued that they had already suffered enough from the tragedies that occurred during their months – five calamities that took place in the month of Tamuz and another five in the month of Av.[15]

When Haman tried to hinge his plot on the *mazal* of Elul, the minister of this month reminded him that Rosh Hashanah for the tithing of animals falls out in this month,[16] and also that

---

[15] Mishna Ta'anis 4:6. The Targum points out in addition that in the month of Av, the generation of the wilderness ceased dying, and this merit was also cited as a reason that the Jews should not be destroyed in this month.

[16] Rosh Hashanah 1:1; the implication of this is that one may not take animals that were born before Rosh Chodesh Elul as a tithe for animals born afterwards.

the construction of the wall of Yerushalayim was completed then.[17] In addition, Moshe Rabbenu went up at this time to receive the second *luchos*.

The month of Tishrei, replete as it is with merits, certainly had no lack of merits to bring up – the *shofar*, the fast of Yom Kippur, the festival of Sukkos. Even the month of Cheshvan managed to summon up the merit of Sarah Imeinu who passed away during that month following the *satan's* report to her about *akeidas Yitzchok*. Her death is a reminder of the merit of the *akeidah*.[18] The month of Cheshvan also cited the merit of Noach who was saved from the Great Flood that began in that month.

The month of Kislev called upon the merit of the days of Chanukah,[19] though it lay in the future, at which time the Jews would light flames to remind us of Hashem's miracles. Kislev also pointed out the merit of the construction of the *Bais Hamikdash* that began during that month. The month of Teves brought up the merit of Ezra who, during that month, separated from their midst the gentile women whom a small number of Jews had married. This month also argued that it had paid its due with the tragedy that the Jews suffered when Nevuchadnetzar began his siege on Yerushalayim during Teves.

Tu Bishevat, the fifteenth day of Shevat that serves as Rosh Hashanah for the trees, was pointed out as a merit by the month

---

[17] Nechemiah 6:15

[18] Aside from that, we already mentioned how two major calamities are not visited on the Jews in the same month (Anaf Yosef, ibid).

[19] Even though the miracle of Chanukah happened many years later, Hashem summoned up its merit already at this point.

of Shevat. Also cited was the fact that on the twenty third day of that month, the Jews gathered, removed Michah's false image from their midst, and battled with the tribe of Binyamin over the incident of the concubine in Givah.

Now, all that remained was the month of Adar, and this month indeed did not succeed in finding a merit in its favor. At that time, before the miraculous deliverance from Haman's decree, the month of Adar was devoid of any festival or celebration, nor did it hold any other special merit.

When Haman discovered this fact, his heart filled with joy. "Marvelous!" he exclaimed. "Finally, I've managed to find a month when no merit will come forward for the Jews to save them from my decree!" But before settling the date finally, he wished to check if the month of Adar was fitting in terms of its astrological *mazal* for the destruction of the Jewish people.

To his gratification, he found that the *mazal* of Adar as well was ideal; it had nothing within it that might rouse a merit for the Jews.

The *mazal* of the sheep – the sign of Nisan – recalls the merit of the lamb that the Jews would offer as the *korbon* Pesach.

The *mazal* of the ox – the sign of Iyar – might rouse the merit of Yosef who is called "*shor*," an ox, as it says, "The firstborn of the ox, he is noble,"[20] as well as the merit of the many *korbonos* offered from oxen.

By the *mazal* of the twins – the sign of the month of Sivan – the Jews might be protected by the merit of Peretz and Zerach,

---

[20] Devorim 33:17

the children of Yehuda from Tamar, about whom the Torah says, "Behold there were twins in her womb."[21]

The *mazal* of the crab – the sign of Tamuz – would be sufficient to raise the merit of Moshe Rabbenu, since just as the crab is found in water, so was the redeemer of Israel drawn from the water.

The *mazal* of the lion – the sign of Av – recalled Daniel, a member of the tribe of Yehuda who is called "the lion's cub."[22] The people of Israel as a whole are also compared to a lion, as Bilaam said in his metaphoric prophecy, "The nation shall rise like a great lion and pick itself up like a young lion."[23]

The *mazal* of the virgin – the sign of Elul – brings to mind Chananiah, Misha'el and Azariah, who were connected only to Hashem.

The *mazal* of the scales – the sign of Tishrei – alludes to Iyov, whose suffering, if it were to be weighed on a scale, would exceed the weight of all the sand on the seashore.[24]

The *mazal* of the scorpion – the sign of Cheshvan – recalls the merit of Daniel who rebuked the Jews even though they fought him like scorpions who sting their enemies from all sides.[25]

The *mazal* of the bow – the sign of the month of Kislev – also reminds us of the merit of Yosef, about whom the Torah writes, "His bow abides in strength."[26]

---

[21] Bereishis 38:27
[22] Bereishis 49:9
[23] Bamidbar 23:24
[24] Iyov 6:2
[25] Yechezkel 2:6
[26] Bereishis 49:24

The *mazal* of the young goat – the sign of Teves – brings up the merit of Yaakov, who used goatskin garments in order to gain his father's blessings, as instructed by his mother Rivkah.

The *mazal* of the bucket – the sign of Shevat – returns us to the merit of Moshe, who drew water for the daughters of Yisro from the well in Midyan.[27]

The only remaining *mazal* was the fish – the sign of the month of Adar – and indeed, no merit could be found in that for the Jews.[28]

"A perfect match!" Haman thought gleefully. "No merit for the Jews can be found in the month of Adar, and even its *mazal* – the fish – does not recall any particular merit. Aha! Now I can certainly carry out my plan and destroy the Jewish people!

"And on top of that, it was in the month of Adar that Moshe Rabbenu, the great redeemer of the Jews, passed away.[29] That is certainly a good sign for me! Just as their redeemer died during

---

[27] Shmos 2:19

[28] Actually, a merit could be found in the *mazal* of this month as well, as we find that Yaakov blessed Yosef with the *bracha*, "And they will multiply like fish" (Bereishis 48:16). Furthermore, the Jews are compared to fish, since just as the entire life source of the fish is in the water, so is the entire life source of the Jews in the Torah which is compared in many places to water (Anaf Yosef, ibid).

[29] Even though we explained earlier that a month in which a tragedy already occurred is not a candidate for another major calamity, Haman was happy that the lot fell on the month of Adar when Moshe Rabbenu passed away. He calculated as follows: Both the year when Moshe died and the present year, when Haman sought to destroy the Jewish nation, were leap years, and therefore each contained two months of Adar. Now, while the decree of Haman was scheduled to take place in the first Adar – since, as we mentioned, it was Nisan at the time and he set his decree for twelve months later – the death of Moshe Rabbenu had taken place in the second Adar. Haman figured that the *mazal* of the two Adars is identical, and that it is a bad *mazal* for the Jews since Moshe died during that *mazal*. On the other hand, the tragedy would not preclude another tragedy, since the death of Moshe actually took place in the second Adar which is a different *time*.

this month, so will they themselves be wiped out in the month of Adar. The *mazal* of the month, the sign of the fish, is also a good omen. Just as the fish in the sea swallow each other, so will I be able to swallow up the Jews during this month!" Haman chose to execute his plan on the thirteenth day of the month of Adar.[30]

But what Haman did not know was that while Moshe *died* on the seventh day of the second Adar, he was *born* on the seventh day of the *first* Adar. Thus, during the first Adar, the Jews were protected by the merit of Moshe Rabbenu's birth, while during the second Adar, the decree could not fall upon them since that month had already suffered a calamity with the death of Moshe (Y'aros D'vash, part 2, derush 2).

The Y'aros D'vash explains the matter from another angle as well. He says that at first, Haman thought Moshe was born in Nisan (since, as we know, Yocheved gave birth at the beginning of her seventh month; that is how she was able to conceal him for three months). Therefore, Haman thought that the *mazal* of Adar was bad for the Jews because their leader died in this month in an unnatural way, since by nature he should have died on the same date he was born. But the truth is that Moshe Rabbenu *did* die on the same date he was born, on the seventh of Adar, and such a natural death does not indicate a bad *mazal* for the month, since everyone dies eventually.

[30] At the beginning of this chapter, we cited the words of the Gra, the Yosef Lekach and the Y'aros D'vash explaining why Haman chose the thirteenth day of the month in particular. Their views do not agree with the words of the Midrash brought in the text above describing the system of the lots. It turns out, therefore, that if we follow the approach of the Midrash, we would still have to explain why Haman chose the *thirteenth* day of Adar in particular, and not any other day in this month that would come up in the lottery.

Regarding this point, the Anaf Yosef (Esther Rabbah 7:17) cites in the name of the Ohr Chodosh that since the merit of Pesach defended the Jews so that Haman could not destroy them in the month of Nisan, Haman refrained from setting the decree for the thirty days preceding the festival as well, since during that time it is customary to study the laws of the festival and therefore they are already considered part and parcel of the festival. If we count back thirty days before Pesach, we reach the fourteenth day of Adar, since there are fourteen days in the month of Nisan until Pesach, and in Adar, which is a shorter month consisting of twenty nine days, there are another sixteen days from the fourteenth to the twenty ninth.

On the other hand, Haman did not want to set the decree for a date before the seventh of Adar, since Moshe Rabbenu died on the seventh; until then, he was still alive and his merit protected the Jewish people. Nor did he want to decree the destruction of Moshe's nation during the seven days following the seventh of Adar, the seven days of mourning for Moshe's death, since during those seven days the merit of the *tzaddik* still defends the members of his generation and his

However, Haman forgot to take two details into account.

For one thing, he forgot that just as the redeemer of Israel passed away in the month of Adar, he was also born in this same month, and this would certainly stand the Jewish people in good stead!

Secondly, while it is true that fish swallow one another, he forgot there are two sides to the coin. Some fish are the ones doing the swallowing, and others are being swallowed! Indeed, at the end, Haman Harasha was swallowed up by the Jews.

In fact, the downfall of Haman was hinted at already at this point, when he cast the lots on the Jews "to terrify and destroy them." The language in the *megillah* reads, "He cast lots – **hu hagoral** – this (literally, '*he,*') was the lot." Hinted here is that the lot fell on Haman himself, designating him to be taken to his death in place of the Jews.

Hashem Wants Repentance

As far as he was concerned, Haman was certain he had found the perfect day on which he would undoubtedly succeed in destroying the Jewish nation. The date chosen had only one disadvantage: Haman had to wait a full year for the day when he could carry out his plan. The lots were drawn in the month of Nisan, while the date for his decimation of the Jews was set for the month of Adar, a year later!

---

congregation. The only day that remained for him to choose was the thirteenth of Adar, the day on which the mourning for Moshe had concluded (since, as we know, part of a day is considered equivalent to a full day in these *halachos*) and the thirty days preceding Pesach had not yet begun.

But Haman was prepared to rally all his patience. It was worth the wait to be able to carry out his plan to perfection!

Still, Haman certainly did not plan to waste the time that remained at his disposal; much work lay ahead of him. He had to persuade the king to agree to the decree, he had to publicize the details of the plan, and so on. All of these tasks would take time – which Haman now had available in abundance.

The Ibn Ezra points out the underlying reason why Haman chose to try to destroy the Jewish people in the month of Adar. "The real reason why the lot fell out in this way is because the judgment was from Hashem, and Hashem extended the time so that the Jews would repent and be saved." The blow they suffered was only meant to rouse them to repent, but at no time did Hashem really intend to destroy His beloved nation!

As Chazal tell us, a *bas kol,* a voice from Heaven, was issued from Hashem, announcing, "Do not fear, community of Israel, and do not be disconsolate. If you return to Hashem, you will be delivered from every sorrow and calamity, and your enemies will take your place and the fate earmarked for you will fall upon them."

HAMAN INCITES THE KING

> *"Then Haman said to King Achashverosh, 'There is a certain nation scattered and dispersed among the peoples in all the provinces of your kingdom. Their laws are different from those of all other peoples, and they do not follow the laws of the king; it is not befitting the king to tolerate them. If it pleases the king, let it be written that they be wiped out, and I will measure out ten thousand silver talents into the hands of those who perform the duties to deposit in the king's treasury.' The king removed the signet ring from his hand and gave it to Haman ben Hamedasa the Agagite, the enemy of the Jews. And the king said to Haman, 'The silver is given to you, and the nation as well, to do with as you see fit.'" (3:8-11)*

The first challenge that Haman faced on the way to his desired goal of destroying the Jewish nation was rallying the king's support for his plan. In order to accomplish that task, Haman used his exceptional talent of persuasion. "There is no greater master than Haman in the art of *loshon hora*, slanderous talk."[1]

Haman opened his speech with the words, *"yeshno am echad,"* there is a certain nation. In this phrase, Chazal[2] find a hint to Haman's first argument to King Achashverosh. The

---

[1] Megillah 13b
[2] Esther Rabbah 7:12

word *yeshno* is interpreted as being related to *shenah*, sleep.[3] Haman claimed to the king that the "*Echad,*" i.e., the one God, is already sleeping and no longer looking after the Jews.

Haman then explained why Achashverosh could only benefit by commanding that the Jews be destroyed.

Haman described the Jewish customs in a demeaning, bigoted tone, defaming their character.[4] He said to King

---

[3] Another interpretation brought by Chazal on these lines is cited in the Gemara (13b), but there Chazal explain that Haman intended to point out that the *Jews* were dozing off from the *mitzvos*, i.e., that *yeshno* is not an allusion to the slumber of Hashem, but rather to the slumber of the Jews. Achashverosh was still concerned, however, since, as he claimed, there must certainly be some *talmidei chachomim* among the Jewish nation who keep all the *mitzvos*. But Haman allayed his fears, explaining that the Jews are *am echad,* one nation, so that even if *tzaddikim* exist, they are held responsible for the sins of the *resha'im* and are destined to be caught up in their blame.

[4] The different commentaries dwell on the simple explanation of the words of the verses, "There is a certain nation scattered and dispersed among the peoples in all the provinces of your kingdom. Their laws are different from those of all other peoples, and they do not follow the laws of the king; it is not befitting the king to tolerate them." What follows is a compilation of their words (Perush HaGra, Yosef Lekach, Minchas Erev and more):

"There is a certain nation" – A nation that is isolated unto itself, without any blood relatives among the other peoples, so you need not be concerned that their relatives will join up with them and resist the king.

"Scattered" – This nation is not concentrated in one location; therefore it would be hard for them to pose any effective resistance to the decree. Consequently, the battle to destroy them should not entail much loss of life on our side. The Gemara also mentions that Haman allayed the king's concern that the decree would leave an unpopulated "bald spot" in the center of his realm since the Jews are not a recognizable entity in any one place.

"Dispersed" – This nation does not intermarry with members of other peoples, so they do not have any marital connections with non-Jews and nobody will come to their aid. The Gemara explains that Haman's intention in using the term *meforad* was to point out that the Jewish nation is like a *pirda,* a mule, who cannot bear offspring, i.e., they are unproductive.

"Among the peoples" – This nation is not considered an independent people; therefore, the honor of the king will not be diminished by people saying that he now rules over one less people.

"In all the provinces of your kingdom" – All the Jews are under your rule, so you are

Achashverosh, "Your Majesty! In the vast expanse of your realm, there is a certain small nation that is scattered and dispersed. As tiny as they are in number compared to the people of the empire, their influence is felt in every place. Their dress is strange, their language is foreign,[5] and all the peoples of the empire suffer from their corruption. This nation is none other than the Jews,[6] and I have an excellent suggestion to discuss

---

in a position to carry out the decree of destruction in the most perfect way possible, without leaving a single remnant or lingering trace of the Jewish nation.

"Their laws are different from those of all other peoples" – That is why the other nations despise them so, and none of them will be inclined to rebel against you or be angered by your action.

"And they do not follow the laws of the king" – They do not take part in the royal work assignments, so no economic loss will be incurred by their destruction either.

"It is not befitting the king to tolerate them" – As regarding their taxation, there too the king need not be concerned for a loss, since they do not pay taxes, and besides, Haman was willing to measure out ten thousand silver talents to the royal treasury to counter a loss of this kind.

The Ralbag brings a slightly different explanation. According to his words, all of Haman's slander revolved around one axle: the damage the king is likely to suffer from the Jews and the lack of benefit derived from them. He points out that they are "one" – that the members of their nation are always of one mind and can easily make a united front to rebel against the king. On the other hand, they are "scattered" and can be found in every corner of the empire, such that it would be easy for them to organize such a plot. "Their laws are different" – they do not decry revolutionary activity; in fact, they might even encourage their members to kill anyone who does not join their ranks.

[5] Malbim

[6] The words of Chazal and the Targum Sheini delineating the specifics of Haman's *loshon hora* seem to imply that Haman related explicitly to the Jewish nation when he spoke, presenting their festivals and their strange customs. But the Perush HaGra writes that Haman spoke only of "a certain nation" without mentioning them by name, since he was concerned that due to the king's close connections with Mordechai, he would refuse to issue a decree of destruction on Mordechai's nation.

The Yosef Lekach takes a similar approach, but he writes that Haman's concern flowed from the esteemed status of the Jews among the nations, a status that might deter the king from killing them out. He adds also that Haman relied on the fact that the king would not be able to verify which nation was under discussion as it would be considered beneath him to do so; the king was expected to weigh each decision on its own merits, not based on the identity of the accused.

with you regarding this people: Let's wipe them off the face of the earth![7] Yes, as simple as that!

---

[7] This is the simple explanation as it emerges from the Midrashim in Chazal. But the commentaries offer other opinions, according to which Haman at first did not ask the king to destroy the Jewish nation. Rather, he slyly veiled his intentions by using ambiguous language in order to test the king's reaction to his request. Only then did he spell out exactly what he wanted to do to the Jews.

This is the approach of the Minchas Erev, who explains that Haman asked the king that it be written regarding the Jews "*l'abdom*," that they be wiped out. This word can be understood in two ways, either as "to wipe *them* out," i.e., to kill the Jews, as was his true intention, or as "to wipe out *from them*," i.e., to divest them of their riches. In fact, King Achashverosh understood that a particular, sinister intention lay behind Haman's ambiguous words, but nevertheless he granted him full authority to do with the Jews as he saw fit.

The Yosef Lekach takes a similar angle, explaining that Haman specifically used the word *l'abdom* since it sounds exactly like the same word with the letter *ayin*, which means "enslaving." Thus, Haman could safely feel out the king's standpoint regarding the Jews, and based on the results, he would decide if he could ask Achashverosh to "destroy, slay and exterminate" all the Jews. If the king would react angrily to the suggestion, Haman could always claim that he never intended to kill the Jews, Heaven forbid, but rather to sell them as slaves so as to enhance the royal coffers. But once again, we see that the king authorized Haman to do with the Jews as he pleased, though he understood full well that his intention was not the least bit innocent.

The Yosef Lekach points out that from here we can see the tremendous kindness that Hashem bestowed upon us. The exchange between Haman and Achashverosh accentuates the deep trust the king bore to Haman Harasha, so much so that it led him to grant the villain a sweeping authorization to do whatever he wanted with an entire population, without any concern for the results! King Achashverosh was convinced that Haman had only the benefit of the king and his kingdom in mind. That being the case, we can begin to fathom the extent of the miracle, when, just a short while later, the king ordered Haman strung up on a tree like a common criminal, after subjecting him to an experience of degrading humiliation in the streets of Shushan!

As we see, the above two commentaries both explain that at the end, the decision to destroy the Jews was mutually accepted by the king and Haman. In contrast, the Megillas S'sorim writes that Haman used the word *l'abdom* which can refer to the destruction of their souls, i.e., spiritual decimation. According to the Megillas S'sorim, even when the king agreed to accept Haman's suggestion, it never occurred to him to physically exterminate the Jews, but rather to destroy their souls, and even this goal he hoped to accomplish in a "civilized manner" – by getting them to willingly convert. Haman, on the other hand, commanded that anyone who would refuse to give up his religion would be killed, taking advantage of the blanket approval given to him by the king who did not understand the true intentions of the enemy of the Jews. The Malbim offers a similar explanation.

"This nation is a people without a home and without a state; their disappearance from the pages of history will not leave any traces behind. Besides, nobody gains any benefit from this people, so they will not be missed by anyone. Why keep them around?

"And if you were to say, Your Majesty, that you see no reason to provoke the Jews and decree their extermination just because you don't see any use for them, I believe you will change your mind when you hear a bit about their way of life and their bizarre customs.

"First of all, 'work' is not in the Jews' lexicon at all. Lazy by nature, they seek nothing for themselves but a life of idleness and pleasures! As soon as word leaks out about a general draft of workers for the State, they quickly hide out in their homes, gripped by the terrible fear that they might have to contribute in some small way to the country they live in. Parasites – that's what they are!

"Even if we manage to lay our hands on some Jew, by some stroke of luck on a day that is neither Shabbos nor a festival of some kind, and we succeed in forcing him to take part in the royal labor force, his work hours will be rather limited. When he wakes up in the morning, he has to say *kri'as shema* for a full hour. Then he has to pray for another whole hour.[8] The third hour of the day is dedicated to *pas shacharis*, a satisfying breakfast, which the Jews are very meticulous about, followed of course in the fourth hour by *birkas hamazon*, the blessing

---

[8] The Yalkut cites that Haman also had a critique on the text of the prayers. He pointed out to the king that the Jews pray for the defeat of the wicked – and it is actually the king they have in mind. They also praise their Creator for being a King Who loves charity and judgment – their intention being to hint at their desire that He pass judgment on the king and his ministers.

after meals. Only in the fifth hour can he begin his work, which concludes already in the sixth.

"The most annoying thing of all," Haman went on to fan the king's fury, "is that the same Jew who didn't do a thing all day, except perhaps for one single hour of unhurried work, comes home in the seventh hour of the day and is greeted by his doting wife who says, '*Oy*, my poor husband! Sit down and let me serve you a hot meal! You must be exhausted after slaving away in the service of this wicked king, may his name be blotted out!' The Jews have the nerve yet to complain about the work that is imposed on them, can you believe it?

"Furthermore, these Jews, who may appear to you to be innocent and harmless, are not really as they seem. Deep inside, they are corrupt, interested in nothing else but undoing the king and his empire![9]

"If you want proof, just try offering any Jew wine that was poured out by his royal Majesty or a dish that was cooked in his royal kitchen. The Jew will reject the offer out of hand, explaining that his Torah prohibits him from eating or drinking anything handled by a gentile.

"See how repulsive we are to them! If a fly would fall into a Jew's goblet, he would scoop it out and drink the remaining wine. But if the king touched his cup of wine, the Jew would immediately spill the wine out on the ground!

---

[9] "And they do not follow the laws of the king" – The commentary Ibn Yichyeh adds also that Haman implied in these words that they do not fulfill the king's most recent and most urgent command – to bow down to him, to Haman, as the king ordered. But if we would think that the king would pick up on the motives of self-interest that lay behind Haman's words, we would be gravely mistaken; he did not relate to this point at all.

"For the very same reason, they do not allow us to take their daughters as wives, nor are they willing to marry our daughters. We are like lepers to them! And I'll tell you something else, confidentially," Haman said with great emphasis, lowering his voice to a rumbling whisper. "When they see one of us, they spit on the ground in contempt!

"Aside from all this, Your Majesty," Haman went on, "you ought to know that these people are constantly celebrating festivals of one sort or another. Almost every month they have a festival or fast day, or some other reason for a party or a mourning session. That's without even mentioning their weekly Shabbos and the festive *Rosh Chodesh* days that occur month after month!

"Now, if the Jews would celebrate their festivals along with observing our holidays, the festivals of the gentiles, one could perhaps excuse them and say that no harm is done by the fact that they keep all their religious rituals. After all, everyone knows that as an enlightened and democratic monarch, you let every people adhere to its own religion.

"But the Jews aren't like that. They celebrate their own festivals in grand pomp and fine style, but when it comes to our holidays, they degrade them, without giving any consideration at all! Isn't that reason enough to sentence them to death?" Haman argued.

But he did not stop there; he kept up his vicious slander. "On top of that, Your Majesty, do you have any idea what these customs are that your Jewish subjects practice on their festival days? Let me tell you a little about them. When you hear, you will be absolutely shocked! Why, it is absolutely outrageous!

"For one thing, every seventh day is Shabbos for them. They don't do a stitch of work on that day, and they certainly evade any labor for the king. You can easily understand why the Jews are so fond of their Shabbos day," Haman Harasha said snidely. "On Shabbos, they pamper themselves with fine foods, meat and fish, and while the food is still between their teeth, they sit and mock us, the gentiles, who work hard for a living every day of the week.

"There are special prayers that the Jews say on the Shabbos day when they take out the Torah scroll and read from it, as well as from the *haftorah*, the Prophets. And all their readings deal with one subject alone - the curses that should be cast on the head of the king!

"Furthermore, they also mark the day of *Rosh Chodesh* with lengthy prayers that don't leave them much time for work. By the time they finish the morning prayer on *Rosh Chodesh*, it is time to take the afternoon break. On their *Rosh Chodesh* days they also read from the Torah, and there, once again, a barrage of curses is fired at the head of our beloved king and his kingdom.

"And if these regular weekly and monthly holidays aren't enough, from time to time they celebrate special festivals, each one once a year. On these festivals they carry out horrible rituals that would make your hair stand on end.

"The first festival is Pesach," Haman reported. "On this festival, which lasts for eight days,[10] the Jews wash all their vessels and burn their *chometz*, unleavened bread, in big bonfires

---

[10] This refers to places outside of Eretz Yisroel, where the second day of *Yom Tov* is celebrated, bringing the total number of days of Pesach to eight.

that they ignite in the streets, polluting the air and wasting precious food that could have sustained many poor families in your realm.

"After that, they take only *matzos* into their homes, saying a special prayer to their God, 'Just as we rid ourselves of all the *chometz* in our homes, so we ask that You rid us of the wicked rule that we suffer, and deliver us from the foolish king, Achashverosh.'

"So that takes care of the festival that falls in the month of Nisan. In Iyar there is no special festival, but soon afterwards comes the month of Sivan, when another festival occurs – the two day festival of Shavuos.[11] On this day, according to the Jews' claim, the Torah was given to their ancestors, and that is what they celebrate," Haman explained, and then he went on to describe the customs of this festival a bit.

"On Shavuos, the Jews have a custom to climb up to the roofs of their synagogues and strew them with apples and flowers, and then to gather what they have scattered and say the following prayer, 'Just as we gathered the apples and flowers, so should our children be gathered from among the wicked gentiles, and not, Heaven forbid, become assimilated among them!'

"After Shavuos, some three months elapse without a festival, but then right after that comes a month that is replete with festivals – the month of Tishrei.

"The series of festivals in the month of Tishrei opens with a two day holiday known as Rosh Hashanah, on which the

---

[11] Here too, he referred to the second day of *Yom Tov* practiced in the Diaspora, and likewise for future references.

Jews blow these strange wind instruments, a sort of trumpet, and pray, 'With the sounding of the *shofar* trumpet, may our memory rise before our Father in heaven for the good, and the memory of the gentiles and their king, be cursed for the bad!'

"Then comes Yom Kippur, which falls on the tenth of Tishrei, one day of the year when the Jews fast, for a change. But the king need not worry," Haman said sarcastically, "on the eve of this festival, on the ninth of Tishrei, they make sure to compensate for the upcoming abstention by eating, drinking, and reveling with their families. After a full day of festive meals, you can imagine that they have no appetite anyway!" Haman Harasha said scathingly.

"On the other hand, even on this day of Yom Kippur the wickedness of these Jews is evident!" Haman went on to tell the king. "On this fast day, not only do the Jews afflict *themselves*, but all their family members as well. Even their little children, including the nursing infants, are forced to fast on this day. The Jews have no mercy in their hearts, not even for their own babies.

"Yom Kippur, they claim, is a day of atonement for their sins. All year long they sin and commit wrongdoings, and then they think that on one day they can shed all their transgressions and become pure and clean as a newborn babe. As for all the sins that were forgiven – the Jews ask that their God should visit these sins upon *our* heads, on the heads of the gentiles and their king, in the hope that we will rot in their sins and be eradicated from the world, just as their sins were wiped away.

"But Yom Kippur is still not the worst of their festivals. The worst one, Sukkos, takes place five days later. If you are wondering, Your Majesty, what is so terrible about this festival," Haman mouthed the words with poisonous emphasis, "let me explain it to you:

"On the eve of the Sukkos festival, the Jews all go out of their homes and up to the roofs where they build *sukkahs*, booths covered by fresh branches, which they chop off crudely from the beautiful trees Your Majesty planted throughout the empire! Any trees that survive the first 'harvest' geared at gathering roofing material for the *sukkahs* are doomed to be chopped up later in the day and bereft of their greenery; the Jews go out to find themselves all kinds of plants that they claim to have been commanded to cut and hold in their hand.

"Out in the orchards, they pluck off the citron fruits that are such a delight to behold – not for the purpose of eating, but simply picking them for the sake of picking. Then they go on to the date orchards and lop off the tops of the palm trees, choosing the youngest branches whose whole future lies before them. Next, they absolutely ravage the myrtle trees planted in the various parks, since they need those branches too. Nor do they have mercy on the willow trees.

"Now, with all these assorted branches - which have no logical connection between them – gripped in their hands, they enter their synagogues, circle the *bimah*, the platform that stands in its center, and cry to their God, '*Hoshana!* Save us!' After these bizarre circuits, they flap the branches in every direction, as the king's legions wave their weapons, explaining that they are metaphorically training to do battle with the gentiles.

"On the last day of that festival, the day when they begin anew each year the reading from their Torah scroll, they again circle the *bimah* of the synagogue, this time without the branches, but dancing wildly, like kid goats.

"And so, these are the Jewish festivals," Haman concluded his speech, replete with absurdities and fabrications. Now he was ready to discuss the practical ramifications with Achashverosh.

"The common denominator in all the festivals I described to you is that in each one, the Jews abstain from useful labor. They do not miss a single opportunity to evade work, and this fact carries with it serious economic consequences that leave their mark on the entire Persian economy.

"And if we have brought up the topic of economics, you ought to know something else. These Jews dabble in every possible occupation, from the simplest to the most respectable and lucrative. But one thing is true across the board - whatever work they do, they do deceitfully! They overprice, cheat and steal, and their conscience doesn't bother them in the least, since they don't see anything wrong in deceiving a gentile, only in doing so to their own fellow Jews.

"On top of that, once every seven years, and again every fifty years, the Jews even take practical measures aimed at ruining the economy and causing the death of all gentiles by starvation! They suspend work on their fields, do not work the land at all, and do not even sell us the fruits that grew spontaneously on their trees, but rather utterly dispose of them! No reasonable explanation exists for this inexplicable behavior – other than the Jews' ardent desire to starve us to death!" Haman clarified.[12]

---

[12] Aggadas Esther

"Furthermore," he went on without a pause, "you should know, Your Majesty, that the Jews are a stiff-necked people. Even though Nevuchadnetzar already exiled them from their land and destroyed their city and sanctuary, their pride was not bowed, nor their spirit broken! They still consider themselves superior to all other nations of the world. At every opportunity they proclaim, 'We are free men, and have never subordinated ourselves to anyone! There is no ruler or monarch whom we are obligated to obey!'

"Since they consider themselves the 'chosen people,' they retain connections with their brethren across the length and breadth of the realm, praying for each other and yearning all the time for nothing less than the decimation of your kingdom and your ministers and our eradication from the face of the earth!

"There is absolutely no doubt about it," Haman summed up his words with a dramatic, suppressed groan, "the Jews are an entire nation of corrupt individuals. There is no solution for the 'Jewish problem' but to wipe them out completely!"

Then Haman tacked on one small surprise for the king. "If you are still bothered by the possibility that destroying the Jewish nation might negatively affect the national economy or cause damage in one way or another, I can put your mind at rest.[13] Due to my deep concern for the benefit of my king[14]

---

[13] The commentary Yosef Lekach explains that Haman did not offer payment from his own pocket in exchange for the destruction of the Jews. Rather, he explained to the king that the taxes on the spoils the masses would plunder from the Jews would amount to some ten thousand silver talents at the very least. When the king declined his offer and said, "The money is yours," he intended, according to this explanation, to grant Haman Harasha as a gift the taxes that would come in from these spoils.

[14] Haman was careful to present matters as if he was merely giving advice for the king's benefit, and that the king was actually the one seeking the destruction of the

and country, I will spare no effort or cost. I will willingly and happily open my pocket and measure out ten thousand silver talents into the king's treasury, a sum which, according to my calculation, amounts to some fifty shekels for each Jew.

"I don't know what the exact census of the Jews is today, so I can't figure out the payment according to the most updated statistics. But one thing I know for sure – when they left Mitzrayim, their number came to about 600,000. If we multiply 600,000 by fifty shekels, we will find that the total comes out to exactly ten thousand talents. This is the amount I will donate as my participation in the costs involved in destroying the Jewish nation," Haman pledged.[15] "Just sign on the decree and I will pay the money on the spot!"

Haman's Missing Information

Haman's lowly offer of this hefty bribe put the finishing touch on the villain's degrading accusatory tirade, bursting with lies.

But Haman did not know that the Jews had already measured out their own shekels into the treasury of the King of all kings, long before this villain offered his silver talents. The half shekel that the people of Israel were commanded to bring each year as their participation in the communal sacrifices offered in the *Bais Hamikdash* preceded Haman's shekels. The merit of these silver coins now stood in the Jews' stead.

Jews. That is why he stressed, "*If it pleases the king*, let it be written that they be wiped out," since he wished to create the impression that the decree was the king's doing and for his own personal benefit (Perush HaGra).

[15] Esther Rabbah 7, 14

Similarly, Haman did not know that he himself brought up the merit of the Jews before their Father in heaven in the course of his prosecuting oration. After all, what was Haman blaming the Jewish nation for? Did he complain about the way they ran their homes? About their outer appearance? About their wisdom or lack thereof? Did he claim that they were murderers or immoral? No! All the arguments raised by Haman related only to the vibrant life of Torah and *mitzvos* that the Jews lived.

In fact, every word of accusation[16] that Haman said before King Achashverosh was transformed by the angel Gavriel into another point in their defense before the King of the Universe. "Look at what Your children are being blamed for," the angel said. "For nothing other than the fact that they observed Your holy Torah!"

Hashem was responsive to the angel's plea. "Don't worry!" He said to Gavriel, declaring unequivocally that He had never abandoned the Jewish people and never would.

As to Haman Harasha, Hashem said, "*Rasha!* You look askance at all the festivals of the Jews? Upon My word, I will bring you to your knees before them and thus *another* festival will be added to them each year, to commemorate your downfall!"

Achashverosh's Folly

We would have expected that Achashverosh, who considered himself enlightened and progressive, would have found the kind of fabrications Haman fed him rather hard to swallow.

---

[16] Esther Rabbah 7:12

Even the simplest person would have entertained doubts as to the reliability of such hateful accusations.

After all, the king should have thought to himself, "How can it be that an entire nation of corrupt individuals has been living in the midst of my realm and I never heard about them? How can it be that all of these wrongdoings never reached my attention?"

And besides, even if the king did not grasp the blatant illogic in the villain's words, he should have at least done the minimum expected of him and checked the matter out! Where in the world do we hear that a decree of decimation should be issued against an entire nation on the basis of the testimony of one single individual?!

Furthermore, did King Achashverosh really think that the suggestion Haman presented to him was fair? Did it seem logical to him to mete out a collective punishment on an entire people, including the tiny infants, without verifying if they had really done anything wrong?

Haman himself had argued that the Jews were so cruel that they tormented their infants by making them fast on Yom Kippur. What, then, did this "great humanitarian" himself come and demand? Did he suggest that children's homes be erected to provide the Jewish children with all their needs? He did not merely seek to afflict them with a one day fast; he wanted to butcher them by committing wholesale genocide! Where was the consistency and logic in his words?

To be perfectly honest, Haman's generous offer alone – his readiness to measure out a fantastic sum to the royal treasury in exchange for the Jews' extermination – should have raised the king's suspicions. But Achashverosh did not think, did not doubt; he merely accepted Haman's words at face value.

Why? As we mentioned earlier, Achashverosh himself wanted the Jews eradicated just as badly as Haman wanted it – and perhaps even more! Therefore, it was convenient for Achashverosh to believe that the Jews were corrupt, deceitful, dishonest, lazy and cruel, and that they sought to undermine his empire. This assumption fit right in with his worldview and with his latent aspiration to get rid of the Jews once and for all.

For this reason, he did not even try to debate the matter with Haman, nor did he cast the slightest of doubts on the authenticity of his report. He accepted Haman's words at face value. The only reason he did not rush to order the Jews' extermination on the spot was because he was afraid – yes, simply afraid.

Had he not been frightened by the revenge that the Jews' God might take against him, he would not have waited until Haman came to him and offered his suggestion. He would have gotten rid of the Jews long before, as soon as he had risen to the throne!

Frightened of the Jews' God

But since Achashverosh was well aware that nobody gets away scot-free after hurting Hashem's children, he was afraid to touch them. The fearful king presented these concerns now to Haman Harasha.[17] "My dear Haman, honored minister,

---

[17] Esther Rabbah 7:13

I agree with every word of what you have said. You cannot imagine how much I wish I could cede your request and exterminate the Jewish people. But I am afraid that the plan cannot be carried out."

"Why?" Haman queried. "What fault did you find in my marvelous scheme?"

The king quickly explained, "Experience has shown that nobody has ever succeeded in destroying the Jewish nation! Their God does not let anyone hurt them, and takes His revenge from anyone who tries to do so! Great kings in the past, mighty monarchs who were stronger and more daring than I, tried starting up with the Jewish people – and they met a bitter end! Please, Haman, don't say another word to me about this matter!"

But Haman would not give up. He brought the subject up again and again, suggested all kinds of schemes, cajoled and persuaded the king more and more, until Achashverosh finally offered a compromise.

"If you want to decimate the Jews, then I have to seek the counsel of my wise men and wizards on the matter. If they approve the plan, then fine; both you and I will be happy. But if they reject it and confirm my concerns," the king said summarily, "then my decision will be final; I will not touch the Jews!"

Indeed, Haman agreed to this suggestion, and the king rushed to assemble all the sage advisors of the nations.

The meeting was opened by King Achashverosh, who proceeded to define the purpose of their assembly. "The suggestion was made to destroy the Jewish nation!" the king presented the facts, and then awaited the opinion of the wise men.

These sage advisors apparently were no greater *tzaddikim* than their king. They did not require any extraneous explanations as to the necessity of wiping out the Jewish people. Nevertheless, they were shaken up at the idea and were quick to unanimously respond, "Who had the nerve to suggest such a thing? What maniac seeks to commit such an outrageous folly? Don't you know that the whole world exists only in the merit of the Jews and the Torah they study? Aren't you aware that the Jewish people are the children of Hashem, His dearest and closest loved ones, while the rest of the world's peoples are considered distant acquaintances?

"That being the case," the sages went on, "do you really think that someone could harm the close relatives of the King, His beloved children, and get away with it? After all, life and death are in the Hand of Hashem; He has the power to raise someone up to the heights or throw him to the depths. Surely He would take revenge from His children's enemies!

"And if you don't believe what we are saying, learn from the experience of those who attempted to provoke the Jews in the past. Look what happened to Pharaoh, who drowned with all his legions in the Reed Sea, or Sisera, who was swept up by the Kishon River, along with his mighty army!" Achashverosh listened intently and the plan was almost dropped.

But then Haman asked for the floor, and in his typical smooth talk, he started persuading those present. "Why are you so afraid of the God of the Jews?" he asked in astonishment.

"Do you really believe that after so much time has elapsed since the days of Pharaoh and Sancheriv His strength is still what it used to be? Since then He has grown old and weak;[18] He can't do anything to us today.

"And if you have any doubt about that," Haman emphasized, "you need only consider what Nevuchadnetzar did to His House in Yerushalayim! If their God still retained His full strength, do you think He would have let the king of Bavel burn down His sanctuary? Would He have allowed Nevuchadnetzar to exile His children from their land?" Haman argued, and amazingly enough, his argument was accepted.

All those sagacious advisors, who, just a few minutes earlier, were astute enough to warn Achashverosh of the great risk he would be taking by attempting to fight against the Jewish

---

[18] In Aggadas Esther, another argument of Haman is cited. Haman claimed that even if Hashem is *able* to save His nation, He doesn't *want* to, since He already despises them. The proof is that He allowed Nevuchadnetzar to destroy their *Bais Hamikdash* and to exile them from their land. In keeping with this opinion, the Megillas S'sorim explains that Haman's words to the king did not address the reasons for destroying the Jewish nation. Haman had no need to convince Achashverosh of that, since he wanted it just as badly as Haman did. Achashverosh was only concerned about the revenge Hashem would wreak on him. In order to allay that concern, Haman explained to him why he is sure that Hashem has rejected the Jewish nation.

Haman said to the king as follows: "There is a certain nation scattered and dispersed among the peoples in all the provinces of your kingdom," and from the fact that they are in such a lowly condition, you can deduce that their God has rejected them and does not stand ready to come to their assistance anymore. And if you want to know why, the answer is, "they do not follow the laws of the king," i.e., they do not keep the Jewish religion, the laws of the King of the Universe, and therefore, "it is not befitting the king to tolerate them" – the King of the Universe has no interest in them.

The Yalkut adds that according to Haman's claim, the Creator loved the Jews only as long as the *Bais Hamikdash* was standing and they would measure out their shekels to Him year after year. "Now, however, He no longer cares for them, and there is nothing to prevent Him from destroying them!" so argued Haman Harasha.

people, suddenly changed their tune and were captivated by Haman Harasha's heretical, nonsensical words!

The Money is Yours

Following the unanimous approval, the king had no reason on his part to reject Haman's proposal. Therefore, the king removed the signet ring from his finger, handed it over to Haman the Agagite, and authorized him to write in his name missives to all the peoples of the kingdom. They were to prepare themselves for the thirteenth day of Adar of the following year, when they would all assemble against the Jewish nation and wipe them off the face of the earth. Achashverosh even ceded the money that Haman offered to deposit into his treasuries.[19] "The money is yours,"[20] the king told Haman, "and you have my full permission to do with the Jews whatever you see fit!"[21]

Why did Achashverosh reject such a generous financial offer? Why give up the huge amount of silver that Haman offered him of his own accord? The simple explanation is that

---

[19] The commentary Yosef Lekach explains that the king did not *cede* the money; he just allowed Haman to *do as he saw fit with these resources.* He bases his explanation on Haman's offer to measure out the ten thousand silver talents *"into the hands of those who perform the duties,"* explaining that the king accepted his offer, and granted Haman the authority to decide what those who perform the duties should do with the money he would measure into their hands.

[20] In the Gemara, Chazal point out the *gematria*, the numerical value, of the words which teach us that the Divine Spirit put these particular words into the king's mouth. *Hakesef,* the silver, has the same numerical value as *ha'etz,* the gallows. Thus, it was as if the king said to Haman, "The *gallows* is yours."

[21] The Midrash Ponim Acheirim explains that at the end, the king was convinced as a result of a lottery that was held between him and Haman – the lottery expert – after they agreed in advance that if the nation falls into the hands of Haman in the lottery, Achashverosh will get the money, and if the nation falls into the hands of Achashverosh, then the money will remain in Haman's possession. In the end, the lottery came out in Haman's hands, but when the king saw that he felt very bad about the money he would lose, he passed up the payment.

Achashverosh was so worked up and eager to decimate the Jewish people that he did not pay attention to anything else, even ten thousand silver talents. But there is another marvelous explanation for this matter as well,[22] that once again reveals the vast kindness Hashem bestowed upon us when He led King Achashverosh to decline Haman's offer of silver.

Had the king accepted the ten thousand silver talents from Haman in exchange for the Jews, he would not have been able to rescind his order later on and abrogate the decree! Everyone in the world would have stood up and asserted that it is not honest to back out of a deal once it is signed and paid for. Therefore, Hashem arranged that King Achashverosh would not accept any payment for the Jews. Thus, he would be free to do as he wished and to rescind the decree when Hashem decided it was time!

---

[22] Aggadas Esther

HAMAN'S LETTERS

"The king's scribes were summoned on the thirteenth day of the first month, and everything was written just as Haman commanded, to the king's satraps, to the governors of every province, and to the officials of every people – to each province in its own script and to every people in its own language, written in King Achashverosh's name and sealed with the king's signet ring. The letters were sent by courier to all the king's provinces, to destroy, slay and exterminate all the Jews, young and old, children and women, all in a single day, on the thirteenth day of the twelfth month, which is the month of Adar, and to plunder their possessions. Copies of the documents were to be sent to all the provinces, published for all the peoples, [telling them] to be ready for that day. The couriers went out speedily by the king's order, and the edict was given in Shushan the capital. The king and Haman sat down to drink, but the city of Shushan was in confusion." (3:12-15)

And so, the terrible decree was finalized. Haman received the king's authorization as well as his signet ring, which granted him broad powers. He immediately summoned the king's scribes to write letters to all the peoples in the kingdom, instructing them to be ready for the thirteenth day of Adar in the following year. On that day, they would have to wage a vicious battle against the Jewish nation, exterminating all the Jews on a single day – young and old, women and children – and also plundering their possessions.[1]

Haman did not waste a moment. He rushed the couriers out on their way the very day he received the king's approval,[2] the thirteenth of Nisan.[3]

But Haman acted very shrewdly. He did not spell out his satanic plot to all the residents of the kingdom. Rather, he split up the missives and sent two separate letters.

---

[1] The Midrash explains (Esther Rabbah 7:18) that Haman Harasha learned from the mistakes of the murderers who preceded him, just as other resha'im before him attempted to do.

The wicked Esav said to himself, "When Kayin killed Hevel, he committed a grave error by killing him in his father's lifetime, a fact which enabled Adom Harishon to bear more children. I, however, will kill Yaakov after the days of mourning for my father are over, and then I will know for sure that he will not bear other sons besides me!"

The villainous Pharaoh also drew conclusions, learning from the mistake of Esav, who sought to kill Yaakov when he was mature and had already had children. "I will kill the Jews the moment they are born!" he decided.

Haman Harasha learned from Pharaoh's "mistake" in leaving the female Jews alive. He sought to exterminate *all* the Jews – young and old, women and children - on a single day, in order to prevent any possibility of the Jewish nation's continued existence.

Gog and Magog, at the end of days, will follow this same practice and learn from Haman's "mistake"; they will attempt to kill the God of the Jews, so to speak, before attacking the Jews themselves. In response to this foolish idea, the most ludicrous of all, Hashem answers, so to speak, "Don't worry, Gog and Magog. I will let you 'play around' a bit, and then – we will close accounts...."

[2] The Malbim explains that Haman rushed to send out the letters that same day, before the king would have a chance to come to his senses and regret his approval of the plan.

[3] According to many commentaries, this was the very same day that Haman cast the lots. However, the way the Targum understands it, it took many days for Haman to convince the king to overcome his fears and agree to the decree, and this agreement was also preceded by consultations with the sage advisors of the nations, in which case we can assume that the lots were cast some time before this date.

One was an open letter[4] forwarded to the officials and governors of every province, and there the entire plan was laid out in its full detail.[5] These are the letters referred to by the *megillah* when it tells us that "everything was written just as Haman commanded, to the king's satraps, to the governors of every province, and to the officials of every people... to destroy, slay and exterminate all the Jews, young and old, children and women, all in a single day, on the thirteenth day of the twelfth month, which is the month of Adar, and to plunder their possessions."[6]

The second letter was published for the general population, saying in an ambiguous manner that all the people must be ready for the thirteenth day of Adar of the following year, at which time they would receive further instructions. These are the letters about which the *megillah* writes, "Copies of the documents were to be sent to all the provinces, published for all the peoples, [telling them] to be ready for that day."

Haman's objective in concealing the information about his true intentions was very simple.[7] He was afraid the Jews

---

[4] The Malbim, on the other hand, maintains that the letters sent to the officials were sealed and meant to be opened only on the thirteenth of Adar, while the common people were sent ambiguous letters telling them "to be ready."

[5] In fact, most of the officials and governors told the Jews about the decree that was about to befall them, as we shall explain later on. Still, since this information was confidential, the Jews could not do anything with it; they could not come and plead with the king to abolish a decree which they were not even supposed to know about, as this would expose the betrayal of those officials who were kind enough to volunteer to them the information (Yosef Lekach)!

[6] The Yosef Lekach explains that Haman wanted to motivate the gentiles to carry out the extermination plan against the Jews, and that is why he promised the plunder, hinging the booty on the successful conclusion of the decimation plan. "Only after you have finished slaying and exterminating young and old, women and children, all in one day, will you receive payment," Haman made very clear.

[7] Perush HaGra. The Minchas Erev cites another explanation for Haman's policy of secrecy. According to him, Haman was afraid that as soon as the nations would hear

would organize themselves meanwhile and use one of the three measures handed down to them from their forefather, Yaakov: prayer, which might abrogate the evil decree, a royal gift, which might get the king to rescind his murderous intentions, or war, which they could certainly prepare themselves for in the lengthy span of time that remained until the month of Adar of the following year. There was also the risk that the Jews might escape and go into hiding, and then it would not be possible to kill them all out and eradicate their name completely. [8]

Copies of the Document

The content of the letters addressed to the general population is written explicitly in the *posuk*, "To be ready for that day." However, we still need to understand the exact nature of the secret letters that were sent out to the officials. Haman wrote these letters, sealed with the king's signet, as if Achashverosh himself was writing them. [9]

They read, "As you certainly know, there is a certain individual in our provinces by the name of Haman, a prominent personage who came to us from the distant city of Yerushalayim. A descendant of Amalek, he hails from a royal family and is one of the most respected people in the land.

"This Haman has requested of me, the king, an insignificant request regarding a particular little people who live among us. These are a lowly and despicable people, a proud and arrogant people, a people that seek the ill of the gentiles constantly,

---

of the plan, they would rush to carry it out before the appointed time. And since the lots clarified that this was the *only* day on which the Jewish nation could successfully be exterminated, they would not succeed.

[8] Malbim

[9] Esther Rabbah 7:13

as they openly declare daily, 'To execute vengeance upon the nations, and punishments upon the people.'[10] They curse the nations at every opportunity, saying, 'Hashem is the King forever – let the nations be eradicated from His land.'[11]

"Now what is Haman's meager request? Really, he does not want much; he only asks to destroy the Jewish nation. On the thirteenth day of Adar of next year, Haman would like us all to be prepared to carry out this goal in the best possible way, so that in one day, we will be able to eradicate the memory of the Jewish nation from this earth![12]

"I, King Achashverosh, have accepted Haman's request. If you want to know why, I'll repeat to you what Haman told me about just a few of the Jews' heinous deeds.

"First of all, they are incomparably ungrateful. Look what they did to poor Pharaoh. Their forefathers came down to Pharaoh's land to purchase food, and he welcomed them hospitably, arranging housing for them in the best area in Mitzrayim, and sustaining them with the finest food gratis during all the years when the land was ravaged by famine.

"And do you know how the Jews paid back this Pharaoh? One day, Pharaoh asked the Jewish people to help him out a bit in building the royal palace but instead of seizing the opportunity, they tried to evade the assignment. When they

---

[10] Tehillim 149:7

[11] Tehillim 10:16

[12] The commentary Yosef Lekach explains that Haman did not reveal to any of the officials that his plan was comprehensive and all inclusive. In the letter that was addressed to each official, the instructions relevant to him were written, i.e., to slay the Jews *in his province* on the thirteenth of Adar. In this way, Haman hoped to avoid the wide scale publicity that would have naturally resulted from a decree dealing with the genocide of an entire nation.

finally gave in to his request and joined in the construction work, their good-heartedness did not last long. After a short time, they came up with a scheme; they asked Pharaoh's permission to go worship their God in the wilderness. When permission was granted, they left and didn't come back!

"But that wasn't the end of it. They did not leave Mitzrayim as upstanding citizens leaving their land and relocating to another. Before they left, they asked their Mitzri neighbors to lend them jewelry and valuable clothing, and the generous Mitzriyim gladly obliged. Each of the Jews leaving Mitzrayim carried with him donkey loads of valuables, and then – they simply ran off with all the Mitzriyim's hard earned possessions!

"When Pharaoh heard that the Jews were not planning to return to his land, he was willing to give them a grand send-off, complete with drums and flutes; all he asked was that they return his subjects' possessions, the valuables that the Jews had deceitfully plundered from them!

"For this purpose, he ran after the Jewish people, but then, Moshe ben Amram, the leader of the Jews, committed a horrific crime. He put a staff under his spell, said a few magic words, struck the sea with it, and split the waters! The Jews went through the sea on dry land. I don't know exactly what kind of magic this was, but that is precisely what happened.

"Then, the Jews pushed the Mitzriyim into the sea using some other sorcery and brought the waters back down on the heads of poor Pharaoh and his army, drowning all the Mitzriyim in the sea! That is how they repaid Pharaoh and his people for all the kindness they did for the Jews – by drowning them in the depths! Did you ever hear of such ungratefulness?!"

Haman conveniently failed to mention that Pharaoh also slaughtered babies in order to bathe in their blood, drowned young infants in the river, and subjected the Jews in his land to slave labor for hundreds of years. He overlooked the fact that when Pharaoh pursued the Jews, his aim was to restore them to a life of slavery in his land.

In any case, Haman went on and wrote, "Then the Jews went out to the wilderness, and there, Amalek, Haman's great-great-grandfather, went out to war against them.

"Amalek sought the counsel of Bilaam ben Be'or, who made it clear that he had to choose one of two alternatives. Either he could wait until, in the near future, the Jews would initiate a fight with him, in which case the Jews would surely win. The other choice was to pre-empt them and engage them in battle, and be assured of victory. Thus, for lack of choice, Amalek was forced into a war which he had no interest in waging, just in order to defend himself against this corrupt, ungrateful nation that left Mitzrayim.

"The corrupt nature of the Jewish people was evident in the way the Jews fought. Moshe chose one of his disciples, a cruel, hard-hearted fellow named Yehoshua, and instructed him to choose people and go out to war with Amalek. Yehoshua duly followed his orders, picked out his men – I don't know if they were warriors or sorcerers – and went out to the battlefield.

"The battle was not fought fairly at all. During the battle, Moshe again took the staff in his hand, said a few magic words and did a bit of sorcery, and caused the courageous and stout-hearted Amalekites to lose their strength and be defeated before the merciless Yehoshua!"

A total rewriting of history.... No mention is made of the efforts to wipe out the Jews or of the battle being waged simply to cool off the effect the miracles done in Mitzrayim had exerted on the entire world!

Haman went on to write to all the nations, "There is another thing you ought to know. After the Jews finished their aggressive, bitter war against the Amalekites, they waged another battle against the kings Sichon and Og, who were renowned as unconquerable fighters. There is no way of knowing how the Jews managed to overcome them, but once again the shocking facts are that the Jews prevailed against Sichon and Og, and even took possession of their land!

"The next battle the Jews fought was against the Midyanites. Once more, it is not clear how, but they won against the people of Midyan as well!

"But all of these battles were no more than a pale introduction to the greatest and cruelest of all, a war that dispossessed entire nations of their homeland by brute force!

"When the Jews entered the land of Canaan, led by Yehoshua, they waged war against the thirty one kings in the land. They didn't suffice with conquering the land and dividing it up amongst themselves; they also killed out all of its occupants without mercy! The fate of those few who were not killed by Yehoshua's sword was not much better, since the Jews took all those who remained alive as their bondservants, dooming them to a life of enslavement!

"After conquering the land of Canaan and killing out its occupants, the Jews took a break from their wars for a few years.

They were satiated for the time being by the blood they had spilled, and lived a life of pleasures in the broad boundaries of the land they had plundered for themselves. But this tranquility did not last long.

"Some time later, Sisera came to fight with them in their land. In some mysterious way, they caused the Kishon River to wash him away along with his vast, mighty army into the Great Sea! You can understand, therefore, how dangerous these Jews are, and how vital it is to rally all our forces in order to eradicate them from the earth, before they exercise their powers once again!

"If you want to have an idea how far the wickedness of these Jews can go, look at what they did to Amalek, Haman's ancestors. As soon as the Jews crowned their first king, Shaul, his first official act was to go out to war against the peace-seeking Amalekite people, slaughtering them all – women and children, the elderly along with the nursing babes!

"Even Agag, the Amalekite king whom the cruel Shaul left alive, was killed at the end by the prophet of the Jews, Shmuel, in a cruel and unusual manner. He slashed him into pieces, and left his flesh as food for the vultures!

"The ensuing kings of Israel followed in the footsteps of Shaul and Shmuel. Outstanding among them was King Dovid, who destroyed empire after empire, without having mercy on a soul!

"After King Dovid, the Jews crowned his son Shlomo as king. He built them a special edifice known as the *Bais Hamikdash*. I don't know exactly what went on in there, but one thing I can tell you for sure. Every time the Jews would go out to war, they would first enter this *Bais Hamikdash*, do some sort of sorcery there, and then proceed to kill and wreak havoc in the world!

"In this house of sorcery, the Jews would pray to their God, and this God would answer them and fell their enemies before them. But that was years ago. Since those days, matters have changed. The Jews sinned to this God Who used to deliver them; He too has grown old and His strength has waned. Therefore, Nevuchadnetzar was able to attack the Jewish nation and burn down their *Bais Hamikdash*, and even to exile them from their land and scatter them among us.

"But don't think that as a result of the blow they suffered, the Jews have repented of their evil ways and begun acting like upstanding, civilized citizens and good neighbors.

"Even today, in exile, the Jews retain their despicable ways. They still scorn us and our beliefs, and seek the ill of the nations all the time.

"That is why, as I stated earlier, I decided to accept Haman's request to destroy the Jewish nation. For that purpose, we cast lots and verified which day would be most appropriate for carrying out the decimation, and the lot came out on the thirteenth day of Adar.

"Know, my beloved subjects, that I, your king, am very happy and absolutely at peace with my decree! I've taken Haman's silver as payment[13] and handed over the Jewish people. My

---

[13] We find a number of opinions in Chazal regarding the question of whether Achashverosh accepted the silver from Haman or not. In any case, this part of the text of the letters appears in Targum Sheini, who apparently understands that the king did not cede the silver.

conscience is perfectly clear! You too should feel free to eat, drink and be merry, just like your beloved king!

"There is only one thing I demand. As soon as these letters reach you, begin your preparations, so that on the appointed day you will be ready to exterminate the Jews – young and old, women and children, all in a single day, without leaving a trace! Do not have mercy on any of them! Those who are experts at the bow should take the bow in hand, those who can draw a dagger should draw it. Everyone together should attack the Jews and wipe them out in all the provinces of my realm!

"I want to make it perfectly clear. I do not want to find even one single Jew alive in the entire length and breadth of my kingdom! To dispel any doubts on the matter, I hereby declare that if a Jew will remain alive anywhere, the heads of the province and the city in which he was found will be slaughtered, so that everyone will see what happens to someone who disobeys the word of the king!

"In conclusion, as a special gesture, I allow everyone from the provinces of my realm to plunder the Jews' possessions for themselves, as fitting recompense for your loyalty to the king's orders!" With that, the letters closed, and Haman was supremely pleased with the final text.[14]

---

[14] In the Midrash Ponim Acheirim, a different style of introduction is cited for Haman's letters. According to this Midrash, he began as follows: "I – the greatest minister of the king, second in command to him, the chief viceroy and the seventh of the chamberlains, the finest of the heads of the empire – have written [this letter]. I, along with all the governors, the officials of the king, the rulers of the provinces and their viceroys, the minor kings and the satraps, have all agreed together, with one mind, one mouth, one word and one tongue, and have written with the authorization of King Achashverosh, irrevocably sealed with his signet ring, regarding the matter of the 'great eagle, whose wings are spread over the entire world' (a reference to the Jews), against whom no bird, animal or beast could stand,

He felt very comfortable with his distorted presentation of history. He was used to such fabrication from the ludicrous slander he had presented to King Achashverosh.

That very day, he rushed to send out the letters with the speediest couriers to every people in each province of King Achashverosh's empire, translated into the language of each people.

It is a Known Fact that Esav Hates Yaakov

What would we have thought had an order been publicly issued by the royal administration requiring us to simply get up one fine day and *destroy an entire nation*? We would most certainly have resisted. We would have debated the issue.

---

until the great lion (Nevuchadnetzar) came and struck the eagle a powerful blow, so that its wings were broken, its flanks plucked and its legs lopped off. Then, the entire world attained tranquility, quiet and calmness, from the day the eagle roved from its nest until this day.

"But now we see that the eagle wants to grow and sprout feathers and flanks, and seeks to cover us and the entire world as it covered and ripped apart our early forefathers who preceded us. Therefore, all the greatest kings of Madai and Paras assembled, under the authority of King Achashverosh, and we wrote to you to join in a united plan to set traps for this eagle, to capture her before her strength grows and she returns to her nest. We want to pluck her flanks, break her wings, and feed her flesh to the vultures, to crack her eggs and wound her fledglings (old and young, women and children), and to uproot any memory of her from the world. Our plan will not be like that of Pharaoh, who issued his decree on the males and left the females alone, and not like that of Esav, who said, 'When the days of mourning for my father come, I will kill my brother Yaakov and leave his children to be my slaves,'" and not like Amalek who pursued the Jews and killed the weak ones, leaving the warriors alive, and not like Nevuchadnetzar who exiled them and let them be and even seated them on his throne, and not like Sancheriv, who exiled them to a land like their own. Rather, we have agreed unequivocally to slay and exterminate all the Jews, young and old, so that there will be no memory, no name and no seed left of them in this world, so that they should not do to us as they did to our forbears, our ancestors, and the illustrious ones that came before us, because anyone who did a kindness for these people was repaid only with a bad turn!" Then he continued in the format we brought above.

Unquestionably, we would have tried to understand what the decree was all about!

Granted, Haman was careful to rewrite the history of the Jews so that their image emerged as that of a bloodthirsty nation who mercilessly destroy everything in their path. But, after all, even the letters themselves reek of a lack of authenticity, since in almost every sentence, Haman admits a lack of understanding.

He doesn't know how Moshe split the sea, how Yehoshua was victorious against Amalek, how Sichon and Og were conquered, how the Jews fought the thirty one kings, how Sisera was swept away by the Kishon River, or why and how Shaul and Shmuel wiped out the Amalekite people. All he knows for sure is that they need to destroy, slay and exterminate the Jews, young and old, women and children, all in a single day.

We might wonder how Haman's words could sound credible to the people. What did Haman think? Did he really expect that the nations would rush to prepare themselves to butcher their Jewish neighbors, the neighbors with whom they almost certainly had some kind of amicable relationship for years?

The answer is yes – that is exactly what Haman thought, and apparently, that is just what would actually have happened, had Hashem not delivered us from the hands of that *rasha* by miraculous means. We see the rule "It is a known fact that Esav hates Yaakov" very clearly.[15] Even if, on the surface, the gentiles appear to be friendly and amicable and retain close neighborly relations with the Jews, still, in the heart of each one of them pulses a deeply rooted hatred for the Jewish people!

---

[15] Sifri, B'ha'aloscha, Piska 11

Haman understood this hatred and knew that the gentiles would be ready and eager to carry out the cruel order. He understood that where there is hatred, there is no logic, and authenticity is unnecessary. Therefore, as soon as Haman finished writing the letters and sending them off,[16] he was ready to celebrate his victory. Confident that the instructions would be carried out when their time came, he sat down with the king to drink.[17] His great joy posed a striking contrast to the general confusion that reigned in the city of Shushan, or, to be more accurate, among its Jews.[18]

---

[16] The Yosef Lekach explains that Haman did not send the letters himself; he just gave over the instructions to the king's scribes – and from that moment on, he was already swept into his gala celebration with King Achashverosh.

[17] Chazal point out (Esther Rabbah 7:20) that the manner in which the decree was issued, i.e., in a spirit of good humor and festivity, was a punishment for the sin of the brothers' selling of Yosef. Just as the brothers sat down to eat right after selling Yosef, so the king and Haman sat down to drink after setting the terrible decree into motion!

[18] This follows the approach of the Minchas Erev, according to which the decree became public knowledge in Shushan the capital, causing the Jews to become confused and concerned as a result. In his opinion, Haman was careful not to publicize the contents of the decree in the provinces, so that the Jews should not initiate an uprising. Since a concern of this kind was not extant in the capital city of Shushan, where the royal army was stationed and would be able to keep the public order and enforce discipline, Haman publicized his plan immediately, in order to give it double strength.

Indeed, the Gra explains that in the other provinces of the king, two letters were sent, as mentioned above – one, an open letter addressed to the masses, and the second, a secret one for the satraps and officers. This was because on the one hand, it was necessary to transmit the instructions that were meant to be carried out on the thirteenth of Adar, while on the other hand, the villain wanted to deny the Jews any possibility of canceling the decree by any means. In Shushan, on the other hand, there was no point in sending out the secret letters, since Shushan was considered to be under the direct rule of King Achashverosh himself, and he, as we know, was well informed regarding the decree in all its details.

The Yosef Lekach adds a different angle. On the contrary, he maintains, the people in Shushan knew even less about the decree than those in the other provinces. In the other provinces, a number of the officers tipped off the Jews about the secret letters that had reached them and the decree these missives contained. Not so in Shushan the capital; there, the king alone was in possession of the full information, and he, as a co-planner of the decree, certainly did not leak anything about it to the Jews.

Regarding that confusion, we find many discussions in Chazal.[19] According to them, the confusion of the Jews in the capital was so extensive that in their extreme bewilderment and distraction, they didn't even realize what they were doing. As an example, there was an incident in which a woman went up to the roof to hang out her laundry to dry, and, in her dazed state, slipped and fell to her death. There were also reports of people who went out to draw water from the well, and in a moment of fluster, fell into the well and drowned.

We can understand the extent of the paralyzing terror that gripped them. It turns out, therefore, that the period of mourning and weeping began now, out of their fear of the decree alone, before it even began to be carried out.[20]

Prophecy of the Three Children

On the day that the letters were sealed, though, Haman suffered aggravation over the Jews.

In any case, according to both the Perush HaGra and the Yosef Lekach, the residents of Shushan knew that a certain decree was set into motion, since the public letters announcing that all the people have to be ready for action were sent to them as well. But they did not know against whom the decree was directed. Therefore, the *entire city of Shushan* was thrown into confusion, since each people was afraid the decree was aimed at them.

[19] Yalkut Esther 856

[20] The Minchas Erev explains that three things expressed the king's determination to carry out the decree: a) The fact that the couriers went out speedily *by the king's order*, i.e., that the king himself gave Haman's decree top priority; b) The fact that the edict was given in Shushan the capital immediately, even though a full year remained until the date of expediting it, and there would be no difficulty publicizing the instructions in the capital city closer to that time; c) The fact that the king and Haman sat down to drink in order to celebrate the decree, an indication of how gratified the king was by it.

As soon as the decree was publicized, the gentiles started degrading the Jews, since they were positive the decree would be carried out; they did not retain even the slightest of concerns that the Jews would remain alive and take their revenge.

Just after Haman left the king's palace, merry and self-satisfied, he noticed Mordechai Hatzaddik walking a bit ahead of him. Haman saw how Mordechai noticed three Jewish *cheder* boys and immediately speeded his pace so as to catch up with the boys.

Curious to know what Mordechai was discussing with them, Haman too increased his pace and heard Mordechai ask each of the children in turn what he learned that day from his *rebbe*.

The first one said he had learned that day from his *rebbe* the *posuk*,[21] "Do not be afraid of a sudden terror, or of the destruction of the *rasha* that may come." The second quoted the verse,[22] "Take counsel together and it will be undone, speak the word and it will not come to be, because Hashem is with us." And the third also mentioned a *posuk*,[23] "Even to old age, I am He, and even to a hoary age, I will carry [you], I have made and I will bear, I will carry and I will deliver you."

Upon hearing the children's response, it was evident on Mordechai's face that he was very happy. This joy caught the attention of Haman Harasha, who rushed to query, "Mordechai, what did the children tell you that made you so happy? Why is your face glowing?"

Mordechai turned towards his arch enemy and said, "Ah, these little children have just given me some good news! Their words hint that I have nothing to fear from the plots you have plotted against the Jewish nation!"

---

[21] Mishlei 3:25
[22] Yeshayah 8:10
[23] Yeshayah 46:4

When Haman heard that, his anger flared. "Even the little children of the Jews are already speaking badly about me and foreseeing my downfall!" At that moment he made a cruel resolution in his heart. "Even before I wipe out the Jewish people in the month of Adar next year, I will first close accounts with these pipsqueaks! The children will be killed first, unrelated to the decree I issued about their nation!"

But in the end, he was not able to carry out his plan. He met his downfall much before he had a chance to harm a single Jew.

MORDECHAI LEARNS OF THE DECREE

"Mordechai learned of all that had been done.
Mordechai tore his clothing and donned sackcloth
and ashes, and went out to the center of the
city and gave forth a loud and bitter cry. He
came until just before the king's gate, since it
was forbidden to enter the king's gate wearing
sackcloth. In each and every province, wherever
the word of the king and his law reached, there
was great mourning among the Jews, and fasting
and weeping and wailing; sackcloth and ashes
were set out for the masses." (4:1-3)

The previous chapter closed with the king and Haman issuing the decree against the Jewish nation. Moments after sealing the letters containing the shocking order to exterminate all the Jews, young and old, women and children in one day, the two villains sat themselves down to drink a toast to their success.

In effect, at this point, the *megillah* switches from focusing on Haman's decree to the beginning of the salvation.

Before embarking on a narration of the events themselves, let us first get an idea of the magnitude of the mourning that spread over heaven and earth.[1]

---

[1] The decree was actually issued on the thirteenth of Nisan, followed immediately by *ta'anis Esther*, the fast of Esther, that continued for a duration of three days, after which Haman was killed. It is unclear, therefore, to which block of time the Midrashim refer when they describe the extreme mourning that took place in

The Jews were paralyzed by the terror that overcame them when they heard word of the decree. Even before the letters reached their destinations, the Jewish people already suffered loss of life as, in their distracted state, people fell from roofs and into deep wells.

As soon as word of the decree was publicized in the capital city of Shushan, the people of the land already began to provoke the Jews.[2] For example, when a Jew would try to buy vegetables or other food items in the market, his Persian neighbor would prevent him from doing so, saying snidely, "Don't fritter away your money! In just a short while, I am going to plunder everything you own. I'm not interested in your wasting money in the meantime!"[3]

Shushan and the other provinces. However, since the matter is described in detail, it is only right to relate this description, which is important in its own right, even though we still have to understand which precise period is being depicted.

It is possible that the description relates to the Jews in the other provinces of the king, at the point when the first letters regarding the decree had already arrived, but the people were not yet informed of the chain of events that took place in Shushan until the second set of letters from the king reached them. (However, this does not seem to agree with the Midrash, where Chazal clearly base their descriptions on the phrase in the *posuk*, "But the city of Shushan was in confusion," indicating that they are referring to Shushan itself. The matter requires further clarification.)

Similarly, we explained in the last chapter, and in this chapter we continue with the same approach, that for the time being, the details of the decree were not known to the general public; they were known only to the officers and governors, and also reached the ears of Mordechai Hatzaddik – with the commentaries differing as to how he became privy to the information. The description of the grief that gripped Shushan and the other Jewish districts does not seem to be consistent with this fact, since if they were not aware of the content of the decree, what would be the meaning of all this mourning? See the footnote above.

[2] See the footnote in the previous chapter where we explained that three points indicated the king's determination to carry out the decree against the Jews. Firstly, the fact that the king himself sent out the speedy couriers, second, the fact that the edict was given in Shushan immediately even though there was no urgency to it, and thirdly, the fact that the king and Haman sat down to drink.

[3] Esther Rabbah 7:25; see also Etz Yosef.

We cannot even begin to imagine how a person must feel knowing that in another year he is slated to be slain along with his family and nation! As opposed to every other kind of mourning, which diminishes as time passes, the situation only became worse from day to day. [4]

Every day, the Jew would despondently mark off on his calendar that another day has elapsed, and would calculate how many days were left for him to live. We can imagine that every evening, as he put his little children to sleep, he would recall that in another few months they were destined to be slaughtered like sheep, and searing tears would flow down his cheeks.

Among the Jews, there were those who, in their great despair, sought an escape hatch by asking their gentile neighbors to acquire them as slaves. "Perhaps if we will become your slaves, the decree will not apply to us!" they explained.

They were refused. "The king specified clearly that even the slaves and maidservants must be killed. If a Jewish slave is found in someone's possession, the master will be subject to the death penalty! We are not willing to endanger our lives!" the neighbors apologized profusely, though they certainly did not feel much sorrow in their hearts. [5]

In general, the neighborly relations between the Jews and the gentiles were very strained during that time. The king's

---

[4] Esther Rabbah 8:2. This is why the mourning is called "*evel gadol*," a great mourning, since it increased from day to day, in contrast to the natural course of events, in which mourning decreases with each passing day.

[5] Indeed, we can attribute this meaning to the words Esther told the king, "Had we been sold as slaves and maidservants, I would have remained silent." She argued that the Jews were not even wanted as slaves and maidservants, since the king had ordered even the Jewish slaves killed.

letters detailed how corrupt and cruel the king considered the Jews, and the gentiles took the report at face value.[6]

Heavenly Efforts to Nullify the Decree

The mourning and sorrow reached the upper worlds as well.[7] The Torah donned widow's clothing, so to speak, and wept loudly before Hashem.

The ministering angels, roused by the Torah's wails, chimed in as well, "Master of the World! If the Jews are wiped out, what purpose is there to our existence?" When the words of the angels reached the sun and the moon, the two luminaries dimmed their glow and donned a mantle of darkness.

At this point, the great ancestors of the Jewish nation tried to abolish the decree. Eliyahu Hanavi rushed in a flurry to the *avos hakedoshim,* the holy patriarchs, and to Moshe Rabbenu and said to them:

"*Avos kedoshim*! Moshe Rabbenu! How can you remain asleep? Don't you realize the terrible calamity that threatens your children? The ministering angels are already standing and pleading before the *kisei hakovod,* the sun and moon have extinguished their glow, the Torah has donned sackcloth, and all this time you remain apathetic?!"

When the *avos hakedoshim* and Moshe Rabbenu heard Eliyahu's words, they hurriedly inquired, "Eliyahu Hanavi, Eliyahu Hatishbi, why was such a terrible decree issued upon our children?" In response, Eliyahu related to them how the Jews

---

[6] Ibn Yichyeh
[7] Esther Rabbah 7:13

had participated in the feast of Achashverosh, and enumerated the many transgressions they succumbed to there.

"If that is the case," the *avos* asked despairingly, "what can we do? If our children sinned and a punishment was decreed upon them, what can we say? Hashem demands payment for His servants' sins!"

But Eliyahu Hanavi did not give up. "Moshe Rabbenu, faithful shepherd, can it be that you are unwilling to speak up on behalf of your flock?[8] Who knows better than you how many times the Jewish people sinned before Hashem and He sought to destroy them, and yet you stood at the breach and mitigated the difficult decree! Why don't you come to the fore now as well, when they are in such dire straits?"

"Tell me," Moshe Rabbenu turned to Eliyahu, "is there any *tzaddik* who can stand opposite me and plead before the Creator from his position in the lower world?"

Eliyahu answered in the affirmative. "Yes, there is a *tzaddik* in this generation, an upstanding Jew by the name of Mordechai!" he said.

"If so, go to this Mordechai and reveal to him the content of the decree!" Moshe instructed Eliyahu. "Tell him that he must stand in prayer below, while I pray correspondingly from above, and with our joint efforts, perhaps we will succeed in annulling the terrible decree!"

---

[8] See Etz Yosef (Esther Rabbah 7:18). He explains there, in the name of the Alshich, that Eliyahu argued before Moshe that he in particular must take a stand, since the date slated for the destruction of the Jewish people was set for the month in which he died, as Haman Harasha sought to take advantage of that fact for the successful execution of his plan.

Eliyahu now informed Moshe Rabbenu of a crucial detail. "Faithful shepherd," Eliyahu said, "be aware that the decree has already been sealed! Immediately after the feast, the *satan* presented a scroll to Hashem. Upon that scroll, the decree was written and even sealed!" the prophet reported.

Moshe Rabbenu urgently inquired, "Tell me, was the decree sealed with a seal of clay or was it sealed in blood?" When Eliyahu replied that the decree was sealed only with clay, Moshe Rabbenu breathed a sigh of relief. "If the seal is only of clay, then Mordechai and I can break it with our united efforts!"

How Mordechai Knew

Without delay, Eliyahu went directly to Mordechai to inform him of the developments. He told him of the decree, revealed the fact that it had been sealed in clay, and went on to describe all that had taken place between Achashverosh and Haman – information that was unknown to anyone else. He concluded by telling him that Moshe Rabbenu himself would be pleading before Hashem,[9] but that he needed back up support from below, and this task had been placed squarely on his shoulders as *gadol hador*.

---

[9] Had Eliyahu not revealed to Mordechai about the help being proffered by Moshe Rabbenu, Mordechai might have despaired of appealing for mercy just as the *avos* had done. Therefore, Mordechai was not informed until Moshe Rabbenu agreed to join him to annul the evil intentions of Haman the Agagite. On the other hand, had Mordechai not been made aware that the decree had been sealed in the heavens as well, he might not have attributed the necessary seriousness to the decree and would have relied on Hashem to deliver His nation from the hands of the *rasha*. Therefore, Eliyahu also updated him regarding the heavenly decree so that he would grasp the extent of the danger (Etz Yosef, Esther Rabbah 7:18).

From here it is clear how Mordechai became aware of the content of the decree.

However, there are a number of additional opinions regarding Mordechai's sources of information. The Targum explains that the information reached Mordechai via *ru'ach hakodesh*. Rashi, in his commentary on the *megillah*, specifies that it was the *ba'al hachalomos*, the master of dreams, who reported to Mordechai all that had taken place.

On the other hand, a different opinion is cited in the commentaries[10] that Mordechai concluded logically what had happened based on the facts. He knew that Haman sought revenge for Mordechai not bowing down to him. Somehow, he heard of the dialogue that had taken place between Haman and the king and of Haman's offer to measure out ten thousand silver talents to the royal treasury in exchange for the Jews. He did not know what the king's response had been to the offer, but when he heard about the copy of the letter that had been issued in Shushan, commanding all the peoples to be prepared for action on the thirteenth of Adar, it was not difficult to arrive at the obvious conclusion – that Haman's suggestion had been accepted and the decree signed and sealed.

Mordechai Tore his Clothing

Immediately after word of the decree reached Mordechai Hatzaddik, he wasted no time in taking the necessary steps to annul the decree. Mordechai's efforts were focused on a number of different fronts at the same time, but the central one was unquestionably the spiritual front.

---

[10] Yosef Lekach

In rent clothing,[11] clad in sackcloth and with ashes on his head, Mordechai went out into the streets, wailing bitterly. He reached the gate of the king, but he could not enter the gate itself in his inappropriate garb,[12] since this was forbidden by law.

As the gist of the decree was not yet known to the masses at that point, they obviously could not pray and plead for its abrogation! Therefore, Mordechai went out into the street with loud cries,[13] wearing sackcloth, thereby publicizing the decree amongst the Jews.[14] Worried that they would focus on material means of annulling the decree, he wore sackcloth and rent his garments. He wanted to make it clear to them that he himself had despaired of all natural means of deliverance, and that he saw no chance of being saved from the decree unless Hashem would have mercy on His nation and bestow His pardon.[15]

---

[11] The Yosef Lekach explains that tearing his clothing was not meant as an act of mourning, since we can see from the words of the *megillah* that follow that Mordechai was suffused with the unwavering belief that the decree would be nullified in the end, as he said to Esther, "Relief and deliverance will come to the Jews." Ibn Yichyeh, on the other hand, explains that tearing the clothing expressed mourning for the decree that was issued above, while wearing sackcloth was a form of prayer and appeal for the nullification of the decree that was issued below.

[12] The Ralbag explains that Mordechai came only *until* the gate of the king, i.e., until the street closest to the gate.

[13] The reason for the *cry* in particular is explained by the Midrash Ponim Acheirim, who states that Mordechai sought to counter the cry that Esav had made when his blessings were taken from him, a cry that led his father to give him a blessing of his own. It was as a result of this blessing that Haman, Esav's descendant, gained his stature (see Esther Rabbah 8:1).

[14] The Malbim, in keeping with his opinion that even the *king* did not know that Haman planned to actually *slay* all the Jews, explains that Mordechai intentionally came to the king's gate in unconventional clothing, so that word of his appearance would reach the king and it would become clear to him what Haman had done with his signet seal.

[15] Megillas S'sorim

Indeed, the commentaries[16] point out that many of the Jews did not fully appreciate the extent of the danger inherent in the decree. They were not aware that their fate had been sealed in the heavens due to their participation in the feast of Achashverosh.

Therefore, there were many among them who figured that it was not necessary to do anything. "Give it a little time and the king will calm down!" they said to themselves. Similarly, there were those who hid behind their declarations of trust in Hashem. "There's nothing to worry about, all we have to do is rely on our Father in heaven to save us from the wicked decree!" they asserted, conveniently forgetting that repentance was necessary to correct the transgression that caused the decree!

On the other hand, others advocated taking practical steps, suggesting that the best move would be to put together a delegation that would come before the king, offer him a gift and plead before him to annul the decree. "We can rally interceders from among the royal staff as well," they added, some of them mentioning Queen Esther explicitly, and pointing out that she should certainly be in a position to ask the king to abrogate the decree issued against her own people.

It was in direct opposition to these opinions that Mordechai took a position at the king's gate, clad in sackcloth. He even took an oath[17] that he would not remove the sackcloth until the decree would be nullified and its danger ended.

---

[16] Minchas Erev
[17] Midrash Ponim Acheirim

Mordechai's conduct and the oath he took made it clear beyond a shadow of a doubt that he saw no hope for deliverance through conventional human effort. Clearly, if he had sought to plead before the king, he would have put on his finest clothing and requested an urgent interview with Achashverosh. Had he wanted to send Esther to Achashverosh, he would have arrived at the king's gate in a manner that would enable him to summon her and speak with her, and not in the manner he presently appeared, which did not even allow him to draw near the gate.

Mordechai's clothing testified to his opinion that all the interceders in the world could not undo the decree. In this way, the Jewish people were given a sharp and unequivocal message regarding the gravity of their position.

Sackcloth and Ashes were Set Out for the Masses

Wherever news arrived of the terrible decree,[18] the Jews gathered together in fasting and prayer clad in sackcloth[19] and ashes,[20] and rousing words of rebuke were delivered by the *gedolei hador* and the *tzaddikim*.

---

[18] The Yosef Lekach explains that the news did not reach all of the provinces, since, in essence, the letters containing specifics of the decree were addressed only to the officers of the provinces. The decree, therefore, reached the Jews only in those provinces where they retained close connections with the ruling powers, who tipped them off about what was happening behind the scenes.

The Malbim explains that the matter became known in all the provinces as a result of the great cry raised by Mordechai, a cry that culled publicity everywhere.

[19] In the Midrash Ponim Acheirim, the opinion is cited that the people *slept* on sackcloth, with the words *yutza larabim* being explained as based on the term "*matza*," bed linens.

[20] The sackcloth and ashes *hutza*, were set out, just for the adults, even though the fast included the children as well (Targum).

The Targum brings a vivid description of the assembly in which Mordechai himself spoke before the Jews of Shushan. Based on this narration, we can imagine that similar events went on in all the other locations.

When Mordechai received word of the decree, he was shocked and terrified, saying to himself, "*Oy!* What a terrible decree has been issued against us – not against a quarter nor a third nor a half of the Jewish nation, but on the entire people of Israel – to slay, exterminate and wipe out our name from under the heavens!"

When the Jews saw Mordechai, their righteous *rav*, crying and wailing, a huge crowd gathered around him. Mordechai stood at the center of the group and cried in a great voice:

"People of Israel, the nation so precious and beloved to its Father in heaven!

"Surely you know about the decree that was issued against us by King Achashverosh and Haman Harasha, demanding that the gentiles destroy us and wipe us all out in one single day – young and old, women and children.

"You are well aware that we have no king to depend on to lead us in war; we have no prophet to plead on our behalf; we have no refuge, no country in the entire globe where we can escape from this villain, because the order was sent to all the provinces![21]

---

[21] Here too, we can sense that Mordechai wished to stress to the people that they have no escape hatch other than the mercies of Hashem, and any other efforts would not be practical and would not generate success.

"We are like sheep without a shepherd, like a ship on the high seas without a captain, like orphans without a father, like nurslings whose mother has died!" Mordechai cried. He ordered that the *aron kodesh* be taken out to the street, the *sefer Torah*, wrapped in sackcloth and flaked with ashes, placed upon it, and the following excerpt read from the Torah scroll, "When you are in trouble, and all these things come upon you in the end of days, and you shall return to Hashem your God and obey His voice, for Hashem your God is a merciful God."

After the Torah reading, Mordechai again stood up and continued his rousing words, "People who are so beloved and precious to their God! Let us consider the people of Nineveh, whose story is described in the book of Yonah. When the prophet Yonah came to Nineveh and gave the shocking pronouncement to the population, 'In another forty days, Nineveh shall be overturned,' the king of Nineveh rose from his throne, removed the crown from his head, donned sackcloth and wallowed in ashes, and announced a general fast in the length and breadth of Nineveh, one in which the entire people would take part, even the animals.

"Indeed, his word was carried out. All the people tore their clothing and languished in the ashes and fasted as their king had ordered. They called out to Hashem with all their might and repented their evil ways, returning the stolen goods in their possession. And Hashem answered them! He saw their repentance and rescinded the punishment that He had planned to give them!

"Let us do as the people of Nineveh did. We too shall call a fast, rend our garments and sit in ashes. If we do genuine *teshuva* and repent fully before Hashem, He will surely have mercy! He will undoubtedly deliver us. We have no other way to be redeemed other than through Him!" Mordechai concluded, and the people were all roused to true *teshuva*.

DEBATE BETWEEN MORDECHAI AND ESTHER

"Esther's maidservants and chamberlains came and reported to her, and the queen was greatly distressed. She sent garments to clothe Mordechai so he would remove the sackcloth he wore, but he would not accept them. Esther summoned Hasach, one of the king's chamberlains whom he had appointed to serve her, and commanded him to go to Mordechai to find out what was going on and why.

Hasach went out to Mordechai, to the city square alongside the king's gate. Mordechai told him everything that had happened to him and about the sum of money that Haman had offered to pay into the king's treasuries in exchange for annihilating the Jews. He gave him a copy of the text of the decree that had been distributed in Shushan saying to destroy them, so he would show it to Esther and report to her, and bid her to go to the king, to appeal to him and to plead with him for her people.

Hasach came and reported to Esther all that Mordechai had said. Esther told Hasach to go back and tell Mordechai, 'All the king's servants and the people in all the provinces of the king know that if anyone, man or woman, shall come to the king, to his inner courtyard, without

having been summoned, there is but one law for
him – the death penalty, unless the king stretches
out to him his golden scepter, and then he shall
live. And I have not been summoned to come to
the king for thirty days.'
They related Esther's words to Mordechai.
Mordechai told them to reply to Esther, 'Do not
imagine that you will be able to find refuge in the
king's palace any more than the rest of the Jews.
For if you remain silent at this time, relief and
deliverance will come to the Jews from some other
place, while you and your father's house will be
lost. Who knows if it was just for such a time that
you attained your royal position!'
Then Esther said to reply to Mordechai, 'Go
gather all the Jews who are in Shushan, and
fast on my behalf; do not eat or drink for three
days, night or day. My maidservants and I will
also fast in this manner. Then I will come to the
king against the rules, and if I perish, I perish.'
Mordechai went and did exactly as Esther had
commanded him." (4:4-17)

Esther's maidservants rushed into her chambers and
informed her[1] that Mordechai Hatzaddik was walking about
the king's gate clad in sackcloth. The queen was shocked

---

[1] The Yosef Lekach infers from here that the connection between Esther and
Mordechai was known, since if that were not the case, why would it have occurred
to the maidservants to tell her about his sackcloth and fasting? Of course, it is
possible that they told her about it without realizing the significance it would have
for her, and it is also possible that since these were Jewish girls, as we mentioned
above in chapter 2 in the name of the Megillas S'sorim, they certainly would have
known of the connection between the two, even if the matter was not common
knowledge throughout the royal palace.

to hear such news, but realized that a good reason must lie behind this strange conduct. She understood that her cousin was certainly not wearing sackcloth simply because he lacked a proper wardrobe.[2]

Regardless of the reason behind this behavior, Esther hurriedly saw to it that Mordechai was sent appropriate garments. She hoped to persuade him to wear them at least *on top* of the sackcloth, so that he could come through the king's gate, speak with her and explain the reason for his mourning and fasting. But the *tzaddik* refused. "I swear that I will not remove my sackcloth even for a moment,[3] nor will I cover it with other clothing, until the decree is undone!" he proclaimed, and his words were transmitted to Esther.[4]

The queen lost no time in summoning Hasach,[5] her confidante.[6] She instructed him to go out to the city square,[7]

---

[2] The Ralbag indeed explains that Esther was concerned that Mordechai had been robbed and his clothing taken from him; that is why she sent him other garments. Only when he refused to accept them did she understand that he was clothed in this manner as a sign of grief, and then she rushed to send Hasach to find out the reason for his mourning. However, the simplest understanding of the *pesukim*, and the approach taken by most of the commentaries, is that Esther understood right from the start that behind Mordechai's unconventional dress lay a sorrowful reason.

[3] Perush HaGra

[4] The Malbim explains that Mordechai was careful neither to remove his sackcloth nor to speak with Esther, so as to avoid creating the impression that he was putting his trust in a human being. He wished to stress that the brunt of his effort was focused on the spiritual plane, while he was turning to Esther only because it was reasonable to assume that she would serve as the medium through which the Heavenly salvation would come about, as he said, "Who knows if it was just for such a time that you attained your royal position!"

[5] As the Yosef Lekach points out, when Esther saw that Mordechai would not give any details to the emissaries with whom she had sent the clothing, she understood that the matter was confidential, and therefore she sent Hasach, whom she could rely on for such a delicate mission.

[6] Malbim

[7] The Midrash (Bereishis Rabbah 74:2) states that Mordechai and Hasach intentionally made their meeting in the city square – a broad, open area - where nobody would be able to eavesdrop on their conversation.

to where Mordechai stood clothed in his tatters, and press him for details of what had happened. "Ask what terrible calamity has come upon my cousin, and what led up to it!"[8] Hasach rushed off on his mission.

This loyal emissary was not just another Persian chamberlain from among the king's royal staff; he was not a gentile, nor even a simple Jew. Hasach was actually none other than Daniel[9] the

---

[8] This is how most of the commentaries understand the *posuk*, "*Mah zeh ve'al mah zeh*," what was going on and why. However, Chazal (Esther Rabbah 8:2) derive a different interpretation for this *posuk*. They maintain that Esther, who lived in the royal palace, surely must have known about the decree that Haman Harasha had issued against the holy nation. However, she wished to find out from Mordechai Hatzaddik what the background was for this decree. "Did the Jews violate the ten commandments that were written *mi'zeh u'mizeh*, on both sides of the tablets? Did they deny the Master of the World, about Whom it is said, '*zeh keili ve'anvey'hu*,' 'This is my God and I shall praise Him?'" she asked, and Mordechai answered her in the negative.

The Meshech Chochma maintains that the intention of her question was, "Are the Jews being punished for prostrating themselves before a false image? If so, the decree would be sealed in blood, since the death sentence is the appropriate punishment for such a violation. Or are they being punished 'just' because they participated in the feast of Achashverosh, for which they would not be deserving of the death penalty, in which case the decree would be sealed only in clay."

"No, Esther the *tzaddekes*. It is the descendant of '*karahu*' – of Amalek who cooled off the fear the Jewish people struck in the hearts of their enemies when they left Mitzrayim – who has set out to annihilate them!" Mordechai explained. In these words, he alluded to the transgression the Jews committed by participating in the feast of Achashverosh, which was meant to trap them into sin, and which had its beginnings in the counsel that Haman Harasha had given King Achashverosh.

[9] Two explanations are cited in the Gemara regarding the name "Hasach." According to the first (Esther Rabbah 8:4), the name alludes to the fact that Daniel "*nech'tach*," was cut off from his high position. In the days of the previous monarchs he controlled a significant segment of the royal matters, while King Achashverosh demoted him from his lofty rank and appointed him to attend to Esther. According to the second explanation, the name actually hints at Daniel's position of power, implying that all royal matters were "*nech'tachim*," determined by his word. The Midrash brings a third opinion, according to which Daniel is called "Hasach" here in particular because he "*chatach*," clarified and drew out from Mordechai what exactly was happening and why.

The Meshech Chochma elaborates on the first explanation and explains that in the past, Daniel merited a high-ranking position due to his unusual devotion to Hashem,

tzaddik. As the loyal attendant of the queen, he was the one she chose to send to Mordechai to verify what exactly was going on.

Hasach Mediates between Mordechai and Esther

When Hasach came to Mordechai, no special efforts were needed to draw out the details that Esther wanted to know; Mordechai immediately provided him with all the necessary information.[10] He told him of the terrible decree as well as what sparked it – Haman's fury that was kindled as a result of

---

evidenced by his being thrown to the lions as a result of his unwavering assiduity in praying three times a day. However now the entire Jewish people was aroused to ardent repentance, abstaining from food and drink for three days, gathering in prayer and learning Torah, and dedicating themselves to the sanctification of Hashem's Name and the observance of His law in such a marvelous way. Consequently, the greatness of Daniel was minimized. It was now obvious how much capacity for self-sacrifice was latent in every Jew; he was not unique in this power.

[10] The Midrash mentions (Esther Rabbah 8:5) that Mordechai also told Hasach about a dream he once had, when Esther was a girl. In the dream, he saw two great sea-giants battling one another (a hint to Mordechai and Haman), and between them, a small people (the people of Israel), while all the other peoples sought to overcome this little nation and wipe its name off the face of the earth. In this little people's distress, they cried out to Hashem while the two sea-giants continued fighting each other, with no one able to separate them (a reference to the battle between Mordechai and Haman, with Haman trying to have Mordechai hung on the gallows, while Mordechai tried to overcome him and subordinate him with his prayers). Suddenly, a small stream of water passed between the sea-giants (a reference to the Jews' repentance) and separated the two contestants. Soon, the stream turned into a gushing river, with a current as strong as that of the Great Sea (saving all the Jews from Haman's decree), sweeping across the entire land. Then the sun came out, shining over the entire world, the small people was raised up, the mighty ones were lowered (as will be explained in the continuation of the *megillah*), and peace and tranquility reigned in all the land. (This commentary follows the Etz Yosef on Esther Rabbah 8:4.)

Mordechai asked Hasach to remind the queen of this dream which he had told Esther in her youth, asking him to give her the message that now, the meaning of the dream is understood. Yes, a terrible decree is hanging over the Jewish people, but they are destined to do *teshuva* and be delivered from their enemies, and Haman's downfall will soon follow.

Mordechai's refusal to bow before him according to the king's command.

Mordechai asked Hasach to convey all these details to Esther, along with an unequivocal order:

"Your mission now, Queen Esther, is to fall at the feet of the king and plead with him to have mercy on your people and annul the terrible decree! Until this point, your instructions were to conceal your family origin. But now circumstances have changed and the moment of truth has arrived – the moment for which you were Heavenly sent to the royal palace. Now you have to come to the aid of your brothers who are in terrible danger, and do whatever is in your power to save them!"

Along with these instructions, Mordechai attached a copy of the text of the decree that had been distributed in Shushan. Although, as we explained,[11] the only letter that had been

---

[11] According to the opinions who maintain that the explicit letters were also publicized already, Mordechai sent Esther a copy of this detailed letter, and went on to tell her orally that he feels a particular obligation to do whatever possible to save the Jewish people, since, in a certain sense, he bears a personal responsibility for the decree, which came about as a result of his refusal to bow down to Haman (Ralbag).

Regarding the reason that led Mordechai to send a copy of the letter and not to suffice with giving the message over orally, the commentary Ibn Yichyeh explains that the letters contained a long-winded treatise of slanderous words, as we described in the last chapter, and it was not feasible to transmit such a lengthy report orally.

In any case, from the responsibility Mordechai assumed for the decree that came about as a result of his actions, we can understand the stature of a true *gadol*. Even now, Mordechai did not retract his position; he did not think that he should have prostrated himself before Haman Harasha. Nevertheless, even though he was sure that he did the right thing by refusing to bow, he still took responsibility for the consequences of his actions and felt a personal obligation to do what he could to save the Jewish people from the decree which his actions played a part in bringing about.

A wondrous light is shed on the matter when we consider the fact that Mordechai was well aware of what was taking place in the heavens. He knew that in fact, the punishment was decreed on the Jewish nation because they had disobeyed him and

publicized at that point was the one ordering all the peoples to be prepared for the thirteenth of Adar, without specifying what was destined to take place on that day, Mordechai filled in the missing details orally[12] and asked Hasach to convey the message and explain it fully to Esther.[13]

Faithfully carrying out his mission, Hasach returned to Esther and conveyed Mordechai's words. But Esther was not so quick to accept her cousin's instructions. She ordered Hasach to go back to Mordechai and explain the illogic inherent in doing as he suggested.[14]

"Mordechai Hatzaddik, forgive me, but it seems to me that it would not be wise to approach the king now. Perhaps you have not been informed, but a new law was recently instituted by Haman.[15] According to this statute, entering the inner

---

participated in the feast of Achashverosh after he had pleaded with them not to do so. Despite all this, he did not exempt himself from the need to exert superhuman effort to save them. "When all is said and done, the decree was instigated by my deeds, and I have to take full responsibility!" he said to himself.

[12] All opinions agree that in addition to the written letter passed over, there was also an oral exchange between Mordechai and Esther, as the *posuk* writes explicitly, "He gave him a copy of the text of the decree that had been distributed in Shushan saying to destroy them, so he would show it to Esther and *report* to her."

[13] Malbim and other commentaries

[14] The Yosef Lekach explains that Esther did not actually send Hasach to *give over* her direct words to Mordechai. Rather, she presented her arguments to Hasach, and asked him to see to it that the gist of it would be passed on to Mordechai. Esther preferred not to give a direct message in this matter, since she did not want to give the impression that she was not interested in taking action for the benefit of the Jewish people. Therefore, she refrained from giving a direct response that would imply her rejection of Mordechai's request.

Following the same approach, the Yosef Lekach explains why this part of the exchange was not transmitted to Mordechai by Hasach. Since Hasach wanted to make it clear that these words were not being sent to Mordechai as a direct quote from Esther, he did not deliver the message himself, but rather through an intermediary. See the later footnote for additional reasons explaining the omission of Hasach from the exchange.

[15] Targum Yonasan

courtyard of the king without an explicit invitation from His Majesty is absolutely forbidden, and will subject the offender to the death penalty, without even recourse to a court judgment! The only way to be saved from death is if the king extends his golden scepter.[16] This is an all-inclusive law, without any exceptions; it applies to the queen herself as it does to all the king's servants!" Esther explained.

Esther then added, "This law is well known both to the king's servants and the general population. Therefore, I cannot possibly claim that I was ignorant of this prohibition! It is reasonable to assume that if I go into the king now, I will be killed, and no benefit will emerge from my foolhardy act.

"Even if the king would wish to pardon me because of his love for me, it would be extremely difficult for him to do so, since I will have committed a blatant violation of an explicit law in the public view. The "Vashti" precedent demonstrates just how sensitive the king is to this sort of offense.

"But even if Hashem were to grant me favor in the eyes of the king, and he would stretch out his golden scepter to me and grant me the gift of life, there would still be nothing gained by my visit in the king's courtyard. After my life will have barely been spared, would anybody imagine that I would have the nerve to make an additional request of the king? I would be eternally indebted to him just for not having me executed on the spot! I certainly would not be able to carry out my mission to undo the decree hanging over the Jewish people!

---

[16] In this way, Esther wished to hint to Mordechai that she might possibly be able to enter the king's court and be miraculously saved from death, if the king would extend his golden scepter to her (Minchas Erev).

"I have not been summoned to the king[17] for the last thirty days,[18] and chances are that I will be called to him very soon. I think it would be preferable to wait patiently. After all, the decree is not destined to be carried out in the near future, but in almost a full year from now. If I wait until I am called, the chances are very good that I will be able to influence the king without endangering myself," Esther argued, and her words were brought to Mordechai Hatzaddik's attention.

Surprisingly, at this point the name of Hasach is left out. Indeed, Haman noticed the communication Esther was carrying on with Mordechai through Hasach, and he was concerned that Mordechai was influencing the queen to act to nullify the decree. The *rasha* found an easy way to sabotage this line of communication; he simply killed Hasach.[19]

Therefore, Hasach's place was filled by the angels Gavriel and Micha'el who were sent down to earth for this purpose;[20] they transmitted the remaining messages between the cousins.

---

[17] The Targum points out that it was not by chance that King Achashverosh had refrained from summoning Esther to him for a period of thirty days. The underlying cause of this seeming estrangement was the ardent prayers of Esther the *tzaddekes*, who begged Hashem that she should not have to maintain any connection to the king, in keeping with the upbringing she was given by Mordechai. "Until now, I acted according to your instructions and did whatever possible to avoid coming to the king. And now, when doing so entails tremendous risk, you ask me to come before this *rasha* of my own free will?" Esther challenged Mordechai. But Mordechai was not dissuaded, as we shall soon explain.

[18] According to the Ralbag, with these words Esther wished to explain her inability to submit to Mordechai's request to enter the king's presence. She wanted to make it clear that she was not summoned to the king frequently, and as proof, she pointed out that for the past thirty days, Achashverosh had not called for her.

[19] Indeed, the Gemara explains that since Esther did not agree to Mordechai's request, Hasach refrained from giving over her reply, since "One does not convey a corrupt response." The Malbim maintains that Hasach was not killed, but that Esther asked that the message be transmitted through someone else, so that Haman should not suspect Hasach and seek to eliminate him.

[20] Targum Yonasan. The Midrash Ponim Acheirim says that from this point on, communication between Mordechai and Esther took place via *ru'ach hakodesh*.

Do Not Imagine You Will Find Refuge in the King's Palace

Mordechai refused to accept Esther's arguments. "I'm sorry to tell you," he sent to Esther, "but you have to approach the king now, without delay,[21] and plead with him for your people. The only reason you were selected as queen was for the sake of saving the Jews!

"Keep in mind, also, that it was the sin of your great-grandfather Shaul who left Agag alive and thereby made possible the birth of Haman Harasha and this decree! If it turns out that you could have saved the Jews and you did not do so, it will be considered as if you killed them with your own two hands![22] If even the fingernail of one Jew shall be harmed, you and the entire house of your forbear, Shaul, will rot in your sin![23]

"As to your argument that we would be better off waiting until you are summoned to the king, you must realize that Hashem does not hinge the deliverance of His children on your actions. If you are lax in carrying out your mission, He will send the Jews deliverance from some other place; Hashem has no lack of emissaries to do His will!

---

[21] The Yosef Lekach explains that Mordechai intentionally insisted that Esther should come to the king for the express purpose of pleading on her people's behalf in a manner that entailed tangible risk to her life, since in this way her words would be more readily accepted. If she would wait to be summoned to the king, and then mention her people's predicament "incidentally," the king would not grasp the full significance she accords to the deliverance of her people. But when he sees that she is willing to risk her life for it, and comes especially for this purpose to the king's courtyard, he will certainly understand that the matter is of paramount importance to her and the chances of his ceding to her request will be greatly increased.

[22] Perush HaGra

[23] Ralbag. See ibid, where he explains that the deliverance of the Jews came about through Esther in particular because she was a descendant of Shaul; that is why the task was placed upon her to correct what her ancestor had corrupted.

"If that happens, not only will you lose the opportunity to come to the aid of the Jewish people in their distress, but you will endanger yourself far more than you would have by coming to the king against the law. Once it is evident that you are not fulfilling the objective for which you were sent to the palace – i.e., the deliverance of the Jews – there will no longer be a need for you, and you and your father's house will perish![24]

"Perhaps you think that the danger hovering over the heads of the Jewish people does not affect you, since you are safely ensconced in the royal palace. But the decree does not distinguish between queen and maidservant. The decree hangs over your head precisely as it does over the rest of your people![25]

"Besides, nobody can promise you that a year from now, when the thirteenth of Adar rolls around, you will still retain your status and your present position. Nobody can guarantee that the king will not die by then or dismiss you. Then your name will certainly be eradicated together with the rest of your people![26]

"Therefore, my dear Esther, go into the king without delay and plead with him for your people. Remember that while Haman may appear to be strong and mighty, he is certainly no more powerful than his forbears, the Amalekite nation, whom Hashem subjugated to Yehoshua when they battled the Jews

---

[24] Malbim

[25] Ibn Yichyeh

[26] The Ibn Yichyeh mentions a similar line of logic, but he explains that Mordechai's intention was to hint to Esther that she should not push off her appeal to the king to a later date, since she cannot know how long she will remain in her position. Recent history proved this when Vashti was brought from the peak of success directly to the gallows.

coming out of Mitzrayim! Nor is he more powerful than the thirty one kings who fell before Yehoshua when he entered Eretz Yisroel, or than Sisera and his mighty army, whom Hashem gave over into the hands of a woman – Yael, the wife of Chever the Kenite! Nor is he stronger than Golias, whom Hashem handed over to His servant Dovid, who killed him with a slingshot!

"Nothing stands in Hashem's way.[27] Plead with Him, beg Him to save you as He saved the Jews countless times before in the merit of the holy *avos*. You'll see – He Who did wonders for our forefathers shall hand our own enemies into our hands and deliver us from the terrible decree!" Mordechai concluded.

The Fast of Esther

"*Ve'es ma'amar Mordechai Esther osah.*" Despite her original misgivings, Esther followed her practice of doing whatever Mordechai said. If Mordechai felt this was the right thing to do, she would carry out his instructions to the letter, especially now that she understood that nothing would be lost.[28] She was assured that even if she failed in her mission, it would not lead to the annihilation of the Jewish people, since "relief and deliverance will come to the Jews from some other place." She was ready to do her part calmly[29] and leave the rest in the

---

[27] In this way, Mordechai wished to make it clear to Esther that Hashem does not truly intend to decimate the Jewish nation, but rather to bring them to *teshuvah*. See above about Mordechai's dream.

[28] Malbim

[29] Esther emphasized, "If I am perish, I am perish." With these words, Chazal explain, she hinted to Mordechai that just as she had lost her family, so she would lose him. As long as she had come to the king only by force, she was not forbidden to Mordechai and could remain married to him. But once she would go to the king of her own free will, she would be forbidden to her husband and would have to give up her marital connection to Mordechai.

hands of the One Who created everything. The risk to her own life did not concern her.[30]

But before doing so, Esther had one request. "I will go into the king as you said," she relayed to Mordechai. "I am willing to do this for my people. But I ask only one thing – that you yourself[31] assemble the Jews in Shushan,[32] and that you all fast for three days.[33] Do not eat or drink;[34] just pray that Hashem should grant me success and enable me to complete my mission properly!

---

[30] Midrash Ponim Acheirim

[31] The Perush HaGra writes that Esther intentionally asked that Mordechai be the one to assemble the Jewish people for the three day fast since he too had to make a personal effort to correct Shaul's sin; Shaul was his forebear, precisely as he was an ancestor to Esther.

[32] The fast was limited to the Jews in Shushan, since it was impossible to inform the Jews in all the king's provinces (Perush HaGra). The Yosef Lekach adds that since the Jews of Shushan were the ones who participated in the feast of Achashverosh which led to the decree of annihilation on the Jews, they were the ones who had to fast and make amends for the matter. The same approach is taken by the Midrash Ponim Acheirim.

[33] The Yalkut (1056) implies that the three days of fasting were not consecutive, but rather for the daytime hours alone; at night the Jews ate so that they could survive. However, the Gemara (Yevamos 121b) clearly maintains that the fast was for three consecutive twenty four hour periods, without a break.

[34] Esther's fast called for abstaining from food and drink alone, not from anointing or wearing shoes, etc., since it was meant as an atonement for the sin of the Jews who participated in the feast of Achashverosh, which naturally featured food and drink. For the same reason, Esther said to assemble the Jews "hanimtze'im b'Shushan," "who are [presently] in Shushan," even if they are not permanent residents of Shushan, to correspond to the feast in which all the Jews, young and old, who were present in Shushan at the time participated (Yosef Lekach; see also Yalkut 1056).

The Yosef Lekach cites another reason why the affliction was limited to abstention from food and drink only. As the *pesukim* explicitly state, this fast included Esther and her maidservants as well. Under the circumstances, Esther and her maidservants could manage to abstain from food and drink while in the palace without attracting too much attention, but abstaining from wearing shoes and such would be more complicated and pose a greater risk of their deeds being discovered and their origin revealed.

"During these three days," Esther the *tzaddekes* went on, "I ask that you withhold food even from the livestock[35] and the nursing infants. The groom should leave his room girded in sackcloth and the bride should step out of her *chuppah* with dust on her head. When Hashem will see our wretchedness, perhaps He will have mercy! Perhaps He will help me find favor in the king's eyes and enable me to influence him to rescind the terrible decree."

The reason for the three day span of the fast, the Targum explains, was to correspond to the three days in which Avraham Avinu made his way to Har Hamoriah to offer up his son Yitzchok. In this way, Queen Esther wished to recall the merit of *akeidas Yitzchok*.[36]

The three days in which the entire nation in Shushan fasted fell out on the fourteenth, fifteenth and sixteenth of Nisan.[37] In effect, that year the Jewish people did not fulfill all the *mitzvos* of the Seder night, including the eating of *matzoh* and *maror*. Indeed, Mordechai pointed this out to Esther, but she

---

[35] Targum Sheini

[36] She also wanted to recall the merit of the *kohanim*, *levi'im* and *yisraelim* – the three segments of the nation who stood at Har Sinai and proclaimed as one, "We shall do and we shall listen." However, it is not so clear how the number three recalls the revelation at Har Sinai in particular.

[37] This is the simple understanding, since the letters were sealed on the thirteenth, as the *megillah* states explicitly, and immediately afterwards Mordechai rent his clothing and sent a message to Esther to come before the king, Esther asked that the people fast three days, beginning from the next day – the fourteenth of Nisan. The Midrash (Esther Rabbah 8:7), however, cites that the Jews fasted on the thirteenth, fourteenth and fifteenth of Nisan. The Alshich explains the words of the Midrash, stating that even though the letters to all the peoples were written by the king's scribes on the thirteenth of Nisan, the text was distributed in Shushan already on the twelfth, the day the decree was issued; only the sending of the letters to the distant provinces was put off until the next day. Therefore, the fast of Esther in Shushan began on the thirteenth of Nisan and continued through the fourteenth and fifteenth. We will deal with this further in the next chapter.

responded, "If there are no Jews, who will eat *matzoh?* Better to give up on fulfilling the *mitzvah* once, so that the Jewish people should do a full *teshuva* before their Creator and merit to be delivered from the decree of Haman Harasha!"[38]

And Mordechai Went

Ceding to Esther's request, Mordechai passed among all the Jews in Shushan and proclaimed the three day fast. He announced that all the Jews must assemble in prayer and beg Hashem to save them from Haman's horrible plan.

Mordechai told the twelve thousand *kohanim* of the Shushan community to go out to their fellow Jews holding a *shofar* in their right hand and a *sefer Torah* in their left and proclaim before Hashem, "We beg of You, God of Israel! Here is the precious Torah You gave us. If Your beloved people will be wiped off the face of the earth, who will study Your Torah? Who will observe Your *mitzvos* and call Your Name? The entire world was created by You just for the Jewish people; what point is there in its continued existence if the holy nation is no more?"

When the *kohanim* finished speaking, they fell to the floor and cried out, "*Aneinu!* Answer us, our Father, answer us! Answer us, our King, answer us!" They accompanied their cries with *shofar* blasts. The people echoed their prayers, until their cries reached Hashem, until all the heavenly hosts cried

---

[38] Esther Rabbah 8:7, and see Etz Yosef ibid. The Yalkut (1056) states that in their discussion, Mordechai raised the problem of calling a fast in the month of Nisan, when fasting is prohibited. It was to that statement that Esther gave the abovementioned response.

along with them, until the bones of the *avos* trembled in their graves!

Mordechai knew that the prayer of little children also had the power to influence Hashem's decision, since the mouths of these young ones were untainted yet by sin. Therefore, he denied them bread and water, clothed them in sackcloth and sat them in ashes. They cried and screamed to Hashem with all their might to deliver them from Haman's decree![39]

Then Mordechai himself raised his eyes upwards and poured forth his prayer.[40] "Father, You know full well that when I refused to prostrate myself before Haman Harasha, it was not my own honor I was protecting. Everything I did was for Your honor, understanding that it would be improper to grant any being of flesh and blood the honor I reserve for You alone![41]

"Had I not been concerned for Your honor, I would have bowed before him and even kissed his feet, anything, as long as he would not harm Your people of Israel! I would not have cared a whit for my own honor.

"Now, Hashem, I beg You to deliver us from the wicked hand of this arch enemy. Let him fall into the grave he dug

---

[39] It was especially in place to involve the children, since Haman had resolved to begin the annihilation project by killing these little schoolchildren, as we explained in an earlier chapter.

[40] Esther Rabbah 8:7

[41] This implies, as we mentioned several times earlier in the name of the commentaries, that there was no *absolute prohibition* to bow down to Haman. Even if he presented himself as a deity, the only prohibition involved in bowing to him would be in a case where doing so would appear to be worship of an image. However, when he is standing nearby and the prostration is obviously a gesture of respect, there is no prohibition against doing so. Nevertheless, Mordechai refused to prostrate himself because he felt it was still improper to bow down to a human being, especially since he was a member of the tribe of Binyamin who had never bowed to anyone but Hashem.

for us and be caught in the trap he set for Your faithful ones. Let him know that You did not forget what You promised us in Your Torah,[42] 'Even when they will be in the land of their enemies, I will not cast them away, nor will I abhor them to destroy them utterly and to break My covenant with them, for I am Hashem, their God!'"

Esther as well, isolated in the royal palace, joined in the general mourning. She was terribly frightened of the tragedy that threatened her people. Removing her royal garb, she wore sackcloth,[43] disheveled her hair, wallowed in the dust, afflicted herself with fasting, and poured out her heart to her Father in heaven.

She pleaded, "Master of the Universe! Please, help me! My dear Father, look at me – I was orphaned of both father and mother, dependent all my life on the mercies of others, never having a warm home to call my own. All my life, I have been accustomed to putting out my hand and begging others for my needs. Now I come before You, my Father, to beg for Your mercy!

"Here I am in a palace, a splendid palace, but I feel as if I am in prison. I wander from window to window, looking towards the heavens where Your Presence lies, and I offer my prayers to You. Please, help me succeed! Deliver Your flock from the enemies who have risen against us; after all, no obstacle can limit Your ability to redeem us!

---

[42] Vayikra 26:44

[43] Midrash Esther Rabbah 8:7. In an earlier footnote, we cited the opinion of the Yosef Lekach, according to which Esther could not afflict herself by abstaining from wearing shoes, anointing herself, etc., in the royal palace, since that might easily give away her national identity. According to this opinion, it is clear that she could not have donned sackcloth either.

"Father in heaven, Father of all fatherless children, come to the support of this poor orphan who relies on Your kindness! Let me find favor before King Achashverosh when I come before him to plead for my people! I admit that I am frightened of him, but I know that You, Who humbles the arrogant, can humble him before me!"

These were the prayers of Queen Esther throughout the three days of fasting, as she prepared to enter the chamber of the king against the rules.

ON THE THIRD DAY

> *"Then, on the third day, Esther donned her royal*
> *robes and stood in the inner court of the king's*
> *palace, facing the king's chambers. The king*
> *was sitting on his throne in the palace facing*
> *the entrance. When the king saw Queen Esther*
> *standing in the court, she found favor in his eyes.*
> *The king extended to Esther the golden scepter in*
> *his hand, and Esther drew close and touched the*
> *tip of the scepter. Then the king said to her, 'What*
> *is your request, Queen Esther? Even if it is half*
> *the kingdom, it shall be given to you.'" (5:1-3)*

On the third day[1] of the fast,[2] Esther took off the sackcloth garment she had been wearing.[3] She donned her royal robes[4] embroidered with gold thread and studded with precious

---

[1] This follows the Midrash, which, as we mentioned in a footnote in the previous chapter, maintains that the fast took place on the fourteenth, fifteenth and sixteenth days of Nisan, and on the third day, the sixteenth of Nisan, Esther came before the king. However, the Targum states that Esther came to the king on the *third day of Pesach*, not the *third day of her fast*. According to this, she did not come to the king until after the three days of fasting were concluded. Rashi in Megillah (16a), on the other hand, says that Esther came to the king on the *third day of the decree*, which was the second day of the fast, so that the next day – when Haman was hung on the gallows – turned out to be the third day of the fast.

[2] The Perush HaGra explains that since Esther needed to "don *ru'ach hakodesh*," it would only be possible after fasting, since *ru'ch hakodesh* will only imbue a body which is broken.

[3] See end of previous chapter.

[4] The Yosef Lekach states that Esther did not don the royal robes in her room, but only when she reached the king's court, so as not to be *poresh min ha'tzibbur*, to set herself apart from her brethren who were afflicting themselves, any earlier than necessary.

stones and pearls imported from Tarshish,[5] slipped on her golden shoes, and placed the golden crown on her head. With a prayer on her lips, she set out to take the decisive and perilous step that would lead either to the Jews' deliverance – or to her tragic end.

The timing of Esther's entrance – the third day – was not by chance. Chazal teach us that even when Hashem is "compelled," so to speak, to strike the Jewish people with painful decrees, these decrees cannot last for more than three days.[6]

An example of this is Avraham Avinu, who had to agonize on his way to Har Hamoriah, not knowing yet where he was to carry out his Creator's commandment. On the third day, "he saw the place from afar."[7] Similarly, the sons of Yaakov who were imprisoned in Mitzrayim by Yosef's command did not remain there for more than three days. The prophet Yonah, too, was delivered from the innards of the fish after three days. Chazal tell us that the suffering that will be experienced at the time of the resurrection of the dead also will not exceed three days.[8]

Here as well, the process of the Jews' deliverance began on the third day, with Esther's entrance into the king's court.

---

[5] Targum Sheini

[6] Esther Rabbah 9:3. See Etz Yosef ibid where he explains that after three days, the calamity would enter the category of *chazoka*, a set state, and it would be harder to deliver them from such a situation.

[7] Bereishis 22:4

[8] See Etz Yosef, who explains that this refers to the pain experienced by the dead who shall come to life before they know if they are among those who have been resurrected for eternal life – or for eternal disgrace.

Clad in Ru'ach Hakodesh

Although Esther donned her royal garb[9] before stepping into the king's court, she did not rely on the beauty these man-made robes lent her to capture the king's heart.[10] Before wearing her elaborate robes, she implored her Creator to endow her with His Spirit,[11] to give her a heavenly charm that would rouse the king's mercies and crown her efforts with success.[12]

"Master of the Universe, I am about to come before this foolish king, but I am not relying on my own merits; I know I have nothing of my own. I am frightened for the fate of Your children! Hashem, You created the entire world in the merit of the Jewish people. If they will be wiped out, who will exalt and sanctify Your Name every day? *That* is why I am about to put my life on the line to beg the king's mercy for my people!

"Please, just as You saved Chananiah, Misha'el and Azariah from the furnace and Daniel from the lion's den, save me from the hands of King Achashverosh and let me find favor in his eyes!" Esther pleaded, her voice suffused with tears and hoarse with her cries.

---

[9] Even according to the Gemara's opinion that Esther "donned *ru'ach hakodesh*," this does not contradict the fact that she wore actual royal clothing when she entered the personal quarters of the king. Chazal apparently derive from the fact that the *posuk* does not say Esther wore "*big'dei malchus*," royal clothing, but just says "*va'tilbash malchus*," she wore "royalty," that the implication is that she donned *ru'ach hakodesh*.

[10] The Yosef Lekach points out that Esther did not use makeup, color her eyes, or take any other measures of *hishtadlus*, human effort, other than wearing the royal robes as was required of her when appearing before the king.

[11] Since the *posuk* states that Esther *donned royalty*, we have to understand that she took some sort of action in order to clothe herself in *ru'ach hakodesh*. Since Chazal (in Targum Sheini) describe Esther's prayer at length, it seems that this is the action she took in order to merit *ru'ach hakodesh*.

[12] Targum Sheini

"Hashem, hear my plea! We have been exiled from our land and distanced from our sanctuary, and, due to our sins, we have been sold to cruel masters who want nothing but to kill and destroy us! Our arch enemy Haman was willing to pour rivers of silver and gold into the royal treasury to acquire the right to slaughter every last one of Your beloved children!

"Please, Father, see Your children, wearing sackcloth and wallowing in the dust as they beg for Your mercy. See the young children who have never sinned. Why should they suffer the consequences of their fathers' sins? And even if the young children are guilty of some transgressions, what could the nursing infants possibly have done?

"Remember the merit of our forefathers – Avraham, whom You submitted to all kinds of trials and who was found to be of pure and ready heart, Yitzchok, who willingly extended his neck to be offered as a sacrifice to You, and Yaakov and all the *tzaddikim* throughout the generations!

"I beg of You, hear our prayers, deliver us from our danger and avenge us from our arch enemy; sever his pride so that he shall never rise again!

"Merciful One, Who forgives sin and keeps His covenant for thousands of generations, answer us as You answer all those who cry to You in desperation! Let the merit of Avraham Avinu escort me as I go to the king, let *akeidas Yitzchok* boost me above him, let the *chesed* of Yaakov be on my lips and the charm of Yosef on my tongue! Do not turn me away!"

Concluding her heartfelt prayer, Esther set out, supported by one of her maidservants, while another walked behind holding up her adornments and robes so that they should not drag on the floor and become soiled.

Imbued with *ru'ach hakodesh*,[13] a heavenly beauty emanated from her. Even someone who did not know her could have pointed her out unerringly: "There goes the queen, glowing with the charm of royalty."

When Esther passed by the building where Achashverosh stored his collection of idols and false images, however, her *ru'ach hakodesh* suddenly left her; a spirit of holiness and sanctity had no place alongside such a place of spiritual defilement. But Esther did not realize the reason for its withdrawal. Certain that the *ru'ach hakodesh* had left because of her sins, she began to agonize if she was at fault for coming to Achashverosh of her own free will, or if she was wrong in using a disrespectful title for the king when she said,[14] "Deliver my soul from the sword, my spirit from the *dog*."

Esther panicked. She knew that without that heavenly charm, she had no chance of gaining the king's good graces. A seventy five year old woman, of greenish pallor, coming after a three day stint of fasting and mourning,[15] could not possibly attract the king by natural means! "If the *ru'ach hakodesh* does not return, my mission is doomed!" Esther understood. She cried out, "'*Keli Keli, lamah azavtani!*' 'Hashem, why did You abandon me?' True, I am going into the king's court willingly,

---

[13] Megillah 14a. The Midrash Ponim Acheirim cites that Hashem clothed her in a "reflection of heavenly royalty."

[14] Tehillim 22:21

[15] The Yosef Lekach makes this point when he explains that Esther certainly did not have a natural beauty when she appeared before the king; rather, she found favor in his eyes only as a result of the heavenly "thread of kindness" that emanated from her.

but can it really be called free will? I have no choice but to do so in order to save Your people! And if I was wrong in calling Achashverosh a dog, I correct my words and beg of You,[16] 'Deliver me from the mouth of the lion!'"

Then Esther added,[17] "Father in heaven, You gave Jewish women three special *mitzvos*; did I violate any one of them? Yet when our matriarch Sarah was taken into Pharaoh's palace for one night alone, You afflicted him with terrible plagues! How about me? I have been in the palace of this wicked king for years against my will, and he still has not been stricken! At least deliver me from his hands!"

In the meantime, Esther passed beyond the house of idols, and the *ru'ach hakodesh* returned to her. She approached the inner court of the king and prepared to take the irreversible and dangerous step.

Esther Reaches the King

Esther had no problem[18] getting as far as the entrance to the courtyard. An ordinary person would have been stopped by the palace guards long before he had reached that point, but as queen, nobody would dare tell her what to do. All the gates were open for her, and she reached the king's court with ease.

The structure of Achashverosh's palace[19] consisted of an outer court, at the center of which stood the royal palace

---

[16] Tehillim 22:22

[17] Aggadas Esther

[18] Ibn Ezra

[19] Malbim. In contrast, Ibn Yichyeh explains that the king had many houses, each one with a courtyard at the front. Each day, the king would choose to reside in one of the houses, depending on the weather conditions, since some buildings were cooler while others were built in a way that made them naturally warmer. Esther,

where the king would sit and administer judgment. From the royal palace, there was access to the king's quarters, where Achashverosh himself lived.

Generally, the king would sit in his inner quarters, not coming out to the royal palace unless a particular need arose. Had that been the case when Esther reached the inner court, the situation would have been rather dire. The king, in his private quarters, would not have known anything about her arrival. Before he would have had a chance to notice her, she would have been caught by the guards appointed to seize anyone who violated the prohibition of entering the court.

But now the amazing Heavenly assistance that accompanied Esther at every step of the way began to show itself. That precise day when Esther came to the palace, the king sat in the royal palace, and not only that; he sat *right opposite the entrance*, so that he noticed the queen the moment she stepped in![20]

The king was not at all shocked to see Queen Esther in his court. He never thought that the law limiting entrance to his court would include the queen! The opposite was true. King

who thought that the king would be in a certain house that day as was his practice at this season of the year, planned to enter the court of another, nearby building, where entrance was permissible, since the king was not presently residing there. She hoped that the king would catch a glimpse of her from his abode and summon her before him, or at least that she would have the opportunity to get somewhat of an idea of his intentions regarding her. However, by Heavenly Providence, the king happened to be precisely in the house within the courtyard Esther chose to enter, and he even sat opposite the entrance. As soon as he saw Esther stepping into the court, he immediately extended the golden scepter in his hand, a gesture that was interpreted as an invitation to come before him.

[20] *Seeing* Esther was a crucial factor, since the king only stretched out the golden scepter after Esther found favor in his eyes, and this favor would not have been possible had he not *seen* the queen (Minchas Erev).

Achashverosh would have been extremely pleased if the queen were to come to him every day![21]

Nevertheless, when the king sensed that Esther was hesitant to proceed and was waiting for his permission, he quickly extended his golden scepter. Esther drew closer and touched the head of the scepter.

Esther's humble behavior – not seeing herself as worthy to appear before the king at any time, but rather waiting until she was called – appealed to the king. He was deeply impressed by her nobility and refinement, and her charm was enhanced in his eyes.[22] This served as an excellent starting point for their entire encounter, since the king immediately gave her a warm and loving reception and made a grand announcement about his eagerness to fulfill all her requests.

This is how many of the commentaries describe the scenario, but not everyone agrees. Chazal provide a conflicting description, which indicates that the king was not at all pleased with Esther's unannounced visit to his court and that she was in fact in grave danger at that moment.

The Midrash[23] depicts the encounter as follows. When the king saw Queen Esther, he was furious that she had disobeyed his order and entered the court without being summoned.[24]

---

[21] As we explained in the previous chapter, Esther prayed all the time that she should not be summoned to the king, and her pleas bore fruit.

[22] Malbim

[23] Esther Rabbah 9:1

[24] The Yalkut (Tehillim 22) brings the opinion that King Achashverosh was sitting in a room within a room within a room – seven times over. Nobody stopped Esther as she entered the first three rooms, but when she got to the fourth, the king glimpsed her and began to grind his teeth in irritation, muttering to himself angrily, "What a shame that this one will perish and I won't be able to find another one like

His eyes flashed with anger and his face contorted in rage. Identifying the danger signals, Esther's spirit dropped sharply. "I am lost!" she said to herself, and her head collapsed hopelessly onto the shoulder of the maidservant at her right.

But at that moment, Hashem, having mercy on His people, saw the pain of this orphan who trusted Him so implicitly and decided to deliver her from danger.[25] Instantly, He improved her outer appearance[26] and granted her favor in the king's eyes.[27] One special angel was dispatched to imbue her with a "thread of kindness," while another was sent for the express purpose of extending her neck and lending her a proper, impressive posture. Achashverosh instantly had a change of heart[28] and extended the scepter to Esther.[29]

---

her. How ironic – Vashti was killed because she disobeyed me and didn't come when I summoned her, and now this one is going to meet her death because she came without being summoned!"

Nevertheless, the king's guards could not yet harm Esther, because the guards at the outer entrance to the palace were not permitted to enter the palace as far as the place where she stood, while the guards in the inner room were prohibited to leave. This fact bought Esther the time she needed to pour her heart out in prayer, as we shall describe.

[25] Both the Yalkut and the Midrash Ponim Acheirim state that the king tried to turn his face away from Esther, but an angel forcibly turned it back. The Midrash Ponim Acheirim also says that when the king saw Esther, his vision improved and his eyes were illuminated.

[26] The Midrash Tehillim (22) tells us that an angel slapped the king on his mouth and forced him to speak gently to Esther and appease her, instead of punishing her as he originally intended.

[27] The Targum mentions that the king saw how sad she was, the tears rolling down her cheeks, and his love for her was aroused by this pathetic sight.

[28] The Yosef Lekach explains that Esther actually prayed for two conflicting things: On the one hand, she asked to find favor in the king's eyes. But at the same time, she pleaded *not* to find favor in his eyes so she would not be forced to be with him. We see that her contradictory request was fully carried out. When Esther reached the *court*, she found favor in the king's eyes, but afterwards, when she *drew close to him*, this charm dissipated and the king did not feel a desire to come near her.

[29] As the Malbim points out, the fact that the scepter was in the king's hands was not a natural phenomenon. The Yosef Lekach adds that the king generally held

It should be pointed out that in order for Esther to be spared the death sentence, the king had to extend the scepter *to her*, i.e., to stretch it out until she could touch it. The problem was that the scepter was short, just two cubits, while, according to one opinion,[30] Esther stood at a great distance – two hundred cubits, more than a hundred meters away from the king. After three days of fasting, Esther had no strength left. She could barely stand, let alone walk that distance. How would she touch the scepter? For that purpose, Hashem sent a third angel who stretched the king's scepter until it reached Queen Esther's hand![31] Esther touched it, and the immediate danger passed.

---

his scepter only when he was walking or leaning on it. When he was seated on his throne, the scepter was always set down at his side. Had that been the case, the king might not have had a chance to reach for it before the servants had executed Esther! Therefore, it was miraculous that the scepter should happen to be in his hand just when Esther walked in, so that he was able to extend it the moment he saw her enter!

Indeed, the Targum Sheini explains that the *sarei hatabachim*, the ministers in charge of execution who stood before the king, wanted to kill Esther as soon as she walked into the court without the king's permission, but the king stretched out his scepter and prevented them. This implies that had the king not extended the scepter at that moment, he could not have prevented the sentence from being carried out, since the law read, "If anyone, man or woman, shall come to the king, to his inner courtyard, without having been summoned, *there is but one law for him – the death penalty*, unless *the king stretches out to him his golden scepter, and then he shall live!*"

[30] The Gemara cites a difference of opinion regarding this point, with different views brought about the distance between the two. The most conservative estimate places it at twelve cubits, while the most extreme opinion places it at two hundred cubits.

[31] Apparently, until the queen touched the scepter, the king could still reconsider. Therefore, a special miracle was necessary to enable her to touch the scepter before the fickle king would change his mind. Otherwise, she could have waited a while until her strength returned and she walked to the king on her own two feet.

This fits right in with the words of the Yosef Lekach that we cited before, according to which Esther's finding favor was limited to the time when she stood in the court, while later, when she drew close to the king, that charm dissipated so that the king would not ask her to be with him. Had Esther drawn close to the king before touching the tip of the scepter, he would have pulled back his scepter when she lost her charm and she would have been doomed.

What is Your Request, Queen Esther?

"Esther, why are you frightened?" the king asked. "The new law was never meant to include you. You are my queen; why don't you speak to me naturally when you come into my court?"

Esther decided to grasp the opportunity and flatter him a bit. "When I saw you, I was so awed by your honor that I couldn't get a word out of my mouth!" the *tzaddekes* responded in her sweetest tone. The king lapped up the compliment. He received Esther with great pleasure and expressed his satisfaction by announcing his willingness to carry out virtually any request she would ask of him.

Actually, as soon as the king saw Esther's face, wan and drawn from fasting, he understood that she had a weighty request to ask of him. Besides, he could have guessed that the queen would not have risked her life to enter the court without permission unless she had something extremely urgent to discuss with the king.

Therefore, he turned to her and said, "What do you want, Esther?[32] Why do you look so ill? Whatever you ask of me, I shall do; even if it is half the kingdom, it shall be given to you!" But in the same breath, he qualified his words, "That is to say, if the request relates to you personally. If your request relates to others, I do not promise to carry it out."[33]

---

[32] Ibn Yichyeh explains that the king meant to ask Esther if her request is to remove her from some sort of harm, which would fit in with the language, "*mah lach,*" – i.e., "what happened *to you.*" Or do you wish to ask for something, as is implied by the language, "*mah she'aylasech,*" "what is your request."

[33] Several commentaries follow this line of thought. However, the Perush Ha'Gr"a disagrees and writes that the king obligated himself to agree to any petition Esther would make, including requests relating to others.

Achashverosh limited his generosity in another way as well. He offered the queen whatever she requested, but only until "*half the kingdom.*" The simple understanding of this phrase is that the king was willing to give Esther even half the kingdom if she wished to share the sovereignty with him – half for him and half for her. More than half he did not agree to give her, since it is not proper to give the next person more than you keep for yourself.[34]

But in addition[35] to this literal explanation, there is a deeper meaning latent in Achashverosh's words. He wanted to emphasize that if the queen intended to request that he should agree to build the *Bais Hamikdash*, he would not be able to fulfill her wishes. "I have already sworn not to do this. I am also afraid that the Jews would rebel against me!"[36] the king explained his unwillingness to fulfill such a request.[37]

Nonetheless, Esther realized that a rare opportunity had fallen into her hands. The king enabled her to make almost any request she wanted, until half the kingdom, and he promised to carry it out!

---

[34] Yosef Lekach
[35] Megillah 15b
[36] Targum Yonasan
[37] It is interesting to note that there was no apparent basis for his assumption that Esther was intending to make such a request. On the contrary! It doesn't seem logical that the queen would take such a risk in order to ask for the construction of the *Bais Hamikdash*. Even if she was a great lover of the Jews, there were other, far more urgent requests she could have made for the Jewish people at that critical time, when they were due to be eradicated from the face of the earth in less than a year! But the king was so horrified at the possibility of a rebuilt *Bais Hamikdash* that he did not forget to emphasize that if, by some far-fetched chance, the queen had in mind to make such a request, he would be forced to deny it.

LET THE KING AND HAMAN COME

> *"Esther said, 'If it pleases the king, let the king and Haman come today to the banquet that I prepared for him.' The king commanded, 'Tell Haman to hurry and carry out Esther's request.' So the king and Haman came to the banquet that Esther prepared. At the wine feast, the king said to Esther, 'What is your request? It shall be granted to you. And what is your petition? Even if it is half the kingdom, it shall be done.' Esther responded and said, 'My request and my petition – if I have found favor in the eyes of the king and if it pleases the king to grant my petition and to fulfill my request – is that the king and Haman should come to the banquet I shall prepare for them, and tomorrow I will do the king's bidding.'"*
> *(5:4-8)*

Given the opportunity to make any request she wanted of the king, Esther chose to invite Achashverosh, along with Haman, his chief minister, to a banquet she had prepared in advance in her own royal house.

Though Esther invited the king along with Haman, she made a point of stressing that the banquet was really meant especially for the king, with Haman just invited to "tag along."[1] This emphasis was made in order to render proper honor to

---

[1] Ibn Yichyeh

the king, and also to prevent him from being irritated by the invitation of a minister to a private, family banquet.[2]

In addition, Esther made it clear that the banquet was all prepared and the food already cooling off; Achashverosh had to come immediately. Her objective was to prevent the king from grasping at an excuse to evade the invitation or postpone it to another time. After the queen had worked so hard and prepared a banquet especially in his honor, it was clear that he could not refuse to attend![3]

To the Banquet I Prepared

As we see, Esther planned the wording of her request carefully, down to the last detail. But the obvious question is why she chose this request at all. Instead of begging the king immediately to have mercy on her people and tear up Haman's evil decree, her urgent petition was that he come to the banquet she prepared, together with the arch villain himself. How can we understand this?

A number of answers are offered to this puzzling question.[4] First of all, Esther understood that the king's generosity had its limits, and after the king had just displayed his largesse

---

[2] In contrast, the Yosef Lekach explains that when Esther stressed that the king should come to the banquet she prepared *for him*, she meant to emphasize that the banquet was meant for the king as opposed to the queen; *she* could not take part in it. As we mentioned at the beginning of the previous chapter, the first banquet took place on the third day of Esther's fast, and therefore she could not actively join in the meal. The Yosef Lekach adds that at the banquet itself, the king wished to drink a toast with his queen, and since she was unable to do so, she informed him that the next day she would hold another party at which she would do the king's bidding and actively participate.

[3] Malbim

[4] Yosef Lekach

by sparing her life, it would be too much to ask him at that moment to spare her people as well.

Therefore, at their first meeting, Esther merely invited the king to the banquet, a request which she knew would bring him pleasure, and thus give him the feeling that he did well by sparing her life. At the banquet, Esther planned to make the true, much more substantial request for which she risked her life to come to the king.

Secondly, Esther knew that even if the king would accept her request regarding her people at this point, her mission would still not be successfully completed, since Haman could easily come and persuade the king to reissue the decree. In order to resolve the problem definitively, Esther understood, she also had to get rid of Haman. The question was, how to do it?

Esther was aware of a basic fact of human nature – when a person dips sharply from a state of extreme joy to a state of anger, that anger is a terrible, consuming one. Therefore, Esther planned to invite the king to a banquet, gladden his heart, and then, just when he was at the peak of joy – tell him of Haman's wickedness. In this way, the king's anger would be so strongly fired up that her enemy would surely get the punishment he deserved.

A third explanation attributes Esther's strategy to her need for a calm state of mind in presenting her true request. Esther knew that when she would enter the king's court without permission she would be so worked up that she would barely be able to get a word out; she certainly would not be able to set out her request clearly and rationally.

Therefore, at this first encounter, she kept the exchange as brief as possible, and just invited the king to her party. At the banquet, she would be much calmer and capable of wording her request in the best way possible.

Let the King and Haman Come

Now we understand why Esther called the banquet and did not make her major request at once. But we are still left with a glaring question. Why was Haman included? Was there no better a guest for the queen to honor with an invitation to her banquet than the villain who sought to annihilate her people?

Chazal[5] offer a lengthy list of explanations.

According to the first reason, Esther's intention was to set a trap for Haman. By giving him the mistaken impression that he was in her good favor, she dulled his alertness. Then, the moment the perfect opportunity would present itself, she would be able to degrade and humble him, when he least expected the attack.

A second explanation maintains that Esther wished to bring Haman to the apex of success. As we know, once a person's *mazal* reaches its peak, it changes direction and begins to wane – which is exactly what Esther was aiming for.[6]

A third view suggests that Esther was afraid Haman would suspect she planned to speak to the king about him, and thus would find a way to sidestep her efforts, or would rebel against the king and implement his decree some other way. Therefore, it was important for her to keep him on the spot.

---

[5] Megillah 15b
[6] See Ibn Yichyeh and Malbim.

According to a fourth explanation, Esther simply wished to conceal her origin. A request for an urgent audience with the king three days after such an unprecedented decree of annihilation was issued would be likely to raise the king's suspicions, and perhaps lead him to refuse to come to the banquet altogether. Therefore, Esther also invited Haman, the one who had initiated the whole thing, so as to put the king's suspicions at rest and give the impression that her invitation had nothing at all to do with Haman's decree.[7]

Yet a fifth view hinges Haman's invitation on Esther's desire to rouse the Jewish people to sincere *teshuva* and fervent prayer, which she accomplished by giving them the clear impression that they could not pin their hopes on their sister in the royal palace. "Look how Esther is buttering up Haman Harasha by inviting him to her banquet with the king in order to save herself. Surely, she will not lift a finger to help us!" they all thought.[8]

A sixth opinion maintains that Esther sought to keep Haman in the close vicinity on the assumption that at some point in the course of the banquet, she would manage to trip him into some inappropriate conduct towards the king, and

---

[7] In fact, as we mentioned earlier, the Megillas S'sorim explains that at first, the king stressed that she could only make a request related to herself, since he was afraid she intended to speak on behalf of the Jews. However, once he saw that Esther had invited Haman to the banquet, he was no longer concerned, and he allowed the queen to ask whatever she wished, including petitions relating to others. He felt assured that she was a hater of the Jews just as he was; after all, she had invited Haman, the Jews' arch enemy, to her party.

[8] According to this explanation, we have to assume that Mordechai gathered the Jews in fasting without mentioning that Esther was the one who suggested the fast or that she intended to go plead before the king.

could then use it as an excuse to incite the king's ire against him.[9]

Besides, Esther wished to close accounts with Haman at the earliest moment; therefore, she needed him close at hand. Indeed, at the second banquet, as soon as the king heard that Haman was planning to decimate Queen Esther's people, and among them Mordechai who had spoken good for the king, he ordered the villain hanged on the spot!

According to the seventh explanation, Haman's invitation was meant to rouse Heavenly mercies. "If Hashem will see to what depths I have reached, that I have to invite the enemy of the Jews to my banquet, perhaps He will have mercy on His people!" Esther thought to herself.

Yet an eighth view asserts that Esther wished to stir up the king's jealousy towards Haman. She hoped that the king would suspect that Haman maintained secret connections with the queen, or that the queen was fond of his esteemed chief minister. This fact would lead him to try and get rid of his competitor as soon as possible. [10] "Even if I lead the king to suspect both Haman and myself, so that he orders both of us executed, as long as I can save my people with my death, I will be satisfied," she resolved.

---

[9] In fact, if we examine the text closely, we will find that the "straw that broke the camel's back" and drove the king to send Haman to his death was the fact brought to the king's attention by Charvona that Haman sought to kill *Mordechai who spoke good for the king*. This followed Haman's apparent efforts to overcome the queen in the king's own home. Thus, Haman was guilty of improper conduct, unrelated to Queen Esther and her request of the king.

[10] Indeed, at the end, the king's suspicions were aroused, when he saw Haman prostrated on Esther's couch.

The ninth answer explains that since Achashverosh was a fickle king,[11] Esther was concerned that even if she were to succeed in convincing him to kill Haman, he might easily change his mind before he would have a chance to implement his decision. Therefore, she wanted to make sure that Haman would be in the area so that the king would be able to carry out his ruling immediately.

According to the tenth opinion, Esther was familiar with the principle *"Lif'nei shever ga'on,"* "Pride goes before a fall." Therefore, she wished to bring Haman to a state of pomposity and pride, so as to guarantee that the "fall" would soon follow.[12]

The eleventh and final explanation maintains that Esther simply based herself on historical experience. She learned from the example of Belshatzar's feast, which concluded with that *rasha's* downfall, that wicked people are disposed of at festive banquets. Therefore, she prepared a banquet for the king and Haman, in the hope that he too would be destroyed in the course of the feast.

These are the explanations cited in the Gemara.[13] The Talmudic sage Rabbah bar Avuha once encountered Eliyahu

---

[11] See Anaf Yosef (Pesichta d'Esther Rabbah 9), where he explains in the name of the Kol Yaakov that it was a great kindness of Hashem to place over the Jews a king who changed his mind all the time – who first killed his wife because of his friend's advice, and then killed his friend because of his wife's advice. Had the king been the type to "stick to his guns," it might have been a lot more difficult to undo the evil decree.

[12] The distinction between this explanation and the second one is unclear, but both are cited separately in the Gemara.

[13] The Malbim and Ibn Yichyeh bring another explanation, according to which Esther wanted to make it clear to the king that she had nothing personal against Haman, the proof being that she invited him to her banquet. Otherwise, the king

Hanavi and asked him, "Tell me, from among all the explanations in the Gemara, what is the true reason Esther invited Haman to her banquet?" Eliyahu Hanavi's response was, "All of them." Every one of these angles was taken into consideration.

Tell Haman to Hurry

Achashverosh accepted Esther's invitation with pleasure. He sent his servants to tell Haman to hurry and come to the banquet immediately, by Esther's order, making it perfectly clear that participation was not only a privilege but also an absolute requirement.[14]

Before long, the king and Haman were seated around a lavishly set table in the queen's quarters, imbibing wine at their pleasure. In the course of the banquet, the king once again

---

might suspect that Esther was slandering Haman for reasons of personal enmity, while he himself was actually pure of any wrongdoing.

Another explanation cited there is that Esther wished to deny Haman the opportunity to set out his arguments and responses before the king. "If Haman will be caught off guard by a sudden attack, without having a chance to give the matter consideration, he will be confused and won't know what to answer," Esther surmised, and her conjecture proved itself to be correct.

A third explanation found in the commentaries is that Esther knew that King Achashverosh could be a very dangerous character when under the influence of wine at a party; the "Vashti precedent" was a vivid example. Therefore, she planned to incite his anger during the wine feast, hoping that in the heat of his fury, he would close accounts with Haman Harasha.

The Targum Sheini, on the other hand, brings a different answer, based on the approach we cited in earlier chapters, according to which Haman had Hasach killed when he suspected him of being the agent between Mordechai and Esther in plotting against Haman. Since Esther was not interested in all her servants being liquidated by Haman, she preferred to give Haman the impression that she had an excellent relationship with him, so that he would not suspect her of plotting against him.

[14] Malbim. The Targum Yonasan, on the other hand, implies that the king merely implored Haman to come to the feast without obligating him. In any case, it is clear that Haman did not require much convincing.

turned to Esther and asked,[15] "Tell me, my dear queen, what is your request? Even if it is half the kingdom, it shall be yours. I understand that you did not risk your life to come into my court without being summoned just to invite me to a wine banquet."[16]

Esther responded diplomatically, in a flattering tone, "My master, the king, nothing is more important to me than to please you. This is my greatest request, and I do not deserve to ask more than that. But if I have indeed found favor in your eyes, and if my next petition also pleases you, I would be happy to invite you tomorrow as well, along with Haman, to another banquet[17] that I will prepare for you."[18]

This time, however, Esther added a little surprise for King Achashverosh. "At that banquet, I promise to reveal to the king the secret I have been guarding so religiously until now – the

---

[15] During the banquet, the king was no longer concerned that something was bothering Esther, since she put on a fine show of a smiling countenance, now that her traumatic experience was over and the immediate danger of death removed. Therefore, this time, he just asked what her request was (Ibn Yichyeh). Besides, the king figured that if something was really bothering Esther, she would not have waited until the banquet to ask for it, but would have requested it immediately when she met him earlier that day (Minchas Erev).

[16] Midrash Ponim Acheirim

[17] See the earlier footnote in which we presented the approach of the Yosef Lekach, who maintains that the need for a second banquet arose as a result of the king's desire that Esther drink together with him, which she could not do at the first banquet since she was still fasting.

[18] Now that she had already proven her affection for the king, Esther was not afraid to imply that the banquet was meant for the king and Haman equally. In fact, from this point on, she preferred to present matters in this light, so as to rouse the king's jealousy of Haman (Ibn Yichyeh). In addition, she wanted to encourage Haman to let his guard down, so she acted as if she felt he was on equal standing with the king (Perush HaGra). Besides, it wouldn't be polite to ignore Haman while he was sitting right there (Minchas Erev).

secret of my roots!" the queen announced. Upon hearing that, the king was the happiest man on earth. Not only was the king thrilled as he left Esther's banquet, but Haman also left the palace that day brimming with delight.

ALL THIS MEANS NOTHING TO ME

*"Haman went out that day happy and exuberant.
But when he saw Mordechai at the king's gate
and noticed that he did not rise or even stir before
him, Haman was infuriated with Mordechai.
Haman restrained himself and came home,
and then he sent for his friends and his wife
Zeresh. Haman recounted to them the glory of
his wealth and his large number of sons, and
how the king promoted him and elevated him
above the officials and royal servants. 'Moreover,'
Haman said, 'Queen Esther invited no one but
me to accompany the king to the banquet that she
prepared, and tomorrow, too, I am invited to her
along with the king. Yet all this means nothing to
me as long as I see Mordechai the Jew sitting at
the king's gate.' Then his wife Zeresh and all his
friends said to him, 'Let a gallows be made, fifty
cubits high, and tomorrow morning, speak to the
king and have him hang Mordechai on it. Then
you can come with the king to the banquet in good
spirits.' Their suggestion pleased Haman and he
had the gallows prepared." (5:9–14)*

The day Haman was invited to Esther's banquet was the
happiest in his life[1] – but his exuberance did not last for more
than a few hours, only from the time he received the invitation

---

[1] Ibn Yichyeh; Malbim

until he exited the king's gate and met up with Mordechai, his mortal enemy.

Haman never felt fully happy with what he had, because the desire always pulsed in his heart to acquire more and more – more glory, more money, more status – in short, more. Now, for a brief moment, he tasted the pleasure of feeling he had everything. But from the minute he encountered Mordechai Hatzaddik, he never again felt that pleasure. His *mazal* had already begun to fade and his end was near.

Actually, we would not have expected Haman to be so happy and serene. Just three days before he had issued a decree, unprecedented in its cruelty, to annihilate all the Jews without any justification. Now, out of the blue, he was invited by Queen Esther to a banquet with the king. Ostensibly, the gears in Haman's mind should have begun to turn. Understanding that he must have acquired many enemies among the Jews, he ought to have been extremely vigilant and regarded every unexpected invitation as highly suspicious.

Of course, even had Haman preferred not to participate in the banquet, he would not have had much of a choice; he was under the king's orders to do so. Nevertheless, why didn't he ask himself the simple question, "Why did Esther decide now, of all times, to make a banquet and invite me to accompany the king to the party?"[2]

The answer is that Haman was so immersed in a feeling of intoxicating self satisfaction that nothing bothered him. On

---

[2] Minchas Erev. However, one could argue that Haman might have figured that Esther herself was a Jew-hater just as he was, and that she was inviting him to a banquet along with the king in recognition for his activities against the Jewish people.

that day he left the palace happy and exuberant[3] – and that is when he met Mordechai the Jew sitting at the king's gate.

When He Saw Mordechai

When Mordechai noticed Haman leaving the palace so gleefully, he decided to accentuate the derision he felt towards him. Not only did he refrain from prostrating himself like everyone else did; he did not even stir from his place a hairsbreadth,[4] demonstrating to everyone that he harbored no fear of this fiend.[5]

Then Mordechai went a step further and actively humiliated Haman. As we mentioned earlier, Mordechai had in his possession a contract that testified to a transaction which had taken place decades earlier, when the two returned from a distant battle. At that time, Haman had sold himself as a slave to Mordechai in exchange for a loaf of bread. Now, when Haman emerged exuberant from Esther's first banquet, Mordechai

---

[3] The Perush HaGra as well as the Yosef Lekach maintain that Haman was aware that Mordechai had reared Esther from her youth. Therefore, until that day, he had assumed that since Esther revered Mordechai, he allowed himself to belittle Haman's honor. That day, however, when Haman realized that Queen Esther had not invited Mordechai to accompany the king to her banquet, but rather himself, Mordechai's mortal enemy, Haman concluded that Esther was not particularly fond of Mordechai, or, at the very least, preferred Haman over him. This was why he felt a particularly great joy that day, and it was for the very same reason that he was so infuriated when he saw that Mordechai would not stir before him. Once he saw that Mordechai did not even enjoy the adoration of the queen, he was furious that Mordechai would so audaciously allow himself to offend the honor of the chief royal official!

[4] The Minchas Erev explains that until that day, Mordechai would rise in Haman's honor, even though he would not prostrate himself. But on that day, in view of the wickedness of this villain who had issued such a horrifying decree on the Jews, he refrained from rendering even this honor.

[5] Malbim; Perush HaGra

made a point of reminding him of this fact, flaunting the proof in his face.

At that, Haman was overcome by a flaming anger. The public humiliation stung his ego like a firebrand, and the feeling of supreme joy that had suffused him just moments before dissipated instantly into nothingness. The humiliation was so great that it completely eclipsed the apex of success that Haman Harasha had attained that day.

Besides, Haman was well aware of the principle, "Whatever a slave acquires, his master acquires." He understood that the contract of sale in Mordechai's hand did not only represent his personal shame and degradation; it also cast his very status into question! "If Mordechai would decide to actualize the rights empowered by this contract and take me as a slave, I would lose my position in the royal court as well as all the possessions I take such pride in!" Haman panicked.

At first, Haman wanted to take his dagger, attack Mordechai and kill him on the spot.[6] But on second thought, he realized that taking action in this way without first putting the matter through a proper trial would be considered murder, and murder committed in broad daylight on a public street, at the king's gate, would tarnish Haman's reputation, to say the least.

"Well, then," Haman thought, "perhaps I should go right back in to the king and register a complaint about Mordechai, along with the recommendation that he be brought to judgment and executed."[7] One problem stood in his way. He understood

---

[6] Ibn Yichyeh, as cited by the Midrash Lekach Tov

[7] Malbim. The Yosef Lekach goes on to say that until that day, Mordechai argued that he was not required to bow down to Haman because the order was addressed only towards the *royal servants*, while he, as a Jew, was not officially numbered among

that it would be beneath his dignity to come crying to the king and admit that a person of his status was upset at being humiliated by an ordinary citizen. Not only that, he knew the offender would in any case not be around for much longer, since he and his entire nation would soon be killed.

Haman decided to restrain himself, go home, summon his circle of friends, and then, in the presence of his advisors, hammer out a satisfactory solution.

Taking Counsel

Forcibly restraining his fury, Haman arrived home and called for his wife Zeresh[8] and his close circle of advisors – 365

---

them. Therefore, until that day, Haman did not want to tell the king that Mordechai was not prostrating himself to him and to ask that he summon Mordechai to judgment. He was afraid that Mordechai would present his arguments successfully, the king would be convinced, and Mordechai would then be legally exempt from the requirement to prostrate himself before Haman. What a terrible embarrassment it would be for Haman if the king would justify his enemy! He wouldn't be able to show his face in his shame.

But that day, when he came out of the royal gate happy and exuberant, he had a new revelation: Haman noticed that Mordechai would not budge "before *him*;" to Haman, he would render no honor at all, but towards the other royal officers, he rendered all the honor in the world. This fact angered Haman to no end and also provided him with material he could use to slander Mordechai before the king. Now he could prove to the king that Mordechai was not refraining from prostrating himself out of his religious constraints, but rather out of a disdain for the king's command. His proof was that Mordechai honored all the other officials, while he expressly refused to do so to Haman, the king's favorite, whom Achashverosh had promoted above all the other royal officers.

[8] Zeresh was the daughter of a person named Tasni, a renowned Jew-hater from across the river. Some commentaries (Ibn Yichyeh) maintain that since Zeresh was not from a family of honorable lineage, once Haman rose to power he thought it was not befitting that he be married to such a woman. Therefore, he divorced her and sent her back to her father's house.

Now, however, when he grasped the extent of Mordechai's humiliating attitude towards him, he began to be concerned that this attitude was based on something. When he tried to determine who could possibly be a partner to a potential plot on

in number.[9] He began painting a comprehensive picture of his grand success.

Haman recounted to his friends[10] his large number of children[11] – 248[12] – and the glory of his wealth. He did not forget to tell them about the honorable banquet in which he had taken part that day, to which, besides the king, Queen Esther had invited only him.[13]

---

the part of Mordechai, he immediately thought of his ex-wife Zeresh. Therefore, he sent his friends to Zeresh to summon her back. She was agreeable to his invitation, and arrived in order to offer him the suggestion we shall soon hear about.

[9] This corresponds to the number of days in a solar year. Apparently, he usually had a special advisor for each day of the year. But this time he summoned all his counselors, as the *posuk* explicitly writes, "Then his wife Zeresh and *all* his friends said to him," in light of the great significance he accorded the subject of the discussion.

[10] Following the simple meaning of the words, according to which Zeresh was Haman's wife all along, it is clear that he did not have to tell her about the number of his children and the extent of his glorious wealth. But according to the explanation of the Ibn Yichyeh cited in the previous footnote, even Zeresh needed to be informed of these details, since from the time she was sent back to her father's house she had not been updated regarding these developments.

[11] The Ibn Ezra is bothered by the question of the necessity of telling Zeresh about the number of Haman's children. He resolves this difficulty by interpreting the words "*rov bonov*" as the *greatness of his sons*, not greatness in number, but rather in *quality and rank*. An alternate explanation brought by the Ibn Ezra simply states that the report about the sons was intended just for his friends, while Zeresh joined Haman in his description of his wealth and power.

[12] This number is in addition to Shamshi, the king's scribe, and the ten honored ones who served as officers and whose names we know well. The number of sons is hinted at in the words "*rov bonov*," *rov* having the numerical value of 208, referring, apparently, to the number of children about whom Haman had to tell. It was not necessary for him to say a word about his famous sons, since everyone was familiar with them already.

We find two additional opinions in the Gemara. One maintains that Haman had "only" thirty sons – the ten we know of who were hung, ten who died, and ten who were not too successful in life and whose only occupation was to go begging. The second opinion agrees insofar as the first two groups of ten are concerned – those who were hung and those who died. However, according to this opinion, there were another *seventy* sons who went begging door to door.

[13] In mentioning the banquet, Haman intended to counter the opinion of those advisors who claimed that Mordechai might be refraining from bowing to him

"Look at my situation!" Haman boasted. "I am elevated above all the royal servants and officers. There is no cause for jealousy. Whom could I be jealous of, if I am at the top?[14] Why, I am almost on an equal status with the king and queen, as my participation in their private party proves. And don't think this was a one-time event; I am invited there tomorrow as well, along with the king.[15]

"Keep in mind," Haman stressed, "that a banquet for the king is not ordinarily held with one official alone present. Usually, all of the upper echelon of officers is invited to join him. Since Esther chose to invite just me, she obviously considers me more important than all the officials put together![16]

"Besides," Haman confided to his friends, "why do you think it was so important for her to invite me? She might have preferred an intimate family dinner with her husband. Why did she choose to include me? I thought about that, and the conclusion I came to is that Esther needs my assistance.[17] She has a request to make of the king and she wants me to help influence him to carry it out. You see that! Even Queen Esther requires my intervention to get what she wants from the king!"

---

because he relied on his close relationship to Esther, whom he raised in his home. Haman rejected this argument, as we mentioned, by pointing out that Esther invited only him to the party, indicating that she is not so fond of Mordechai. Even when the advisors tried to argue that Esther might be setting a trap for Haman by inviting him to the banquet, Haman refused to see any truth in their claim. He based his view on the fact that he was invited to another party the next day, a clear indication, in his opinion, of the queen's "deep affection" for him.

[14] Minchas Erev

[15] Ibn Yichyeh

[16] Malbim

Haman then went on to delineate his problem. "The problem is that all of this greatness means nothing to me;[18] all my success cannot outweigh[19] the fury I feel when I see Mordechai the Jew sitting at the king's gate and not budging in my honor. I have to endure his enjoying a certain degree of status in the king's court while he degrades me at every opportunity![20] All the success in the world is in the palm of my hand, yet I can't enjoy it, since Mordechai's derisive behavior does not give me any peace. Can you imagine how I am suffering?[21]

"Besides,[22] what use is all my success if it can be taken away from me at any moment? That contract of sale that I was forced to sign years ago, which Mordechai waves at me every time I pass by him, does not only trample my honor, it actually threatens my future. If Mordechai should choose to actualize the contract and take me as his slave, what will be left of my sweeping success?"

Haman was not recounting his glory just for the sake of pomposity,[23] even though he surely drew great pleasure from

---

[17] Ibid

[18] The Gemara further cites that Haman carried the list of all his money and possessions in his front pocket at all times, in order to feel a rush of pleasure by glimpsing at this impressive list from time to time. Now he pointed at the list and emphasized that "*zeh*," *this* means nothing to me, as long as I see Mordechai the Jew sitting at the king's gate.

[19] Ralbag

[20] Ibn Ezra

[21] In this way, Haman wished to make it clear to his friends that he could not possibly allow himself to wait until the thirteenth of Adar, when he would anyway be rid of Mordechai along with all of his fellow Jews. "Every day that I see Mordechai, I experience indescribable suffering that does not allow me to enjoy my success at all! Do you think I can go on like that, without doing anything to change matters, for almost a full year?" he asked (Minchas Erev).

[22] Ibn Yichyeh. He adds that Haman did not mention to his friends the fact that Mordechai wasn't bowing down, because he felt it would be beneath his dignity to mention this fact even to them, as if he attributed any significance to it at all.

that too. A description of his lofty status was absolutely necessary as a preface to his problem, since it was his greatness that lay at the root of his dilemma.

"You have to understand, my friends," he said to his advisors, "if I would be a simpler person, I could have just gone to the king and told him what was bothering me. I would have asked him to kill Mordechai, and everything would have worked out just fine. But since I am so prominent and honored, it is beneath my dignity to deal with such trivialities. How would it look to the masses if the chief royal officer found nothing better to busy himself with than some Jewish rabbi who refuses to bow down to him? And what would the king think of me?" Haman finished bemoaning his troubles, and looked towards his friends, awaiting their response.

Although Haman's question was addressed towards his friends, it was Zeresh who leaped forward and answered first,[24] due to her great hatred for the Jewish people and their revered leader, Mordechai.[25] Besides, as Chazal teach us, among all the 365 advisors, there wasn't a single one who was able to advise Haman as well as his wife Zeresh did.

---

[23] The Perush HaGra adds that Haman had to recount his greatness, so that the pleasure he would find in relating it would dull his pain and anger at Mordechai's degrading attitude. He was afraid that if he did not salvage his lost honor, if he did not devote some time to describe his great success, he might just die of sorrow.

[24] The Midrash Ponim Acheirim says that Zeresh actually advised Haman not to start up with Mordechai, since nobody gets off scot-free after getting involved with people of his kind. But Haman announced that he was willing to lose everything he had, if he could only succeed in causing harm to Mordechai. He did not heed Zeresh's counsel, and directed the question to his friends, who suggested to him the idea of the gallows.

[25] Ibn Yichyeh

Let a Gallows be Made

Zeresh said as follows, with all the advisors egging her on.[26] "Since this fellow you are asking about is a descendant of the Jews, you have to proceed with great caution and forethought, because the God of the Jews has already demonstrated in the past that He can deliver His beloved *tzaddikim* from the most hopeless of situations. Therefore, I advise you to find a way to kill him that no Jew has ever been submitted to before, so that there is no guarantee that his God will be able to save him from it.[27]

"Now, let's think," Zeresh continued. "If you try to throw Mordechai into a burning furnace, that's no good, because Hashem saved Chananiah, Misha'el and Azariah from such a situation.

"If you try to have him thrown into the lions den, his God can deliver him from that too, as He delivered Daniel.

"If you imprison him, his God can do as He did for Yosef the *tzaddik*, whom He elevated to royalty directly from the dungeon.

---

[26] Esther Rabbah 9:2; Targum

[27] This just goes to show the foolishness of Zeresh and the depth of stupidity to which heresy can lead a sinner. Here Zeresh was enumerating the long list of deaths from which the Creator had delivered His children, and searching for a form of death for which Hashem had not yet proven, so to speak, His power to save the victim from. How ridiculous! Did she really think that the God Who could save someone from the burning furnace could not save him from the gallows? Is that more daunting a challenge than saving someone from the jaws of hungry lions? But Zeresh did not think into what she was saying. All she knew was how to deny the Creator's strength, even when doing so was utterly contrary to simple logic. But in the end, the Creator's mighty Hand was sent to save His *tzaddik*, proving to all that there is no plan or counsel that can stand up against Hashem's will.

"If you try to put him into a cauldron and ignite a fire beneath it until he is cooked, Hashem will do a miracle for him as He did for Menashe whom they tried to kill in this way.

"If you are thinking of casting him into the desert, well, I don't have to tell you that the Jewish people are experienced in surviving under such conditions; they spent forty years in the desolate wilderness on their way from Mitzrayim to the land of Canaan.

"If you are considering blinding him, better consider first the case of Shimshon, who caused immense damage and the death of huge numbers of Plishtim even after his sight was taken from him.

"If you want to toss him into the depths of the sea, remember that this body of water already split in the past at the bidding of Mordechai's God, and his entire nation walked through it on dry land.

"If you would throw him to the dogs, keep in mind that these creatures might not touch him, just as they held their tongues when the Jewish people left Mitzrayim.

"If you try to kill him by the sword, it might just boomerang against you, as happened when Pharaoh tried killing Moshe Rabbenu when he heard what Moshe did to the Mitzri who struck his fellow Jew.

"Even if you place a knife to his neck, he will be protected by the merit of his forefather Yitzchok, who had the slaughtering knife at his neck when Hashem saved him from death at the last moment.

"Therefore, you have no choice but to hang him on a gallows. I can promise you one thing – there is no record of Hashem saving anyone from the gallows. So, have a gallows prepared, have the king string Mordechai up on it, and your problem will be solved once and for all,"[28] Zeresh advised.

She then added a few more recommendations. "Since you made it clear that it would be beneath your dignity to reveal how bothered you are by Mordechai's attitude towards you – a position which I fully support – you will have to carry out your plan against Mordechai in a carefully calculated manner.

"First of all, you have to get up early and approach the king at the crack of dawn[29] so that he will hang Mordechai in the

---

[28] The commentary Ibn Yichyeh brings another two reasons why Zeresh advised killing Mordechai by hanging him on the gallows, and on a tall one in particular. The first reason was so the matter would get the necessary publicity; everyone would see how he paid for his defiance and be afraid to do likewise. The second reason was that she thought the power of the *tzaddikim* and the source of their deliverance came from the powers of sorcery. Since it was known that sorcerers only have power when they are standing on the ground (see Sanhedrin 45b – the incident of Rabbi Shimon ben Shetach and the sorcerers), Zeresh figured that it would be best to detach Mordechai from the ground and hang him in the air, on the assumption that the higher he hangs, the weaker his powers will be. (See ibid, where the matter is explained on a deeper level, according to the fifty *sha'arei kedusha*, gates of holiness.)

The Anaf Yosef (Esther Rabbah 9:2) writes an idea similar to this second explanation, but he adds that Zeresh based her words on the opinion of Haman, who, all his life, was sure that the strength of the Jews' deliverance came through sorcery, as we can deduce from the slanderous words he wrote about the Jews in his lengthy letters, as delineated above in the chapter "Haman Incites the King."

[29] The Perush HaGra explains that Zeresh advised Haman to come to the king early in the morning, before any of Mordechai's friends would have a chance to get there, since that could endanger the outcome of the meeting. The Yosef Lekach, on the other hand, maintains that the reason for making the meeting with the king early was so that no one would know that Haman made the request of the king to hang Mordechai, for the reason mentioned earlier – that it was beneath his dignity. Zeresh thought that it was not enough that the people should understand that *Haman asked the king to hang Mordechai for the honor of the king*; it was necessary to create the impression as if *the king himself, on his own initiative, decided to do so* as a result of information that he received from his sources.

morning hours, counter to the common practice of hanging criminals in the afternoon, after their case has been brought before the judges in the morning. Secondly, you need to have Mordechai hanged on a gallows fifty cubits high,[30] unlike the gallows usually used for hanging common criminals.

"In this way, it will be clear to everyone that Mordechai is not being hanged because of your concern for your personal honor, but rather as a public warning to all those who violate the king's order. Hanging him on an especially tall gallows will facilitate the greatest possible publicity, as will the time chosen for the execution, which coincides with the hour when the people go out to work. Thus, everyone will be able to see what happens to such an offender and will learn a lesson," Zeresh concluded.

He Had the Gallows Prepared

Haman was pleased with the suggestion, so much so that he decided to begin implementing it immediately.

The commentaries teach us that even though the intention of Zeresh was that Haman should instruct others to prepare the gallows, the villain volunteered to set it up himself,[31] since, as Chazal say, "Hatred changes the normal way things are done."

---

[30] The Perush HaGra writes that Zeresh's recommendation regarding the height of the gallows was intended to enable Haman to see the hanging of his mortal enemy, even though at the time, he would certainly be occupied in carrying out his regular duties in the palace. It was actually Divine Providence that planted the idea in her head, since just as it enabled *Haman* to see the gallows from the king's court, it also enabled *the king* to see it, and it was through seeing the gallows at the right moment that matters developed such that Haman was hung on that very same gallows, as we shall see.

[31] See Yosef Lekach, Perush HaGra.

On the other hand, the Targum cites that Haman hired carpenters to construct the gallows, but he organized grand festivities around the project. He gathered his sons around the gallows, and all of them together – he, Zeresh and his sons – reveled and hooted, danced and played musical instruments.

The construction of the gallows was completed that very day; Haman would not go to bed until the work was finished. He wanted to approach the king at the first light of dawn, just as Zeresh had advised him. Only after the gallows was ready to his satisfaction, and after he had even checked if the size was adequate by matching it to his own measurements,[32] which apparently were identical to the dimensions of Mordechai, Haman allowed himself to catch a bit of sleep.

The job of erecting the gallows was no simple matter. First they had to find a suitable tree, but no tree[33] was willing to volunteer itself for this lowly purpose, since it was known that in the end Haman himself would hang from the gallows. It was no great honor for any tree to have this despicable character hanging from it.[34]

Therefore, Hashem summoned all the trees of creation and asked, "Who will come forward and agree to have this *rasha* hanged on him?"

---

[32] Esther Rabbah 9:2. A voice from heaven proclaimed, "The gallows is perfect for you, and was prepared for you from the six days of Creation."

[33] Esther Rabbah 9:2

[34] Etz Yosef (Esther Rabbah 9:2). However, the Etz Yosef himself cites there the opinion of the Yefei Einayim who understands the matter precisely in reverse. All the trees *wanted* to volunteer that the gallows be made from them, since they knew that Haman would eventually be hanged on this gallows, and they all wanted to merit a part in this *mitzvah*. According to the approach of the Yefei Einayim, each tree boasted its particular merit, arguing that because it is important or serves for some *mitzvah*, it would be most appropriate to utilize it for another *mitzvah* – hanging this despicable *rasha*.

But the trees resisted, each one in turn. The fig tree said, "I, from whom the people of Israel give *bikurim*, first fruits, should allow this *rasha* to be hanged from me?"

The grapevine protested, "Surely not on me, to whom the Jewish people are compared, as the *posuk*[35] says, 'You shall transport the grapevine from Mitzrayim.'"

The pomegranate tree claimed, "Nor on me, to whom the Jewish people are likened, as it says,[36] 'Your temple is like a segment of pomegranate fruit.'"

The nut tree said, "How could I, to whom the people of Israel are compared, as it says,[37] 'I went down to the nut garden,' allow this *rasha* to be hanged from me?"

The citron tree echoed, "Nor could I, the tree from which the Jewish people take an *esrog* for the *mitzvah* of the four species on Sukkos."

The myrtle tree protested, "I, to whom the people of Israel are likened, as it says,[38] 'He stands among the myrtles in the deep waters,' could never have such a *rasha* hanged from me."

The olive tree resisted, "Nor I, to whom the Jews are compared, as it says,[39] 'A fresh olive tree, fair, with goodly fruit.'"

The apple tree asserted, "Never would I, to whom the people of Israel are likened, as it says,[40] 'Like an apple tree among the

---

[35] Tehillim 80:90
[36] Shir Hashirim 4:3
[37] Shir Hashirim 6:11
[38] Zecharia 1:8
[39] Yirmiyahu 11:16
[40] Shir Hashirim 2:3

trees of the forest, so is My beloved among the boys,' and,[41] 'The scent of your nose is like apples,' allow this *rasha* to be hanged from me."

The date palm tree challenged, "I, to whom the Jews are compared, as it says,[42] 'Your stature is like a palm tree,' should allow this *rasha* to be hanged from me?"

The acacia and the cypress trees said, "And what of us, from whom the *mishkan* and the *Bais Hamikdash* were constructed?"

The cedar and the date tree objected, "We, to whom the *tzaddik* is compared, as it says,[43] 'The *tzaddik* shall blossom like the date tree, and flourish like the cedar of Lebanon,' should agree to have this *rasha* dangle from us?"

The willow said, "Nor I, to whom the Jewish people are likened, as it says,[44] 'Like willows on the streams of water,' and from whom they take branches for the *mitzvah* of the four species with the *lulav*!"

At that moment, when no willing volunteer could be found to provide the gallows upon which Haman Harasha would be hanged, the thorn bush stood humbly before Hashem and said, "I – who have no merit, no asset, and no *mitzvah* performed with me – shall submit myself to the indignity of having this repulsive scoundrel be hanged on me. Besides, this fiend is like a painful thorn, and what could be more appropriate than a thorn being hanged on a thorn bush!"

---

[41] Shir Hashirim 7:9
[42] Ibid 7:8
[43] Tehillim 92:13
[44] Yeshaya 44:4

And so, at the end, the bramble, a thorny bush, was chosen to be the one from which Haman took the wood to use for erecting the gallows for Mordechai – and upon which he himself would eventually be hanged. Chazal[45] cite other opinions as well, according to which the cedar was the one who volunteered to have the *rasha* hanged on him.

In any case, finding a tree fifty cubits high – a height of approximately twenty five meters – was no simple matter. Where did Haman locate such a towering tree?

Chazal[46] explain that the tree in question was actually ready and waiting in Haman's possession. His son Parshandasa, who served as the ruler of the province of Kardonia, had once brought him a piece of wood this size from the remnants of Noach's ark.[47] Haman originally included this unusually long plank in the construction of his house, but now, for the sake of such an honorable goal as hanging Mordechai, he was even willing to dismantle his home and extract the board.

The gallows erected, Haman went to sleep, ready to enter the king's quarters at the earliest possible moment the next morning.

---

[45] Targum Sheini

[46] Yalkut, Midrash Ponim Acheirim

[47] The Yalkut explains that this board was preserved from the ark so that there would be an eternal remembrance of the Great Flood, just as the wife of Lot remained as a pillar of salt to serve as an eternal remembrance.

THAT NIGHT

> *"That night, the king could not sleep. He ordered that the record book, the annals, be brought and read before the king. It was found written there that Mordechai had reported on Bigsana and Teresh, two chamberlains of the king, among the guardians of the threshold, who had plotted to assassinate King Achashverosh. 'What honor or dignity was conferred on Mordechai for this?' asked the king. 'Nothing was done for him,' the king's pages replied. Then the king said, 'Who is in the court?' Haman had just come into the outer court of the palace, to speak to the king about hanging Mordechai on the gallows he had prepared for him. The king's pages told him, 'It is Haman standing in the court.' And the king said, 'Let him enter.'" (6:1-5)*

Before describing the events that transpired when the king's sleep eluded him, let us preface with some background.[1]

The day that Zeresh gave Haman the advice of preparing gallows for Mordechai and asking the king for permission to hang him on it, Haman decided to go see what Mordechai was occupied with at the time. To Haman's consternation, he found Mordechai sitting with his young students, 22,000 in number,[2] immersed in Torah learning as if nothing was going on.

---

[1] Esther Rabbah 9:4

[2] Corresponding to the number of ministering angels that descended with Hashem at the giving of the Torah (Etz Yosef).

Haman could not tolerate this inexplicable tranquility. Mordechai's apparent apathy and the fact that he displayed no fear – or at least far less than this *rasha* expected to see – absolutely infuriated him. He craved immediate revenge; he could not wait until the thirteenth of Adar, the far off day when his decree would go into effect.

Therefore, he had the children shackled in iron chains and appointed guards to make sure they would not attempt to escape. "Tomorrow morning, when I go to the king to ask him to hang Mordechai," he said to himself, "I'll have him order all 22,000 of these young children killed. Only after I finish off these intolerable urchins will I close accounts with Mordechai and have him hanged; let him first have a chance to see his precious students slaughtered!"

When the mothers of these children got wind of Haman's plans, they rushed to the *bais midrash* to offer their young sons food and drink. "Dear children, eat something before you die! At least let the last hours of your lives be free of the pains of hunger!" the mothers pleaded tearfully, but in vain.

The children lay their hands on their books and proclaimed with deep emotion, "Our dear mothers, thank you for your devotion, but we swear by the life of our teacher Mordechai that we will not eat or drink; we would rather die fasting!" All present burst into tears.

The cries of the tender children roused a great commotion in heaven. Their wails reached Hashem, and that is when the turnabout began. Hashem arose from His Seat of Judgment and went over to His Seat of Mercy, as He inquired from His angels, "What is the meaning of this great noise I hear, the sound of bleating goats and lambs?"

The angels, who understood that the Creator expected them to come to His children's defense so that He could deliver them from danger, responded, "No, Master of the Universe, it is the sound of Jewish children, young students of Torah, who have not touched a bite of food for three days, and whom Haman wishes to slaughter tomorrow like lambs and kid goats!"

As soon as Hashem heard the words of defense presented by the ministering angels, He immediately ripped up the decree that had been issued against His loved ones and sealed in clay. He began accelerating their deliverance, with the first step being King Achashverosh's unexplained insomnia.

The King Could not Sleep

That particular night, King Achashverosh logically should have fallen into a deep sleep, having freely drunk wine at Queen Esther's banquet, but Hashem saw to it that sleep would elude him. That night the Jews could not fall asleep, worrying about the terrible, unprecedented catastrophe that was destined to overtake them, worse even than what they underwent at the hands of Pharaoh in Mitzrayim.[3] Hashem decided that it wasn't right for King Achashverosh to slumber peacefully.[4]

Achashverosh was not the only one who suffered from sleeplessness that night. Chazal explain[5] that even the "sleep" of Hashem, so to speak, eluded Him that night. We know

---

[3] See Targum Yonasan.
[4] Minchas Erev
[5] Megillah 15b; Esther Rabbah 10:1

that Hashem never really slumbers, as the *posuk*[6] tells us, "The Guardian of Israel shall neither slumber nor sleep." But when the Jews sin, He conceals His Countenance from them, as if He were sleeping.[7] But that night, Hashem could not "slumber"; He rose like a warrior, garnering great strength to save the Jewish people.[8]

That night, Mordechai Hatzaddik could not sleep either,[9] because of an unpleasant event that had taken place that day. All the Jews had assembled around him and accused him of being the cause of Haman's terrible decree, since he had refused to prostrate himself before Haman as commanded. "Had you bowed before that *rasha*, this whole tragedy would not have come about!" they claimed. However, once Mordechai explained to them that the reason he refrained from bowing to Haman was because an idolatrous image was engraved on his robes, in front and in back, in order to trick all those who bowed to him into violating the prohibition of idolatry, the Jews accepted his explanation and were silent.

Haman, too, spent a sleepless night, busy as he was with the construction of the gallows for Mordechai, not realizing that he was actually building the gallows for himself.

That night, sleep eluded Queen Esther the *tzaddekes* as well, since she was occupied preparing the banquet that was to take place the following day for Haman and Achashverosh.

And, of course, Achashverosh could not sleep, bothered by thoughts that gave him no rest. Much as he tried to fall

---

[6] Tehillim 121:4
[7] Targum Yonasan; the same is implied in Esther Rabbah ibid.
[8] Etz Yosef and Anaf Yosef Esther Rabbah ibid
[9] Targum Yonasan

asleep, he was unable to do so. Finally, he turned to his officers and said to them, "I do not have any pleasure from what I ate or drank today. I feel that the heavens are upset with me. I cannot understand why I am so restless. Did I promise to give a tax exemption to some province or another and not keep my word? Or perhaps," he suddenly thought, "my rest is bothered by the question of why Esther invited Haman to join me at her banquet?

"Really, what is the meaning of this invitation?" the king started wondering to himself.[10] "Perhaps Haman and Esther are conspiring against me? Or maybe Esther has started to prefer Haman over her husband the king?" he thought in horror. The angel Micha'el, the great advocate of the Jewish people, was sent down from heaven to support his suspicions.

In order to calm himself, the king ordered the book of chronicles brought to him, where the deeds of the great kings of old were recorded.[11] But when the officers started reading to the king, Micha'el suddenly appeared before him in the guise of a poor person and said to him, "Your Majesty, you must know that Haman is planning to kill you and crown himself king in your stead![12] If you do not believe me, I will give you a

---

[10] Ibid; also brought in part in Megillah ibid.

[11] The Targum, which is the source of this expansive description, implies that the officers read to the king about the history of the monarchs who preceded him, but it could be that after hearing the angel Micha'el's warning, the king asked to hear about the recorded events from his own time, so as to figure out who it was that once saved his life and whom Haman seeks to hang. That is how it came about that they read to him about Mordechai's deed.

[12] See also Esther Rabbah ibid. However, the Midrash maintains that the king saw Haman in a dream, coming to him with sword drawn and threatening to kill him. According to this opinion, the Midrash continues, the moment the king heard that Haman was standing in the court, this confirmed his dream. We can understand that this fact had a decisive effect on the attitude Haman received from the king later on.

sign. Tomorrow morning, Haman will come to your court and ask you to hang a man who once saved you from death. Now, take my advice. When Haman comes, ask him what should be done for the person whom the king wishes to honor. You will see that he will suggest that you give that person the king's robes, the royal crown and the horse that the king rides upon – since this is actually his own hidden desire, to kill you and acquire all of the royal trappings!"

Bring the Book of Chronicles!

At this point, the king was absolutely unnerved.[13] "Could such a plot have been hatched without anyone knowing a thing about it?" he wondered to himself.[14] "Haman and Esther must have accomplices in the royal court! But if that is the case, how can it be that no one tipped me off about the conspiracy?"

Then, suddenly, he understood everything – or to be more precise, he thought he did.[15] "Someone must have once done

---

[13] In Midrash Abba Guryon ch. 6., we are told that at first, the king thought that the cooks or the wine butlers had put fatal poison in his food, or some other poison that causes illness and sleeplessness. Therefore, he ordered all the cooks, bakers and wine butlers killed. In the end, however, they managed to convince him that this was absolutely illogical, since Haman and Esther had eaten together with him, yet they felt fine and were healthy and hale.

[14] Megillah ibid

[15] The Perush Hagra brings another, slightly different explanation, according to which Achashverosh was actually concerned that he would be compelled to do a big favor for Mordechai the Jew. He understood that Esther was interested in asking him for something, and seeing that she had endangered herself for that purpose, he concluded that it was no simple request. He tried to guess, "What could the queen have in mind?" After a great deal of thought, he decided that she must be interested in asking for a big favor on behalf of Mordechai, who had raised her. Achashverosh also interpreted the invitation of Haman to the banquet as a ploy to have him on the spot to help her push through her request to the king. He was not aware of the deep personal hostility that existed between Haman and Mordechai.

me a favor, and I did not repay him in kind. That's why my servants aren't cueing me in about the current plot![16]

"If they would feel certain that I award a hefty prize to those who protect my life, their attitude would surely be entirely different. They would prefer to reveal the plot rather than cooperate with the plotters." Immediately, he asked that his servant read to him excerpts from the book of annals where all the events of his life were recorded, so that he could figure out who it was that once saved his life and was not properly recompensed.[17]

The king surmised that if Esther wanted him to do something for Mordechai, it probably would not be absolutely undeserved, since it would not be fair to make such a request. "Mordechai must have once done *me* a favor, and now Esther would like me to pay him the reward he earned," Achashverosh said to himself. He was not particularly interested in doing too great a favor for Mordechai, since, after all, he was a Jew, and the king was not especially fond of that people. Therefore, he decided to check in the book of annals to see what exactly it was that Mordechai had done for him and in what way he had been repaid so far.

King Achashverosh hoped to discover that Mordechai had already received his reward, so he could reject Esther's request. If that was not the case, he hoped at the very least that the deed itself would be insignificant and would not require an inordinate gesture of appreciation. The king intended to acquire the necessary information that same night so that he would be able to take counsel and figure out how to explain to the queen that the favor was not so great and did not justify such extensive compensation. We will address how matters evolved, according to the Gra's approach, in later footnotes.

[16] As the Minchas Erev explains, the king was concerned that his servants were afraid to reveal Haman and Esther's plot because they were intimidated by Haman, whom the king had promoted to a position above all the other officers. Therefore, he wished to reward Mordechai in a way that would make it clear that the king is honoring his benefactor *more* than Haman, and that he is even *humbling* his chief officer before the one who saved his life. "When the servants and the common people see this, they will understand that they have nothing to fear from anyone when coming to give over information that might save my life. Then, if Esther and Haman are really conspiring to kill me, somebody will certainly come forward and tip me off about such a plot," the king thought to himself.

[17] According to the commentary Ibn Yichyeh, the king was afraid that one of his officers was harboring a grudge against him for his not having shown him proper appreciation for some good deed. Therefore, he wanted to check in the book of

In the Madai and Paras empire, two record books existed. One was the expanded, comprehensive volume that contained a detailed description of all the events, and the other was a kind of index, where the events were recorded briefly, with references to the corresponding place in the complete volume. When the king asked his servants to read to him, the large book of records was not available. The only book that was handy was the condensed version with the skeletal outline, and that is what the king asked to have read to him.[18]

Now, had it been up to the servants in charge of the reading, the episode with Mordechai certainly would not have been read, since they were not particularly fond of the Jews. In fact, Chazal say that they were sons of Haman, and they intentionally skipped over the page where Mordechai's deed was mentioned, so they would not have to mention their father's enemy to the king.[19]

But Achashverosh noticed the attempted evasion, and insisted that they read at whatever spot the book opened for

records to see if he remained indebted to someone who had once benefited him. The Ibn Ezra writes that the king was afraid his insomnia was a form of punishment for having made a promise and not carried out his word; therefore, he wished to check out this point in the book of records. But the simple understanding is as Rashi explained. It was common practice for kings to have the book of annals read to them on those occasions when they could not fall asleep.

The Yosef Lekach challenges that statement, however, since stories tend to draw a person's heart and heighten his alertness; they do not make him drowsy and put him to sleep.

[18] Perush Hagra. The Malbim, on the other hand, explains that indeed there were two record books. One was a large tome dealing with the history of the kings of Madai and Paras throughout the generations, and was not generally in the king's possession. The second was a special book for each king in which he would write the things he had to remember or take care of. Since the king wanted to check if he owed a reward to someone, as mentioned, he asked that the *record book* be brought to him, i.e., the smaller book that dealt with the period of *his reign* – and so it was.

[19] Aggadas Esther, and see Gemara Megillah 15b.

them. They tried opening to a different spot, again and again, but each time, the book opened by itself to the same place – "that Mordechai had reported on Bigsana and Teresh." In the end, the written words read themselves out on their own,[20] and the servants had no control at all over what was being read.

Another miracle took place here as well. Shamshi, the king's scribe and son of Haman Harasha, had long ago seen to it that Mordechai's name was erased from the book of records. He was not interested in any honorable mention remaining regarding this *tzaddik*. But Hashem, Who wanted the text to read as it did originally, found a simple solution. He sent Gavriel, the angel, to restore the records to their original form, which included the name of Mordechai and a detailed description of his deed.[21]

---

[20] Midrash Ponim Acheirim

[21] The Minchas Erev explains that Shamshi indeed erased Mordechai's deed from the book of records, but he could only eradicate it from the big book of records, since in this book, the subjects were not arranged in proper order, and it was possible to erase one piece or another without its absence being conspicuous. But in the book of the "outline," on the other hand, it was not possible to erase anything, and it also was not accessible to Shamshi. Therefore, in this book, the incident of Bigsan and Teresh still appeared, though in brief form. Now, as Divine Providence arranged it, the king requested that the *book of records* in particular be brought to him, i.e, the outline, and as a result, he came across the information about Mordechai's deed.

There was another advantage to the smaller book, from Mordechai's standpoint. While in the detailed text the entire incident should have appeared, mentioning specifically that the vital information was passed on to the king at the time through Esther, in the smaller text, where the matter was recorded in short, all that was written was that "*Mordechai* had reported on Bigsana and Teresh," indicating clearly that the king's deliverance was chalked up to Mordechai's merit alone.

Had the king read the story in the detailed book, he certainly could have reached the conclusion that it was *Esther* who did most of the work, and that the debt of gratitude is towards *her*, a conclusion that would have discharged him from any obligation whatsoever, since he could not do more for Esther than he had already done by choosing her as his queen!

The truth is that, originally, the king had figured that it was not necessary to reward Mordechai too much, since as he understood it, Mordechai did not relate the information expressly to benefit the king; he merely related the incident of Bigsan and Teresh to Esther incidentally, and Esther was the one who brought his

The facts were read before Achashverosh, relating how Mordechai was the one who informed the king that Bigsan and Teresh were seeking to kill him, an accusation which was found to be true, and which led to the two being executed.[22]

"Aha, so this is the anonymous hero who saved my life," the king realized. "And what honor or dignity was conferred on Mordechai for this?" he urgently inquired of his servants.[23]

---

words to the king's attention. As proof for this opinion, the king pointed at the fact that Mordechai did not give the information over to him personally, but rather transmitted it through Esther. But now, when only Mordechai's name was recorded in the book, the king understood that he had been responsible for this favor, and therefore, he wanted to give him his just reward.

As we pointed out, Haman rose to stature as a result of his advice regarding the execution of Vashti, advice that turned out retroactively to have been extremely efficacious, since it led indirectly to Esther coming into the palace, and to the king being saved by her from the plot of Bigsan and Teresh. Now that it became clear to the king that Esther's part in that incident was a more minor one than that of Mordechai, he understood that he need not feel any particular gratitude towards Haman anymore in this context. Therefore, he sought to elevate Mordechai in rank in place of Haman.

The Malbim, on the other hand, goes on to interpret the sequence of events according to his abovementioned approach, explaining that Haman rose to greatness after he gave King Achashverosh the impression that *he* was the one to uncover the conspiracy involving Bigsan and Teresh. According to the approach of the Malbim as well, the king was interested in granting Mordechai all the favors he had inadvertently showered on Haman, as we shall soon explain.

[22] The Minchas Erev explains that the chroniclers rewrote history. In order to detract from the value of Mordechai's noble deed, they altered the facts slightly, and instead of writing that Mordechai reported about Bigsan *and* Teresh, a sentence that would clearly indicate that Mordechai had exposed the assassination conspiracy to the king, they wrote that "Mordechai reported about Bigsan *or* Teresh," implying that Mordechai only uncovered the plot of one of the chamberlains, and then that one confessed and revealed the name of his partner in crime.

But Hashem arranged for the inscription to be changed to conform to the clear and true facts. The change was done by appending the letter *alef* of the word *oh*, or, to the name of Bigsan, so that his name would read Bigsana (the final *nun* also changed to a regular *nun*), while the letter *vav* of that same word joined the name of Teresh, so that it was written *and* Teresh.

[23] Even though there was no mention in the book of records of Mordechai being awarded any sort of recompense, the king hoped that, somehow, he had paid Mordechai his just reward, and for some reason the matter was forgotten and not recorded. Therefore, he addressed this question to his servants, who were able to say

"Was he awarded some special honor or given a valuable prize at the expense of the royal treasury?"[24] the king asked.

"Nothing was done for him at all," the servants were quick to reply. "Mordechai received absolutely no reward in return for the tremendous service he did for the king."[25] Chazal[26] tell us that the servants were not particularly interested in Mordechai's benefit, but they were eager to hurt Haman,[27] and how better to do so than to have the king elevate Haman's greatest enemy!

Now it became clear to the king that he was greatly indebted to Mordechai, and he wanted to pay his debt for his own reasons. Therefore, when Haman arrived at the royal court at the break of dawn to ask the king to order Mordechai hanged on the gallows, the king stopped him before he had a chance to say a word and asked his advice regarding a fitting reward for someone whom the king wishes to honor.

---

unequivocally that no favor was bestowed on Mordechai following his saving the king's life. This fact led the king to be concerned that Mordechai might be seeking to take revenge on him for that at this time (Ibn Yichyeh).

[24] Perush HaGra. He explains "y'kar" as honor and "gedulah" as wealth.

[25] Mordechai did acquire a certain degree of status in the royal court, as indicated by his regular seat at the king's gate, but this benefit did not constitute a reward for his deed; it was an outcome of his special connection with the queen, since it was known that he had raised her from her youth (Malbim).

[26] Megillah ibid

[27] The servants' malice towards Haman may have been sparked by the obligation incumbent on them to prostrate themselves to him, an order that offended their honor. The matter becomes even more striking in light of the words of the commentaries (Yosef Lekach and others), who maintain that the law regarding bowing to Haman affected only the *royal servants* who were at the *king's gate*. According to this opinion, it is clear that these servants would feel degraded and humiliated, being required to prostrate themselves to Haman. Here too, we see the Hand of Divine Providence that arranged matters such that the ordinance that brought such pleasure to Haman was the very one that played a role in his downfall, since it led the king's servants to tell the king that Mordechai did not receive any reward for saving his life.

HAMAN ENTERED

"Haman entered, and the king asked him, 'What
should be done for the man whom the king wishes
to honor?' Haman thought to himself, 'Whom
could the king wish to honor more than me?' So
Haman said to the king, 'For the man whom the
king wishes to honor, have them bring royal robes
that the king has worn, and the horse upon which
the king has ridden, that the royal crown was
placed on his head. Let the robes and the horse be
given into the hand of one of the king's most noble
officers, and let them dress the man whom the
king wishes to honor, and parade him on the horse
through the city square, proclaiming before him,
"This is what is done for the man whom the king
wishes to honor!"' Then the king said to Haman,
'Hurry, get the robe and the horse just as you said,
and do all this for Mordechai the Jew who sits at
the king's gate; do not omit a single detail that you
mentioned!'" (6:6-10)

Before Haman even had a chance to open his mouth
and explain why he had come,[1] the king turned to him and,

---

[1] As the Minchas Erev explains, Divine Providence arranged matters such that
Haman would not have a chance to speak with the king about hanging Mordechai.
Had Haman said a word on this subject, the king – who at this point was likely to
interpret every suspicious move as a sinister conspiracy – would have immediately
come to the conclusion that Haman and Esther were plotting together to murder
Mordechai, so that Mordechai would not be able to reveal to the king their plans to
assassinate Achashverosh.

following the advice he had received from the angel Micha'el, asked him, "Honored Haman, most exalted chief officer, my most esteemed advisor! Tell me your opinion, what is the most appropriate favor I can bestow on the man[2] I wish to honor?"[3]

Such a conclusion – as baseless as it sounds – might have led the king to order Haman executed on the spot, along with Queen Esther, his presumed partner in crime! To prevent such a scenario, Hashem set things up such that Haman would not even have a chance to say why he had come, and so that the information regarding the gallows Haman had prepared for Mordechai would be transmitted to the king only later that day, by Charvona, after Esther would already have made her abhorrence of "this terrible Haman" perfectly clear. At that point, the king would no longer have any reason to be wary of Esther, and certainly would not suspect her of being an accomplice of her people's mortal enemy.

[2] The Gra, following his approach that the king thought Haman was extremely fond of Mordechai and was even planning to help Esther ask the king to do her a great favor, explains that the king intentionally did not mention Mordechai's name since he was afraid Haman might go overboard and suggest granting Mordechai the kingship itself.

According to the opinion of the Malbim and others who take the approach that the king expressly wished to give Haman's glory over to Mordechai, it is clear why he did not mention Mordechai's name; he wanted Haman to be misled into thinking that the intention was for himself, as we shall explain in the next footnote.

[3] It should be emphasized that when the king inquired as to whether Mordechai had received a reward for his deed, he asked, "What y'kar u'gedulah, honor or dignity, was done for Mordechai?" indicating that he wished to give him both of these. In contrast, when the king asked Haman's advice, he did not mention his desire to grant Mordechai dignity, but focused only on, "What should be done for the man whom the king wishes to honor?"

The Malbim and the Minchas Erev, following their approach mentioned above, explain that when speaking to Haman, the king intentionally put aside the matter of dignity, since it implies a lofty and dignified position. If the king would say that he wants to know what dignity to accord the man he wants to honor, Haman would immediately understand that he is not the subject of the question, since it was not possible to raise him to a higher position than he already held. Therefore, the king mentioned only the honor he wished to accord his benefactor, so that Haman would think the king was talking about him and would honestly respond with a proper answer for the king's question, suggesting the reward most appropriate for the one who saved the king's life.

However, the commentaries who maintain that the king did not really and truly want to benefit Mordechai (Gra, Yosef Lekach and others) claim that it was by Divine Providence that the king omitted the term "dignity," so as to mislead Haman and have him fall into the trap.

Knowing that when he left the palace the previous night the king had mentioned no such idea[4] of conferring benefit on anybody, Haman had no doubt that Achashverosh intended to do this favor for none other than himself. He assumed the idea must have occurred to the king at night, when he could not stop thinking of Haman's welfare.

Therefore, the moment he heard the question, Haman unctuously replied, "Your Majesty, if someone once had the privilege of doing you a good turn, and because of this you wish to pay him back in kind, your very desire to bestow a reward upon him is such a vast honor in itself[5] that you do not owe him another thing!

"The only problem is, as long as this person has no knowledge of the king's favor, he cannot derive any pleasure from the king's desire to benefit him. Therefore, in order to *reveal* Your Majesty's wish to honor this individual, I recommend you do as follows:

"Have the royal robes brought for him – robes which the king himself has worn.[6] Bring the horse that the king has ridden on – not just at any time,[7] but the one he rode on the

---

[4] Ibn Yichyeh

[5] Malbim. Therefore, the first *posuk* concludes with the words, "the man whom the king wishes to honor," while the details follow only in the next *posuk*, "have them bring royal robes, etc."

[6] The Yosef Lekach explains that Haman stressed that the robe has to be "*l'vush malchus*," "royal robes," i.e., robes that the king uses at this time, and in addition, "*asher lavash bo hamelech*," not a new garment hanging in the wardrobe, but a robe which the king himself has made use of. Furthermore, this use should have been after "the royal crown was placed on his head," i.e., since he began his reign.

[7] According to other opinions, Haman recommended that they take the horse that the king rode on while the crown was on his head. Only on rare occasions, when esteemed officers would go riding with the king, would he ride with the crown on his head, and at that time, he would use the finest horse (Ralbag, Malbim). The Ibn

day of his coronation, when the royal crown was placed on his head!"[8] Haman specified.

"Now, the robes and the horse should not be brought by any ordinary servant, but rather by the most noble of the king's officers.[9] Then the man whom the king wishes to honor should be attired in the royal robe and paraded on horseback[10] through the streets of Shushan, while proclaiming before him,[11] 'This is what is done for the man whom the king wishes to honor!'"[12]

Ezra, in contrast, explains that the crown under discussion is not the *king's* crown at all, but rather the crown that was put on the head of the *king's horse*, and which made it clear to all that this was the king's special steed that no one else was allowed to ride upon. Rashi brings the simple explanation (Midrash Abba Guryon, Parsha 6), according to which Haman advised the king to place the royal crown itself on the head of the person who deserves his benevolence. Later on, though, he rescinded the suggestion when he saw how the king's face grew hot with rage when he mentioned it the first time.

[8] Koheles Rabbah 5, 1

[9] The custom at that time was that the most noble royal officer would himself lead the king's horse out of the stable, not one of the stablemen (Perush HaGra). But when it came to mounting the man on the horse or attiring him, Haman did not suggest that one of the officers carry out the task, since that was not accepted practice at all. Therefore he did not say, "Let *him* dress him," or "*He* should parade him on the horse," which would imply that the same royal officer should carry out these duties, but rather said, "Let *them* dress him," and "*They* should parade him," in plural, implying that the servants should tend to these duties.

[10] The Ibn Yichyeh adds that Haman did not seek for himself any ordinary honor. Haman knew that according to the laws of Madai and Paras, certain specific powers were granted to the person who wore the king's robes and rode on his horse – among them, the authority to kill anyone who humiliates him without a court judgment. Haman was very interested in acquiring this authority, since that would in essence spare him the need for the king's approval in order to hang Mordechai.

[11] The Aggadas Esther states that Haman suggested to the king that they should proclaim before the man that anyone who does not prostrate himself this time shall be killed on the spot and his possessions plundered. Since Haman had no doubt that all this honor was meant for him, and that *he* would be the one riding on the horse, he wanted to set a trap for Mordechai, who would be forced to bow to him – or be killed on the spot.

[12] On a simple level, this proclamation was meant as an honor for the person upon whom the king wished to bestow honor. However, the Minchas Erev adds another

With this, Haman concluded his colorful description, which actually provided a glimpse into what was in his own heart.

"Aha, that old man was justified in his warning," the king thought to himself, referring to the angel Micha'el. "Indeed, Haman, who is convinced that the honor is meant for him, does not ask for silver or gold, nor for a palace or any other privileges. All he covets are my most personal royal accessories. He must have been eyeing them for a long time. Indeed, he wants to kill me and usurp the throne!" The realization trickled into the king's consciousness and began to fan his anger.

"So that is your suggestion?" he asked Haman, and upon receiving an answer in the affirmative, he gave Haman his just deserts.[13] "Well, my esteemed officer, if that is what you think, then you are cordially invited to put your suggestion into action at once."

---

dimension, saying that when Haman saw how displeased the king was with his suggestion about the crown, he wanted to demonstrate his deep concern for the king's honor. He did so by suggesting that this proclamation be made before the rider on the horse, to make it clear that his honor is not on par with that of the king; on the contrary, his glory flows only from the fact that the king wishes to honor him.

[13] Following his approach, the Gra explains that the king was not angry at Haman; he simply asked him to finish the job he had begun and to carry it out himself. According to the Gra, the king was afraid that Esther was planning to ask him to grant Mordechai some huge favor for having saved the king's life and he was concerned that Haman was in agreement with her on this subject. Therefore, when Haman made it clear that, in his opinion, it was not necessary to give this person any tangible and lasting reward but rather some minor benefit of royal honor, the king grasped at his suggestion eagerly and asked Haman to hurry and pay off his obligation before Esther would ask for any greater benefit to be bestowed on Mordechai.

In his desire to give Mordechai a reward that would not leave Esther any opening to make more requests on his behalf, the king instructed Haman himself to personally carry out all he had said. This way, the king's obligation towards Mordechai would be taken care of in the best possible way, leaving Esther no claim against him in this area.

Chazal describe to us the elaborate details of Mordechai's honor that the king demanded of Haman to carry out.[14]

"Hurry over to the king's storage chambers, and take from there a royal garment – a purple robe and a fine, striped tunic, studded with diamonds and pearls, with four golden bells hanging on its four corners, alternating with decorative pomegranates on all four sides.

"Also take from my treasure house the golden crown that was brought to me from the province of Macedonia on the first day of my reign,[15] as well as the sword and armor that were brought to me from the land of Kush. Take two officers along with you and dress them in royal uniform, dotted with African diamonds. Then continue on to the stables.

"Take from there my finest horse, the one called Shiffergoz, that I rode the day I was crowned as king and stepped up to the throne.

"Once you have collected all the necessary items, I want you personally[16] to go to Mordechai, attire him in the robes, put him on the horse, and do for him everything you said a few moments ago.

---

[14] Targum Sheini

[15] The king was not interested in having an outsider don the royal crown on his head, and therefore he said to bring the crown that he had once received as a gift but that was never used as the royal crown. Apparently, the royal crown was not stored in the treasure house, but rather in a more convenient and accessible location, since it was in daily use.

[16] The Malbim explains that the king expressly told Haman to do all these gestures of honor for Mordechai by himself, as compensation for the honor he had appropriated for himself all these years, after he gave the king the mistaken impression that he was the one who had given him the information regarding Bigsan and Teresh.

"Follow my instructions without leaving out a single thing,"[17] the king added. He knew his chief officer well, and suspected that he might conveniently "forget" some detail[18] or try to swallow some of the words in his proclamation in order to minimize the honor accorded to Mordechai.[19]

One can imagine how Haman felt after hearing the king's orders. His face turned colors, his eyes darkened, his mouth quivered, his thoughts raced, his knees knocked and his legs nearly buckled under him. In desperation, Haman asked the king, "Your Majesty, there are many people in Shushan named Mordechai. How will I know to which one the king is referring?"[20]

The king replied, "I mean Mordechai the Jew!"

"But even among the Jews there are many who are called by this name," Haman persisted.

The king responded unequivocally, "I mean the one who sits at the gate of the king, the one who spoke good on my behalf and whose name was recorded in the book of annals."

---

[17] The Aggadas Esther adds that the king even appointed two chamberlains to check that the order was being properly carried out and to make sure that Haman did not miss any detail.

[18] Ibn Yichyeh

[19] Minchas Erev

[20] Apparently, Haman, who was so absolutely certain that he was about to hang Mordechai on a tall gallows that very day, simply could not believe what he heard. He hoped that he had not heard correctly or had not properly understood the king's words – in particular, that this Mordechai that the king wanted Haman to lead through the city square was a member of the Jewish people against whom Achashverosh himself had sanctioned the terrible decree to kill, slay and exterminate! Therefore, he tried asking all the questions in the world, in the hope that he would discover he was mistaken in his original understanding, and that the king was really referring to some other anonymous "Mordechai" whom Haman did not know.

"But Your Majesty, have you only one gate?" Haman kept hunting for some loophole.

But to his dismay, the king went on to define Mordechai's precise location. "I mean Mordechai the Jew who sits at the king's gate that leads from the palace to the harem!" he roared, eliminating Haman's last excuse.

Haman understood clearly that the king deliberately wanted to humiliate him before his enemy, Mordechai. Now all he could do was try and persuade the king to rescind this intention. And try he did.

"Your Highness," Haman said to the king, "didn't you yourself issue together with me a decree of destruction on Mordechai's people? How can you ask me now to humble myself before him?"

The king was not convinced by his argument. "Do not omit a single detail that you mentioned!" he reiterated.

"But Your Majesty, this Mordechai is *my greatest mortal enemy*! How can I degrade myself before him and grant him such vast honor? I am willing to pay him ten thousand silver talents, if I could only be excused from this vexing obligation!" Haman offered.

But the king could not be dissuaded. "No problem. Do as you said; give him ten thousand silver talents. In fact, he will even be appointed master of your household and all your possessions – but all that does not excuse you from rendering him this honor as I commanded!"

"Well then, let's consider another suggestion," Haman tried his luck once more, this time attempting to entice the king himself. "I have ten successful and talented sons. I am willing to give them to the king as slaves, to run before his horses and pay him homage; just let me off the hook and excuse me from honoring Mordechai!" the villain pleaded, but the king stuck to his position.

"Just as you say – you, your wife and your sons will become slaves to *Mordechai*, but that still does not excuse you from rendering him all the honor as you were commanded," the king stated definitively, in a determined tone.

"If the king wants so badly to honor Mordechai, I have another suggestion that is ten times better!" Haman attempted to argue from a different angle. "For Mordechai, who comes from a background of poverty, it would be better to reward him by appointing him governor of a province or district. In this way he will gain permanent status, as well as regular income! In contrast, the honor which the king wishes to give him is transient. When Mordechai gets home, not a thing will remain of all this honor!" the *rasha* tried to persuade the king.

Achashverosh repeated his stand. "Leave that to me. I will appoint Mordechai ruler over many provinces and countless districts. All the empires on the continent will bow to his authority – but all that does not dismiss you from your obligation to give him the honor I ordered you to render to him!"

"I understand that the king wishes to punish me for some reason," Haman sighed. "All right, then. I am prepared to offer the following: I am willing to grant Mordechai the esteemed status I enjoy today, my fame and high rank,[21] so that he will gain public acclaim throughout the provinces in my stead; all I ask is that I not have to undergo this horrifically humiliating experience," Haman pleaded, but the king would not budge from his position.

"A man who saved his king's life indeed deserves to get all the honor and rank you presently enjoy, but once again, without detracting in the least from your obligation to grant him all the honors we talked about!"

Haman was down to his last offer, the most painful one of all. "I am even prepared to give up on the achievement of my life, on my greatest dream, the decree to annihilate the Jewish people, Mordechai's people. All I ask is that the king in turn excuse me from the obligation to degrade myself before this Jew!"

Haman begged, but the king said for the last time, "Don't worry, the decree against Mordechai's people I'll nullify myself, but as for you, not another word, go do exactly what I commanded for Mordechai the Jew!"

After that, Haman had no choice but to leave the king's chambers that very minute and carry out his instructions precisely. Who knew better than he what kind of punishment awaited a person who dared defy the king's orders? After all, it was he who had advised the king to send people to their deaths at every opportunity for such crimes.

---

[21] The Targum stresses Haman's "fame," which will be replaced by Mordechai's "fame." But apparently this is merely a detail that indicates a greater generality, since it is not possible to "publicize" a person without him having gained the status that would justify his renown.

The above exchange gives us a glimpse into the extent of this Amalekite's wickedness and the depth of his poisonous hatred. As we saw, Haman offered the king a variety of suggestions in order to get out of his humiliating assignment. Only after all these suggestions were rejected did he make his final offer – to forgo the annihilation of the Jews. Haman was willing to give up on a huge sum of money, and even to sell his own children as slaves, to see Mordechai honored as governor of a province, as long as he could express his hatred for the Jewish people and destroy them!

HAMAN TAKES THE ROBE
AND THE HORSE

"So Haman took the robe and the horse, attired
Mordechai, and paraded him through the city
square, proclaiming before him, 'This is what is
done for the man whom the king wishes to honor!'
Then Mordechai returned to the king's gate, while
Haman hastened home, mourning and with his
head covered. Haman told his wife Zeresh and
all his friends everything that had happened to
him. Then his advisors and his wife Zeresh said
to him, 'If this Mordechai, before whom you have
begun to fall, is of Jewish descent, you will not
prevail against him, but will surely fall before
him.' While they were speaking with him, the
royal chamberlains arrived, and they hurried
to bring Haman to the banquet that Esther had
prepared." (6:11-14)

Like it or not, Haman had no choice but to do everything
precisely as the king instructed. Taking the necessary items
in hand, he trudged out to Mordechai, who sat at the king's
gate.

When Mordechai saw Haman approaching him,[1] he was
certain that his enemy was coming to take him to his death or
to trample him under the hooves of the horse he was leading.[2]

---

[1] Esther Rabbah 10:4; Megillah 16a
[2] Midrash Ponim Acheirim

Turning to his students, he said, "My dear *talmidim*, I see that Haman is on his way here to kill me. I beg of you, escape! Run for your lives! Why should you suffer because of my sins and be singed by the flame of my punishment?"

But, needless to say, the students refused. "If you die, we shall die with you!" they informed their esteemed teacher. "We will not leave you in your time of trouble!" Mordechai understood that they would not be convinced otherwise.

At the time, Mordechai and his students were deeply engrossed in their learning. Their lives of Torah carried on as usual, unaffected by the looming decree, due to go into effect in less than a year. In fact, when Haman approached, Mordechai was in the midst of delivering a lecture on the subject of the *mitzvah* of *kemitza*, or to be more specific, *kemitzas ha'omer*, taking a handful of the barley offering.[3] But when his devoted students made it clear that they would remain at his side and were ready to give up their lives for the sanctification of Hashem's Name, he cut his lecture short and announced that it was time for prayer.

"Let us all *daven* together, and then we will at least know that we met our deaths while standing before Hashem!" Mordechai explained. The *rav* and his students opened with a heartfelt prayer, certain that this would be the last *tefillah* of their lives.

---

[3] The Gemara explains that they were involved in the subject of *kemitza*, while the Midrash implies that they were studying the *mitzvah* of the *omer* or *kemitzas ha'omer*. Rashi in Megillah ibid mentions that they were involved in the relevant topic of the day, since the date was the sixteenth of Nisan, the day the *omer* was offered. Apparently, Rashi saw no disagreement between the opinion of the Gemara and the Midrash, since they were clearly studying the laws of *kemitza*, but with a focus on the *mitzvah* of *kemitzas ha'omer*, the current topic.

Many tears were shed during that *tefillah*; the cries undoubtedly reached the very heavens, shaking each soul to the core and melting every heart. Neither the *talmidim* nor their great teacher knew that deliverance was just around the corner. They certainly did not guess that the villain had come, not to kill them, but to degrade his own honor and take the first step towards his downfall.

Haman reached the *yeshiva* just as they were pouring out their hearts in prayer, and he had no choice but to wait until the lengthy, emotional *tefillah* drew to a close before he could tell anyone what he had come for.

As soon as the prayers concluded, the *rasha* hastily approached one of the students and inquired what subject they were involved in. He was told that Mordechai and his *talmidim* were studying the laws of the *omer* offering and its auxiliary details.

At first, before he understood the meaning of this strange word, "*omer*," he thought it must be some offering of gold or silver that the Jews would bring to their God, or at least a gift of quality wheat.

When the students explained to him that the *omer* offering was composed of simple, cheap barley, he was certain that they at least had to bring a generous amount of the grain, amounting to the value of several silver talents. But again, they corrected his mistake and explained that the value of the barley amounted to no more than a few coins.

When Haman heard that, he got up and announced, "Unbelievable! Your handful of barley, your measly *omer* offering, has prevailed over my ten thousand silver talents![4] In the merit of this handful of barley, it appears that your God is going to save you from my hand and pay me what is coming to me!"

Now, Haman proceeded to carry out the king's orders.[5] He went over to Mordechai and said, "Rise, Mordechai Hatzaddik, son of Avraham, Yitzchok and Yaakov. Shake off your ashes so I can attire you in these royal robes. Then get up and mount the king's horse!"[6]

---

[4] The Anaf Yosef in the Midrash Rabbah ibid cites the obvious question here. What do the ten thousand silver talents that Haman had measured out for the king's treasuries have to do with the *omer* of barley that was offered to Hashem? Did Haman expect that his ten thousand silver talents would cause the Creator to favor him? What special virtue did these talents have that made Haman think that the handful of *omer* would have trouble standing up against them?

The Anaf Yosef replies that the king had told Haman to do with these ten thousand silver talents *as he saw fit*. However, he did not authorize Haman to take them back for himself, only to do with them as he wished *in the king's name*. Haman, being aware of the power of *tzedaka*, charity, distributed that huge amount of ten thousand talents to the poor, hoping that in the merit of this good deed, his plot against the Jews would succeed. Now, Haman was surprised that a single handful of barley should outweigh the grand charitable act he had done with his ten thousand silver talents; *this* was the source of his amazement.

But, the Anaf Yosef adds, he had no reason to wonder at this, as the Gemara goes on to bring Mordechai's reply, "*Rasha*, when a slave acquires property, who owns the slave and who owns the possessions?" With this, Mordechai hinted to him that all of Haman's gold and silver actually belong to Mordechai who acquired him as a slave, as we mentioned in earlier chapters. Consequently, the silver that was measured out also did not belong to Haman, nor to Achashverosh, but rather to Mordechai Hatzaddik! The act of *tzedaka* that was done with that silver is counted, therefore, to the merit of Mordechai and to the merit of his people, saving them from the one who sought to destroy them.

[5] This description is based on the words of the Gemara ibid, the Midrash and Targum Sheini.

[6] The Targum Sheini explains further that Haman even brought Mordechai food and drink that Esther had sent for him, and anointed his flesh with cosmetics and perfumes in order to revive him from the lengthy fast. However, the text above is based on the opinions maintaining that Mordechai was still immersed in fasting – either the third day of the fast called by Esther, or an additional fourth day of

At first, Mordechai simply did not believe him. "I understand that you are planning to torture me before you take me to my death," he said to the *rasha*, making it clear that he did not intend to cooperate.

Haman, who found the whole situation extremely uncomfortable, was forced to explain the entire sequence of events and persuade Mordechai to agree to do as the king had said – to don the royal robes and ride the king's horse.

"There's no way out," Haman explained forlornly. "My bad luck! I got the gallows ready for you, but your God prepared the royal crown. I prepared ropes and nails,[7] but your God summoned for you regal robes. I came to the king to ask him to hang you on the gallows I prepared, but he commanded me to mount you on the horse instead of on the gallows!"

At this point, Mordechai began to understand that Haman was serious. Once he realized that his prayer had been accepted and the tide was beginning to turn, he decided to milk the situation for all it was worth.

Turning to Haman, he patiently explained to him, "Listen here, Haman, you surely understand that it would not be proper for me to put on the royal robes right after taking off my sackcloth and getting up from the ashes! I might soil the valuable robes, or damage them in one way or another, and then how could I face the king? No, before I get dressed, I must wash up!" he insisted.

---

fasting that he took upon himself – and according to these opinions, he obviously did not eat anything that day.

[7] From which he apparently constructed the gallows.

Haman had no objection to the idea. "Wash up? What could be so bad about that?" the villain thought to himself.

But soon enough, he understood that it could be bad for him indeed, *very* bad. To his surprise, he discovered that all the bathhouses in Shushan were locked and barred,[8] and that all the bath attendants were holed up in their homes, by the order of Queen Esther, who wished to harass this murderous *rasha* a bit.

For lack of a viable alternative, Haman went home, brought washing materials, got a hold of the key to one of the locked bathhouses, and warmed up the water so that Mordechai could wash up.

Haman thought that with this he had finished his share of humiliation for the day, but he soon discovered how mistaken he was in this assumption. When Mordechai emerged from the bathhouse, he made it clear that he still did not consider himself ready to don the royal robes.

---

[8] The Perush HaGra explains that Esther sealed off the bathhouses supernaturally, through the use of Holy Names, since by nature it is not possible that Haman could not have found even one servant who could have taken his place and carried out the degrading task of washing Mordechai Hatzaddik.

However, the Etz Yosef on Esther Rabbah (ibid) explains that one of the servants certainly could have done the job instead of his master Haman, but Mordechai himself would not hear of it. "First of all, I want someone professional to take care of me, and I have already heard of your expertise in this area," Mordechai insisted. Then he added a winning argument, "If you were to harm me 'accidentally,' so to speak, you know perfectly well that the king would have your head. Therefore, I am confident that you will not do so. In contrast, one of your servants might easily take the opportunity to kill me by your command, because I am certain that the punishment the servant would later receive from the king would not bother you in the least! That is why I want you and you only to take care of me, and if you won't do so, I shall refuse to get on the horse, and you will have to answer to the king why you did not carry out his orders!"

"What now?" asked Haman.

Mordechai pointed at his head of hair. "What do you suppose the king will think when he sees a person who looks so neglected and unkempt parading around wearing his royal clothing? He will surely be incensed!" Mordechai therefore insisted on a haircut.

The same scene repeated itself. Haman searched high and low for a barbershop that was open for business, but discovered that all the barbers had been locked up by Queen Esther. Once again, left with no choice, he grudgingly went home, took a pair of scissors, and set out to give Mordechai a proper haircut.

The sighs of Haman in the throes of his humiliation could be heard loud and clear, but Mordechai Hatzaddik was not overly impressed. "Why are you groaning?" he asked his enemy in feigned innocence. Haman replied that it cut him to the quick that a man of his rank should have to sink to such depths, serving as a bath attendant and a lowly barber. "What's so terrible?" Mordechai retorted. "Were you always such an important personage? To the best of my memory, you served as the barber of the village of Kartzom for twenty two years! Isn't that true?" Indeed, Haman was forced to confirm his words.

Now that Mordechai was immaculately clean and his hair neatly trimmed, he was finally willing to don the royal robes. But when it came to mounting the horse, a new problem arose. Mordechai Hatzaddik was physically weak, enervated by his three day fast.[9] It was difficult for him to lift himself up and climb onto the horse's back.

---

[9] According to the simple understanding, this should have been the day after the three day fast, and Mordechai was still weak in its wake. But, as we shall see later, after Mordechai's "stroll" with Haman through the streets of Shushan, he resumed his

He related this problem to Haman, and even offered a solution. "If you bend down to the ground, I can step onto your back, and from there, climb up onto the horse with ease!" the *tzaddik* suggested,[10] and Haman unhappily complied. He bent over, Mordechai stepped onto him, and before swinging himself up onto the horse's high back, he did not forget to give his mortal enemy a hearty kick.[11]

"What was that for?" Haman winced, and then added a learned objection, "Don't you Jews have a principle that[12] 'When your enemy falls, do not rejoice?'"

Mordechai was not impressed by this argument. "Before you start quoting *pesukim*, you have to learn a bit!" he admonished Haman. "This *posuk* refers only to an enemy who is a fellow Jew. But for a non-Jewish enemy such as yourself, we are permitted, and even commanded, to rejoice, as the *posuk* says,[13] 'You shall trample his high places!'"

Mordechai was finally seated on the royal steed, and Haman strode before him, blowing the trumpet[14] and proclaiming,

---

sackcloth and fast. The commentaries there disagree as to whether this was actually an additional day of fasting, beyond the prescribed three days, which Mordechai took upon himself alone, or if it was still within the framework of the three day fast.

[10] The Midrash (Esther Rabbah 10:4) explains that Mordechai attributed his difficulty to his old age, and when Haman tried to argue that he too was no youngster, Mordechai responded, "What do you want from me? Is it my fault that you brought this trouble upon yourself?"

[11] The Etz Yosef explains that Mordechai used every possible pretext to irritate Haman, in the hope that Haman would get so angry that he would kill him on the spot, a fact that would undoubtedly rouse the king's fury against him and lead him to kill his chief officer and nullify his decree. Mordechai was willing and happy to sacrifice his own life to save his fellow Jews, and that is why he chose this tactic.

[12] Mishlei 24:17

[13] Devorim 33:29

[14] Targum Sheini

"This is what is done for the man whom the king wishes to honor!"

Haman was not the only one walking before Mordechai's horse.[15] Another 27,000 pages were sent from the palace, all wearing fine uniforms and holding goblets of wine in their hands. They all marched together before the steed, calling out in a great voice, "This is what is done for the man whom the king wishes to honor!"

The king's pages were soon joined by all the Jews of Shushan, who, seeing the great honor being accorded to Mordechai, chimed in with a proclamation of their own, similar to the one being announced by Haman and the pages, "This is what is done for the man whom the King – the King of the world – wishes to honor!"

This strange parade made its way through the streets of Shushan. The Jews of Shushan took the lead, followed by 27,000 royal pages in uniform. Haman Harasha trudged behind them, his face lowered in shame, holding the horse's reins, and finally, atop the majestic horse, sat Mordechai Hatzaddik, praising his Creator.

"I shall exalt You, Hashem, for You have raised me up from the depths, and not let my foes rejoice over me. Hashem, my God, I cried out to You and You healed me! Hashem, You have raised up my soul from the Lower World, You have preserved me lest I descend to the Pit!"[16] Mordechai publicly praised Hashem.

---

[15] Ibid

[16] See Midrash Rabbah 10:5, where Chazal homiletically explain that whole chapter of Tehillim, "A psalm and song, on the dedication of the House of Dovid," (Tehillim 30) as relating to this incident. They explain that Mordechai Hatzaddik said the

From the window of her room in the palace, Esther too noticed the parade making its way slowly through the streets, and when she saw Mordechai sitting on the horse in royal garb, she raised her eyes heavenward and offered her thanks to Hashem above for this deliverance. She called out to Mordechai, "In you, the words of the *posuk* have been actualized, 'He raises the poor from the dust and lifts up the destitute from the trash heaps, to set them among princes!'"[17]

Esther was not the only one looking out her window. Haman's daughter was doing the same, as she waited with bated breath to hear about the king's agreement to hang Mordechai on the gallows her father had prepared for him.

When Haman passed by his house, his daughter, from her spot at the window, heard a herald announcing something before an important personage riding the king's horse, wearing royal robes and a crown upon his head.

The girl did not have a shadow of a doubt who was the rider and who was the herald. She was absolutely certain that her father was taking the opportunity to humiliate Mordechai before hanging him on the gallows he had prepared. Therefore,

---

first two verses cited above, to which his *talmidim* responded, "Sing to Hashem, His devoted ones, and give thanks to His holy Name! For His anger endures but a moment, life results from pleasing Him." Haman Harasha then said, "I said in my serenity, 'I will never falter,' but Hashem, it was Your goodwill alone that supported my greatness with might. When You concealed Your face, I was terrified!" Esther prayed and cried out, "To You, Hashem, I shall call, and to my God I shall plead. What gain is there in my death, in my descent to the Pit? Shall the dust acknowledge You? Will it tell of Your truth?" The Jewish people then proclaimed, "Hear, Hashem, and favor me; Hashem, be My helper! You have turned my lament into dancing; You undid my sackcloth and girded me with joy." *Ru'ach hakodesh* responded to them from the heavens, saying, "So that my soul might sing to You and not be stilled; Hashem, my God, I shall thank You forever."

[17] Shmuel I 2:8

in her eagerness to help her father degrade the *tzaddik*, she took the sewage pail from its corner and promptly emptied out its disgusting contents onto the head of the herald – who she imagined was Mordechai Hatzaddik.

Only when she looked out the window to survey the outcome of her deed did she grasp her terrible mistake. When the herald glanced upwards to locate the source of the repulsive shower to which he had just been treated, she saw that it was her father's face glaring at her, burning with anger. His clothes were filthy and the stench unbearable.

When she understood what she had done, the daughter of Haman was terribly distraught. In her confusion she fell from the upper story window to the ground and died instantly.[18] Now, a feeling of mourning was added to Haman's deep humiliation, as the *megillah* itself relates, "Mordechai returned to the king's gate, while Haman hastened home, mourning and with his head covered." Chazal expound on this *posuk*,[19] "'mourning' for his daughter, and 'his head covered' in humiliation over what had happened to him."

When Haman got home that day, he could "boast" at having mastered four professions;[20] he had served as bath attendant, barber, stableman, and herald – all in one day.

---

[18] However, in Esther Rabbah 10:5, we are told that the daughter of Haman jumped from the window when she saw her father leading Mordechai, implying that the humiliation itself caused her to take her own life.

[19] Megillah 16a

[20] The Targum Sheini explains that Haman came home with four tools of the trade – the scissors with which he had cut Mordechai's hair, the basin in which he had washed him, the reins of the horse he had led, and the trumpets with which he served as herald.

Mordechai Returned to the King's Gate

The Jewish community in Shushan was rippling with excitement and anticipation. Finally, they perceived a spark of hope. Their prayers had taken effect, and their venerable *rav* was publicly exalted in stature.

The only one who did not join in the general aura of excitement was Mordechai. As soon as Haman finished leading him around the length and breadth of Shushan, Mordechai went right back to his sackcloth and fasting.[21] He was not swept up by the rare honor that had been rendered to him and did not allow himself to lapse into a feeling of calm and complacency. Instead, he resumed praying and pleading to his Creator to have mercy on His people and speedily redeem them from their enemies.

As for Haman, he hastened home. While his usual practice was to stride slowly through the streets, taking small, measured

---

[21] Esther 10:6; Megillah ibid. However, some of the commentaries derive from the choice of words in the *posuk* that Mordechai returned to the *gate of the king himself*, to which entrance was prohibited when garbed in sackcloth. From this they conclude that Mordechai removed his sackcloth at the conclusion of the three day fast, apparently because he was confident in Hashem's deliverance once he saw that Hashem had saved him from the hands of the enemy who sought to take his life (Yosef Lekach). On the other hand, the Minchas Erev explains that the words of the Midrash and the implication of the *pesukim* do not contradict one another. It could be that Mordechai resumed his sackcloth, but concealed it beneath his regular clothing so that he would be able to enter the king's gate. Mordechai implemented this "leniency" only now, after his oath not to remove the sackcloth until he would see the Jews' deliverance was no longer applicable, since he had already seen the beginnings of the deliverance, including Haman hurrying towards his home, i.e., towards the *gallows* by his home.

Regarding the fast, most of the commentaries understand that this was the day following the three day fast, and Mordechai alone, as the *gadol hador*, remained immersed in fasting. However, we already cited above the opinion of Rashi (Megillah 16a), who maintains that this was the third day of the fast, and that is why Mordechai resumed fasting.

steps and deriving boundless pleasure from the sight of the masses bowing before him, today was different. Today, he wanted to get home as soon as he could, to escape the contemptuous looks that pierced him from every direction.

When Haman got home, he immediately assembled his friends once again, as well as his wife Zeresh. This time, however, Zeresh was more restrained; after all, her last suggestion had not achieved overly impressive results.

Haman opened his statements in a rather optimistic tone,[22] saying, "Everything that happened today is nothing more than unfortunate happenstance!" He delineated the strange circumstances that brought the situation about. "At this point, it seems to me that nothing more should stand in my way of asking the king to hang Mordechai on the gallows I prepared. He has already received his reward, and now he is an ordinary civilian once again – actually worse than that, since after all the kindness the king dealt him, he still refuses to follow his command!"[23] Haman explained to his advisors. But they simply shook their heads at him.[24]

---

[22] Malbim. He explains that Haman wanted to allay the concerns of his advisors, who thought that Haman had come to the king that morning and asked to kill Mordechai, and that the king had found that justice was with Mordechai and therefore instructed Haman to render him a great honor. "Had that been the case," Haman said, "I too would agree that things were hopeless. But the king did not hear me out at all; he simply latched onto things I said by chance, in order to reward Mordechai, since, as it happened, that night he had read about how Mordechai saved him from Bigsan and Teresh!"

[23] The Gra has a similar explanation. However, in his opinion, the king did not instruct Haman to do all this for Mordechai as a punishment for Haman, but rather in order to prevent any chance of Esther making a greater request on behalf of her righteous cousin. It is clear why Haman thought that it was no more than coincidence; the king remained on good terms with him as usual, but simply ordered him to be the emissary to pay Mordechai his reward! Nevertheless, Haman's advisors insisted that there is no happenstance and no mistake here. By the Jews, everything takes place

"You are mistaken, and you will realize your mistake soon enough!" they began. "Perhaps you are not familiar with the nature of the Jewish people. Allow us to acquaint you briefly with them. First of all, by the Jews, there is no such thing as happenstance; everything comes about through Divine Providence. If their God has decided to deliver them, you won't be able to stand in His way no matter what you do!

"Besides," the advisors continued, "the Jews are compared to the dust and also to the stars. This indicates that when they fall – they fall as low as the dust, but by the same token, when they rise – they rise as high as the stars.[25] Therefore, once we see that you have begun to fall before this Mordechai,[26] we regretfully have to inform you that there is no chance you will be able to overcome him.

"The only thing we can suggest is that you refrain from starting up with Mordechai from this point on. You can be pretty sure that if you don't hurt him first, he will not harm you. But if you take even the slightest step against this *tzaddik*,

---

as the result of precise and pre-planned Providence, and if Haman has begun to falter, he may as well take down the gallows he prepared for Mordechai already. But Haman refused to do so, and at that point, the chamberlains walked in. This too was an act of Divine Providence, to summon him with such urgency, so he would have no time to consult his advisors and perhaps decide to dismantle the gallows, since it was through this gallows that his downfall came about, as we shall see later on.

[24] As the Gemara goes on to say, Haman's advisors explained to him that if Mordechai was a member of the tribe of Yehuda, Binyamin, Efraim or Menashe, he had no chance of prevailing against him, since these tribes were granted a special ability to resist their enemies, as Chazal derive from various *pesukim*.

[25] According to a slightly different explanation presented by Ibn Yichyeh, the advisors said that when the Jews sink as low as the dust, from that point they begin to rise until they reach the stars.

[26] The proof is that you fell before Mordechai without his even having made any effort in that direction. Another proof is that you faltered, while he did not fall at all. In a typical battle, both sides suffers some losses, but in this case, you were utterly degraded while Mordechai came out of the encounter untouched (Malbim).

you can expect to find yourself in a downward spiral, suffering fall after fall.[27] And if you are foolish enough to still try to hang him on the gallows you prepared, your end will be a bitter one!" they warned him.

Just as the advisors concluded, the king's chamberlains arrived to hurriedly and urgently fetch Haman to the banquet Esther had prepared,[28] without allowing time for any questions or explanations. The king knew that Haman's day had not been an easy one, but he was not willing to spoil Esther's party for such a trivial reason.

Haman had not even had a chance to wash up properly from the filth of the sewage that his daughter had poured on his head.[29] When he got home, he had rushed to gather his advisors, and while the meeting was still going on, the chamberlains arrived to take him without allowing him to tarry even a moment.[30]

The last sentences that were exchanged between the advisors and Haman were overheard by the chamberlains as they entered; this information later played an important role in the way matters evolved.

---

[27] However, the advisors agreed that there was still one way in which he could overcome Mordechai – if Mordechai would fall before him and subordinate himself of his own free will. Then, perhaps Mordechai would set aside his sackcloth and prayers and distance himself from his God, and Haman Harasha would be able to defeat him. But even they realized that the chances of such a plan succeeding were very small, so they did not even try to consolidate it into a practical program.

[28] Megillah 16a

[29] Rashi Megillah ibid

[30] The Ibn Yichyeh explains that Haman completely forgot about the banquet in his great distress, and that is why the king sent the chamberlains, furious that he was being kept waiting by Haman, who was late to the party.

AN ADVERSARY AND AN ENEMY

"The king and Haman came to drink together with Queen Esther. On this second day at the wine feast, the king again asked Esther, 'What is your request, Queen Esther? It shall be granted to you. And what is your petition? Even if it is half the kingdom, it shall be done.' Esther replied, 'If I have won Your Majesty's favor and if it pleases the king, let my life be given to me as my request, and my people as my petition. For I and my people have been sold to be destroyed, slain and annihilated. Had we merely been sold as slaves and maidservants, I would have remained silent, for it's not worth the king's damage.' 'Who is it? Where is the one who had the audacity to do so?' demanded the king. 'An adversary and an enemy – this wicked Haman!' Esther replied, and Haman trembled in terror before the king and queen. The king rose in a rage from the wine feast and went out to the garden court. Meanwhile, Haman got up to plead with Queen Esther for his life, because he saw that the king's evil intentions towards him were final. When the king returned from the garden court to the banquet hall, Haman was sprawled on the couch where Esther was. 'Would you dare assault the queen while I am in the house?' roared the king. As soon as the king uttered these words, Haman's

*face showed his humiliation. Then Charvona, one
of the king's chamberlains, said, 'Furthermore,
the fifty cubit high gallows that Haman prepared
for Mordechai, who spoke good for the king, is
standing in Haman's house.' 'Hang him on it,' the
king ordered. And so, they hung Haman on the
gallows he had prepared for Mordechai, and the
anger of the king abated." (7:1-10)*

Now, as the pieces fall into place, we will see in retrospect how all the necessary moves had been set into motion to facilitate Hashem's deliverance of the Jews and His revenge against the villain who sought to annihilate His beloved children.

After Haman was rushed to the palace, he and the king sat down to dine with Queen Esther at the second wine feast.[1] At a certain point, the king turned to Esther and asked her once again, "Queen Esther, tell me please, what is your request and your petition? Just say what you would like me to do;[2] even if it is half the kingdom,[3] I shall do it for you!"

---

[1] As we mentioned earlier in the name of the Yosef Lekach, at the first banquet Esther was not able to eat or drink, since she was still in the third day of her fast. We explained there that this was also the reason Esther gave for holding the second party, at which she promised to drink together with the king as he had asked her to do at the first one. However, the Ibn Yichyeh differs and explains that at the first banquet, Esther refrained from eating because she was afraid that if she would participate freely, the king – who was known to be very envious, in keeping with the Parsi nature – might suspect that she was a bit too chummy with Haman, and his envy would be roused. At the second party, on the other hand, Esther knew that she had already allayed the king's concerns about their relationship, and therefore, she allowed herself to drink in Haman's presence.

[2] The Yosef Lekach explains that the king was now willing to fulfill only a request relating to Esther herself, and that is why she made sure to explain to him that it would not be sufficient for him to save her life; it was necessary to save her entire people, since she herself could not bear to see the tragedy that would befall them.

Esther got directly to the crux of the matter. "My master the king, Your Highness, I do not ask for much – only for my life and the life of my people![4] That is all! We were sold[5] to be destroyed, slain and annihilated, and it is this decree that I plead with Your Majesty to nullify!

"I assure you, Your Majesty," Esther stressed, "that had we merely been sold as slaves and maidservants[6] by the command

However, many of the commentaries disagree on this point and maintain that at this second banquet, the king agreed to carry out any request, even one that did not relate to the queen personally.

[3] See above, at the description of the first banquet, where we brought two possible explanations for this addendum: either that the king was willing to fulfill any request that did not include more than half of his kingdom, or that he wished to emphasize that if Esther would petition for the construction of the *Bais Hamikdash*, he would be forced to reject her request.

[4] In the Minchas Erev, we find an explanation of why Esther first asked for herself, and only afterwards for her people. There is a known principle that "A prisoner cannot free himself from his prison." That being the case, Esther was forced to ask that she be freed herself first before attempting to save others.

[5] As the Perush HaGra explains, even though the king did not actually receive the silver in hand, it is considered as if they were sold, since the king never *gave up* the silver, he just *returned it as a gift* to Haman. However, we have already cited other commentaries according to which the king did actually receive the gift and *did not return it at all;* he simply left the decision up to Haman as to *what to do with the silver* in the framework of the royal budget.

According to the Minchas Erev, Esther explained to the king that the transaction was null and void, for two reasons: First, because it was an erroneous transaction to begin with, since the king certainly would not have been willing to sell his queen and her people. Second, because the transaction was based on deceit; though Haman agreed to pay ten thousand silver talents in exchange for the Jews, their value is actually far greater, as the taxes the king could obtain from them over the years would accrue to a much higher amount.

The Yosef Lekach maintains that Esther did not mean to argue that the Jews were literally *sold,* since this would cast aspersions on the conduct of Achashverosh himself, as if he had been willing to destroy the Jewish people in exchange for a monetary bribe. Esther rather argued that her people were *given over* to be destroyed – another possible meaning included in the term "we were sold."

[6] We discussed earlier the approach of the Yosef Lekach, according to which Haman presented his request to the king with the implication that he merely intended to enslave the Jews. Following this approach, the Yosef Lekach goes on to explain that here, Esther argued to the king that had matters really been as Haman had

of our enemy, I would not have opened my mouth.[7] I would have said to myself, 'At least this vile scoundrel is concerned for the benefit of our beloved king; who am I to object?' But this rogue gave no thought to the king's welfare.[8] He did not sell us as slaves, but rather ordered us destroyed. What benefit could that possibly bring the king?"[9] Esther demanded.

---

presented them in his request, she would have remained silent, but since Haman actually misled the king, and indeed sought to annihilate the Jewish people, she must come forward and plead with him.

[7] According to the Ibn Yichyeh, there were two arguments here. One related to the severity of the decree – that Haman did not suffice with enslaving the Jews but rather sought to destroy them. The second addressed Haman's obvious disregard for the king's good, since had he kept the king's benefit in mind, he would surely have opted for enslaving the Jews and enriching the royal coffers.

In contrast, the Ralbag explains that this was all part of one argument. Esther explained that she understood the king had received the formidable sum of ten thousand silver talents in exchange for the decree. Therefore, had it only been a decree of enslavement, she would not have intervened, since she would have understood that it was worthwhile for an entire people to be enslaved in order to yield such a huge profit for the royal treasury. But since the decree was to destroy the Jews, she could never tolerate it, no matter what the profit. Therefore, even though nullifying the decree would involve a major monetary loss, she was compelled to plead with the king.

The Malbim, on his part, explains that Esther's first argument was that Haman actually was seeking to kill *her*, and that is why he was provoking her people. Besides, she added, the decree to destroy and slay a nation, rather than to sell them into slavery, is degrading to the king, since it should be beneath his dignity to annihilate an entire people without their having committed a capital crime of any sort.

The Malbim also points out that Esther wished to reveal Haman's deceit to the king. As we mentioned earlier, according to the Malbim, Haman intentionally did not mention the name of the people under discussion, but rather said in a general sort of way, "There is a certain nation." Similarly, he chose the wording, "*k'abdom*," to decimate them, which the king interpreted as a request to force the Jews to abandon their beliefs. Now Esther clarified to the king that the anonymous "people" that Haman spoke about was her people, and he deceitfully concealed this fact from the king so that he would not refuse Haman's request. The other deceit was that Haman slyly did not let out that the decree was to physically annihilate the Jews, not just to impose on them spiritual destruction, as he originally presented it.

[8] Since Haman had argued that the Jewish people do not bring the king any benefit, and that they are constantly seeking the ill of the king, Esther emphasized the fact that Haman himself is the one who does not have the king's benefit in the forefront of his mind.

When the king heard Esther's words, he was horrified. "Kill the queen? Destroy her people? Who is it? What person would want to do such a terrible thing?[10] And what could possibly motivate him to want it?"[11] he stuttered to the queen,[12] tripping over his tongue in his consternation.[13]

---

[9] Most of the commentaries seem to imply that Esther argued that a decree of enslavement would not be so severe as to warrant her pleading to the king, as opposed to a decree of destruction. However, the Minchas Erev explains otherwise, maintaining that had the decree been one of enslavement, Esther would not have said a word to the king because she would have relied on the fact that he himself would not allow anyone to take his queen and her people as slaves. In contrast, once the decree was one of destruction, which could be carried out in a moment and would not involve so much degradation, the decree could have been executed before the king had a chance to consider its significance; that is why it was so urgent for her to talk to him about it.

[10] The Perush HaGra explains that the king intended to ask Esther, "*Who is it* who seeks to kill you and your people, and, for that matter, *what is* your nation? Didn't you yourself say that you do not know your national origin and that you grew up as an adopted orphan in Mordechai's house?"

[11] Malbim. He explains further that Esther's response to the king answered both questions. "It is an adversary and an enemy" – and that is the reason why he seeks to destroy my people. As to the question of his identity, the answer is – "this wicked Haman." Later on, we will see that according to the Gemara, Esther explained to the king that Haman envied her and therefore sought to kill her. According to the approach of the Malbim, we can say that these words too served as an answer to Achashverosh's question regarding the villain's motives.

[12] The Gemara explains that once the king heard from Esther that she was a Jew, a member of the Chosen People and a descendant of the royal lineage of King Shaul, he immediately related to her in an entirely different fashion. Until now, he had spoken to her via an emissary, since it would not be proper for a king to speak directly with an ordinary person. Now, he addressed her directly (Megillah 16a).

[13] That is how the Ibn Ezra explains the double language, "King Achashverosh said, he said to Queen Esther." However, the Ibn Yichyeh and other commentaries explain that there were two separate statements made, one to the servants, Haman among them, and a second to Esther. Regarding the argument that "it's not worth the king's damage," the king asked the servants, since this argument did not relate to Esther but rather to his kingship. Regarding the argument that "I and my people have been sold," he asked Esther herself. The Malbim, however, explains that at first the king addressed the question to his entire household, including Haman, and when they had nothing to answer him, he turned to Esther and asked her to explain her words.

Esther lost no time in pointing a finger at Haman and saying, "A man who is an adversary and an enemy, none other than this wicked Haman[14] who stands before you and pretends to be your dearest friend! Yes, the same one who was not ashamed to ask you today to put the royal crown on his head and have him led through the streets of Shushan, clad in *your* robes and mounted on *your* horse![15]

"This Haman was jealous of Vashti, your first queen, and therefore counseled you to kill her. Now he is jealous of me, the new queen, and seeks to do away with me as well![16] Haman does not seek your benefit – only your detriment!"[17] Esther declared.

In the course of this conversation, which appears entirely natural, an open miracle actually took place. As Esther spoke, she tangibly sensed that she was standing and presenting her points before the King of all kings. She was so totally focused on Him that inadvertently, she began to point her finger at King Achashverosh himself as the one responsible for the decree, since that was actually the truth. Such an act would have been perceived as a proclamation of the king's wickedness and hardheartedness; its ramifications would have been devastating. Therefore, a heavenly angel had to be sent to shift her finger in Haman's direction.[18]

---

[14] Esther emphasized, "this wicked Haman," to stress that his wickedness is an intrinsic part of his character; this was not a one-time wicked act (Ibn Yichyeh).

[15] Targum

[16] Megillah 16a

[17] As the Minchas Erev explains, Esther argued to the king that Haman actually seeks to kill *b*, and since he is afraid that Esther and Mordechai might save him as they saved him from the plot of Bigsan and Teresh, he first wants to get rid of them.

[18] Megillah ibid, according to the Perush HaGra.

The King Rose in his Rage

In any case, the king understood beyond a shadow of a doubt who was the dastardly villain to whom Queen Esther was referring. He concealed – or perhaps conveniently "forgot" – the fact that he too had always nursed the latent aspiration to destroy the Jews, and had refrained from doing so to this day only out of fear of their God's retribution.

The king's rage flared up, and Haman easily identified the signs of his familiar fury. Well aware that this fury generally did not bode well for its target, he was so frightened and confused[19] that all he could do was stare motionlessly at the raging king and queen.

Besides, in the present situation, there was not much that Haman could say in his defense.[20] Had he faced the king alone, he could have managed. Were Esther by herself, perhaps he could have found a way to assuage her anger. But with the two of them sitting side by side and glaring at him, there was no way for him to conciliate them.

If he were to appease Esther by saying that he did not know that it was her people, and that he would nullify the decree and speak up on their behalf from that point on, this would only have aggravated the king's rage, since it would imply that all along he had been motivated merely by his personal hatred of the Jews. The proof: now he was willing to promise that he would not repeat his words. Had his arguments been genuine and with the king's benefit in mind from the start, how could he now suddenly refrain from reporting them to the king?

---

[19] Ibn Yichyeh
[20] Malbim, Perush HaGra

On the other hand, if he were to try and allay the king's fury by arguing that he had spoken the truth all along, he would merely intensify the queen's anger by denigrating her people and plotting their destruction right in her presence.

Therefore, Haman had no choice for the time being but to remain silent. Only after the king stormed out of the banquet in a rage and went out to the garden to get some fresh air and allow his searing anger to cool down a bit,[21] did Haman find the right moment to try and appease Queen Esther. Now, while she was alone,[22] he would beg her to have mercy on him and ask the king to spare his life.

"My honored Queen Esther, I swear that it never would have entered my mind to harm your people! Had I been given the slightest hint as to your family origin, I would have glorified your people and rendered them immeasurable honor! But I did not have any inkling that you were a member of this nation. I did not act maliciously, the offense was absolutely unintentional, and therefore, I beg of you to forgive me!" Haman pleaded, but Esther firmly rejected his pleas.

While Haman tried unsuccessfully to win Esther's good graces, the king, walking through his beautiful and well-cultivated garden, was witness to miraculous visions geared

---

[21] As the Yosef Lekach explains, it was Divinely orchestrated that the king should leave the banquet before its conclusion, so that Esther should not be forced to drink *yayin nesech* with him. When he returned, he might have been too worked up to give thought to drinking with the queen, or perhaps Esther was able to pretend that she had already had a drink in his absence and could not imbibe another drop.

[22] The Ibn Yichyeh explains that Haman, being quite familiar with Achashverosh, knew that he would not be able to gain his mercies. He knew that when the king was in a temper, he did not have compassion on anyone. Therefore, he preferred to approach the queen, in the hope that she would be a softer target, as is the nature of women.

to accelerate Haman's sharp descent. Achashverosh noticed a number of workmen – actually heavenly angels sent down in the form of laborers[23] – methodically uprooting tree after tree in the king's ornamental orchard.

"What are you doing?! Have you gone mad? Who gave you permission to enter the royal garden, and why are you pulling out the trees?" the king screamed hysterically, unable to restrain himself at the sight of his lovely gardens being destroyed.

The "laborers" replied, "Haman authorized our entrance to the garden, and he also commanded us to uproot the trees and bring them over to his yard!"[24]

The workmen's reply aggravated the king's fury to no end. Better to do without the fresh air, he decided, and instead, to go back inside. He could not allow himself to remain there and lose all control at the tremendous audacity of this "trusted" officer who shamelessly ordered his favorite trees yanked from the ground.

But when the king stomped furiously into the banquet hall, he did not have much chance to calm down, since a rather unpleasant surprise awaited him there. In those days, the practice at festive meals was to recline on couches. In order for Haman to beg the queen to spare his life, he had to get up from his couch and approach Esther's couch.[25]

---

[23] Megillah 16a. The Midrash Ponim Acheirim writes that Achashverosh imagined he saw Haman's sons chopping down the trees. Similarly, the Pirkei D'Rabbi Eliezer says that the angel Micha'el chopped down the trees, and when the king asked him what he was doing, he replied, "I am one of Haman's sons; this is what he commanded me to do!"

[24] The Perush HaGra explains that since Haman had spoken loshon hora about the Jewish people that was absolutely devoid of any truth, it was decreed that his own downfall should be intensified through loshon hora devoid of any truth.

[25] Ibn Yichyeh

When the king walked in, the picture that greeted him, therefore, was that of Haman crouched over Esther's couch. The first thought that entered his mind was,[26] "Aha, Haman is trying to do what he could not accomplish through the decree!"

"Aren't you ashamed?" he roared. "To kill the queen in my own home?![27] Even people who have been sentenced to death and run to the palace for refuge are safe there from execution. Yet you dare to try and assassinate the queen in the very place that is the symbol of pardon?"[28] Achashverosh sputtered in anger. Haman understood that his fate was sealed.[29]

Chazal tell us that in fact, Haman himself tried to get up and move away from the queen as soon as the king entered the room. He sensed that the general picture would not be especially pleasing to Achashverosh. But he was Divinely prevented from doing so; in order to intensify his downfall,

---

[26] The commentary Yosef Lekach points out that Haman's well thought out plan to wait and beg Esther for mercy only after the king would leave the scene, when he could convince her in a private conversation, merely turned against him. Had he pleaded with Esther in the king's presence, perhaps his words would not have been accepted, but at least they would not have increased the king's wrath. Now, however, when Haman prostrated himself before Esther while the king was in the garden, his act was interpreted as an effort to attack the queen, and this made Haman's situation many times worse.

[27] The Ibn Yichyeh explains that the king actually understood that Haman was pleading with Esther for his life, but he expected Haman to hide his face in shame, to mourn and agonize, not to have the audacity to get up and make requests. Therefore, when he saw him pleading before the queen, he became even more incensed, and the results were not long in coming.

[28] Malbim

[29] The Yosef Lekach explains that Haman did not even manage to get a single word of apology out of his mouth. He could not utter even one syllable that might have shed light on the goings on and clarified to the king that he had no malicious intentions towards the queen, and only wished to plead for her mercies.

an angel was sent who pushed him back again and again, not allowing him to leave his compromising position.[30]

As soon as the king uttered these words, the servants knew that they had better act quickly in order to calm the royal temperament. Achashverosh was so worked up that they feared for his health. Therefore, they quickly covered Haman Harasha's face so that the king would not see his countenance and thus, his fury would not increase and intensify any further.[31]

At this precise juncture, Charvona came and "hammered the last nail into Haman's casket." There are differing opinions in Chazal regarding the identity of this Charvona.[32] Some maintain that he was none other than Eliyahu Hanavi himself, in the guise of a royal chamberlain, and that he was Divinely sent especially to report about the gallows Haman had built in his courtyard. Others[33] claim that the speaker was an actual chamberlain by this name, who, for reasons of his own that we shall soon delineate, decided to provide the king with this information.

Charvona stood before King Achashverosh and said, "Your Majesty the king, do you know who this Haman is? You should be aware[34] that standing in Haman's courtyard is the gallows

---

[30] Megillah ibid; Esther Rabbah 10:7. The Midrash also mentions that Esther even cried out to the king, "Save me! Haman is trying to assault me!" rousing the king's anger yet further.

[31] The Ibn Ezra, Ralbag and others explain the *posuk* in this way. However, the Gra explains it in its simpler sense – that Haman hid his face in his great shame.

[32] Esther Rabbah 10:7

[33] Megillah ibid

[34] According to the Yosef Lekach, and as we shall soon point out in the text, Charvona knew about Haman's plans as he had overheard Haman's dialogue with his advisors when he came to fetch Haman to Esther's party. In the course of that dialogue, the advisors tried to convince Haman to dismantle the gallows, but he

upon which he planned to ask you to hang Mordechai[35] – yes, Mordechai the Jew who saved the king's life!"[36] Charvona clarified, leaving no room for doubt.

Where did Charvona acquire this information regarding Haman's plan? Chazal[37] explain that at first, Charvona himself was in league with Haman. He helped him construct the gallows, and eagerly anticipated the downfall of Mordechai, against whom he apparently harbored some grudge. But now that Charvona understood what a bitter fate awaited Haman after having been caught ostensibly trying to kill the queen, he sensed which way the wind was blowing and realized that it would be wise to place himself on the winning side.

Therefore, Charvona jumped in to save his skin by exposing Haman's guilt to the king, telling him about the gallows that

---

was not persuaded, since he still thought there was a chance he would succeed in hanging Mordechai. Following this approach, the Yosef Lekach points out that Charvona wished to stress that the gallows was standing *even now*, i.e., even now, after learning that the king owes a debt of gratitude towards Mordechai, he still seeks to kill the king's benefactor.

[35] The Perush HaGra explains that Hashem put into Charvona's mouth these precise words, which the king interpreted in a slightly different manner than they were intended. Charvona said, "There is the gallows that Haman prepared for Mordechai who said good for the king," while the king understood that he meant to say, "There is the gallows that Haman prepared for Mordechai, (and that) he said, 'Good for the king!'" meaning that Haman deemed the gallows proper and fitting for the king himself!

[36] In his statement, Charvona wanted to emphasize that at the very moment that Haman led Mordechai on the horse through the streets of Shushan, the gallows stood ready in his courtyard, so that in essence, the proclamation he announced before Mordechai by the king's command was actually a form of deep humiliation for the king. It was as if he was saying, "This is what is done for the man whom the king wishes to honor – and I plan on hanging that same man on the gallows!" (Malbim). The Yosef Lekach adds that Charvona wanted to say that Haman sought to kill Mordechai *because* he spoke good for the king, and this is a terrible *chutzpah* that reveals the true colors of this wicked *rasha!*

[37] Megillah ibid; Targum Sheini

Haman had built, while intentionally covering up his own participation in the matter.

The commentaries offer another answer to the question of Charvona's source of information.[38] As we mentioned in the previous chapter, when Haman was late in coming to the banquet, a cadre of chamberlains was sent to fetch him, Charvona among them. As he walked in to Haman's house, Charvona managed to overhear bits of the conversation, from which he understood that the tall gallows set up in the courtyard was meant for Mordechai the Jew.

Now, Charvona transmitted this information to the king, and Achashverosh needed no further convincing. Without thinking twice, he ordered the chamberlains who were present, "Take Haman away and hang him on the gallows that he prepared for Mordechai!" In doing so, he made use of the broad powers bestowed upon him several years earlier by Haman himself.

Haman was the one who had recommended passing a law endowing the king with the authority to judge and rule even in matters that affected him personally. This law gave the king broad powers to execute rebels without having to bring them to judgment. And that is precisely what the king did now – he ordered Haman executed on the spot, without giving the *rasha* recourse to a court judgment, at which the judges might perhaps have had mercy on him and spared his life.

The commentaries explain that the execution of Haman's sentence was given over to the chamberlains, among them Charvona, the one who had testified to Haman's construction of the gallows. However, in Targum Sheini we are told that

---

[38] Gra, Malbim, Yosef Lekach

the task of sending Haman to his death was entrusted to Mordechai himself.

Chazal, in Targum Sheini, go on to say that Haman had the audacity to plead before Mordechai to have mercy on him and not to repay him in kind. He begged Mordechai at least not to submit him to the humiliating death of hanging on the public gallows, but rather to kill him in a more respectable fashion, such as by the sword. At the same opportunity, Haman declared his acknowledgement of the open miracles that Hashem did and has always done for His people, and in particular, the most recent miracle that revolved around him.

But Mordechai did not take the bait. The arch enemy's smooth talk did not move him in the least, nor did the profuse apologies Haman "remembered" to offer once he saw that his fate was sealed. Mordechai did to Haman exactly what the *rasha* intended to do to him – he hanged him on the gallows.

With that, a life replete with wickedness came to an ignoble close, with Haman hanged in full display on the fifty cubit high public gallows, his name engraved for eternal infamy.

That day, for the first time since Vashti had violated the king's will, Achashverosh found peace of mind. All the pent up anger that had accumulated in his heart for years he took out on Haman's head,[39] and now he finally felt calm. The circle had been closed; the advisor who had counseled him to kill Vashti had found his death as a direct outcome of his own advice.

But, at this point, Haman's decree had not yet been nullified! The letters sent out in the king's name, ordering his subjects to

---

[39] Esther Rabbah 3:15

destroy, slay and exterminate all the Jews, were still making their way to the various provinces and districts, and mediatory efforts would still be required to abrogate the decree.

ESTHER SPOKE YET AGAIN

"That day, King Achashverosh gave over the estate of Haman, enemy of the Jews, to Queen Esther. Mordechai came before the king, as Esther had told the king what his relationship was to her. The king took off his signet ring that he had removed from Haman and gave it instead to Mordechai, and Esther appointed Mordechai over Haman's estate.

Then Esther spoke yet again to the king. She fell at his feet, cried and begged him to avert the evil intent of Haman the Agagite and the malicious plot which he had hatched against the Jews. The king extended the golden scepter to Esther, and Esther rose and stood before the king. She said to him, 'If it pleases the king, and if I have won his favor and the proposal seems proper to the king and I am pleasing to him, let it be written to recall the letters devised by Haman ben Hamedasa the Agagite, in which he wrote to annihilate the Jews in all the king's provinces. For how can I bear to see such a calamity befall my people? How can I bear to witness the destruction of my family?'

Then the king said to Queen Esther and to Mordechai the Jew, 'Behold, I have given Haman's estate over to Esther, and he himself was hung on the gallows for having plotted against

the Jews. Now, write about the Jews as you see
fit, in the king's name, and seal the letter with the
king's signet ring, for an edict which is written in
the king's name and sealed with the royal signet
cannot be revoked.'" (8:1–8)

Once Haman was hanged on the gallows, the king began to distribute his possessions. He gave Haman's estate and all his money to Queen Esther, since all money belonging to executed rebels goes to the king's coffers. Achashverosh wanted to make it perfectly clear that Haman had been killed for rebelling against the queen and for seeking to annihilate her people, and therefore his wealth was put in her hands.[1]

At this point, Mordechai was formally introduced to King Achashverosh in the palace. Esther took this opportunity to explain to the king how she was related to Mordechai, and told him of their family lineage.

Duly impressed, the king promptly granted Mordechai a promotion in rank, appointing him as viceroy in place of Haman, and entrusting him with the royal signet, effectively making him responsible for all royal matters.[2]

Achashverosh also authorized Mordechai to come before him at any time, without having to wait to be summoned by

---

[1] Malbim

[2] See comment in the next chapter, where we will explain that the commentaries differ on this point. Some maintain that as soon as Mordechai presented himself before the king, he was immediately appointed as the king's viceroy and given full control in political matters (Malbim), while others maintain that at first the king put Mordechai in charge only of *his household*. Only with time did he continue to rise in rank until he was appointed viceroy to the king (Yosef Lekach).

the king and without being dependent on his good graces – whether he stretched out his golden scepter or not.[3]

Esther, on her part, also gave Mordechai a valuable gift.[4] She put him in charge of Haman's estate, instantly endowing him with massive wealth. The commentaries disagree as to whether Mordechai was appointed merely as administrator of Haman's estate on Esther's behalf,[5] or whether it was given over to him as a personal gift.[6]

The fact that Esther and Mordechai inherited Haman's glorious wealth and lofty position[7] constituted sweet revenge against the *rasha* for all he sought to do to them. Hanging the arch villain, on the other hand, was a form of retribution *for "the king's damage"* – for having attempted to act against the interests of his illustrious king.

To Avert the Evil Intention of Haman

Now the moment of truth had arrived. Until this point, the king had seen to it that Mordechai and Esther were personally taken care of. He saved Mordechai from the gallows that Haman Harasha had prepared for him, hanging him instead, and granted Haman's vast possessions to Esther and his rank and honor to her righteous cousin.

But nothing had been done to resolve the real problem in question - the terrible decree that had been issued ordering the king's subjects to destroy, slay and annihilate the Jewish people!

---

[3] Malbim
[4] Ibn Yichyeh
[5] Ralbag
[6] Ibn Yichyeh
[7] Malbim

This decree was still in effect; on the thirteenth day of Adar in the following year, the people of Achashverosh's realm were due to let loose against the Jews! What would be?

At first, right after Haman's execution, Esther thought that the king had not yet calmed down from his fury, and was not ready to deal with nullifying the decree. But days went by and the king still did not say anything at all about the mortal threat that was hanging over the Jewish people.

"Surely the king will summon me any day now, and then I will be able to offer him my petition and beg him to spare my people from Haman's terrible decree!" Esther hoped. But the days continued to pass, and still she was not called to the king.[8]

Esther was especially bothered when she received Haman's estate as a gift from the king, since she thought to herself, "I did not ask the king for wealth or property. Nor did I ask him to take revenge against my enemy. I asked only that he *save my people and my family*! If King Achashverosh had planned to fulfill my request, he would not have bothered to grant me such trivial gifts; he would have focused on what I asked – the deliverance of my people and nullification of the decree!

"But Achashverosh did not do so. He gave me Haman's estate; he granted my cousin influence and high rank. Consequently, I have to assume that in regard to the *crux of my request*, he has no intentions of complying! In that case, what did I accomplish? What did I gain by risking my life to come before him uninvited?"

---

[8] Ralbag

Esther had no choice but to take her life in her hands once more. Again she entered the inner court without having been summoned, again she risked her life for her people, and again King Achashverosh extended his golden scepter and allowed her to say what was on her mind.[9]

Esther cried and pleaded. Collapsing at the king's feet, she begged for mercy on her people, saying, "Your Majesty, how can I bear to see the tragedy that would befall my people and the destruction of my family? This petition is not a request on behalf of others that you can dismiss out of hand; it is a request for my own life, because to live with the knowledge that my people are slated for destruction – is not living at all!"

An Edict Written in the King's Name

Esther presented her pleas to the king over and over,[10] until he finally acceded to her request; he was prepared to rescind the decree. Still, a serious problem remained. The first missives, dealing with the destruction of the Jewish people, had been sent in the king's name and sealed with the royal signet. The laws of Madai and Paras clearly stipulated that such an edict could not be redacted! Therefore, with all his good intentions, what could he do?

Esther was not naïve. Well aware of the aforementioned law, she expected the king to grasp at it as a last straw and hinge his

---

[9] Ralbag, Ibn Yichyeh. However, Malbim implies that Esther entered the king's presence legitimately. However, she collapsed at his feet in tears, and then the king stretched out the golden scepter to authorize her to present her petition in detail.

[10] Ibn Yichyeh. He implies that even after Haman was killed and Mordechai promoted, the king still intended *not to nullify the decree against the Jews*, due to his deep hatred towards the holy nation.

refusal to nullify Haman's decree on the legal limitations. But she was not deterred.

"Your Majesty, I grant that a just edict – one that was sent at the king's initiative and which expresses the king's wise judgment – indeed may not be rescinded. Doing so would constitute contempt of the king's honor, and that is the last thing I would want. But could the law possibly apply to these hateful letters, which were written without the king's knowledge, and whose content the king would never have agreed to? On the contrary! If the decree would not be retracted, then *that* would constitute the greatest disgrace for the king and his regime!" the queen argued.[11] But the king did not accept her words.[12]

"I am terribly sorry, my dear queen, but an edict written in the king's name cannot be retracted under any circumstances

---

[11] Ibn Yichyeh

[12] Following his approach that the detailed letters were sent only to the officers with attached instructions not to open the letters until the thirteenth of Adar, and the general public was only informed in a general way to be prepared for this day, the Malbim explains that Esther argued to the king that there was no reason not to rescind the decree. As far as the king himself was concerned, there would be no disgrace in nullifying a decree that was not sent with his full knowledge (as the Malbim explained above), i.e., since it was actually *machsheves Haman,* Haman's idea, and not the king's proposal. As far as the officers were concerned, they didn't know anything about the content of the letters, and if new letters would be sent to them with attached instructions to replace the first letters, they would never know that the decree had been altered. Thus, the whole matter would remain in the form of "Haman's idea" – merely a thought. But, as mentioned in the text, the king did not accept Esther's argument.

According to the Minchas Erev, Esther's argument was that disgrace would only be incurred to the king if he rescinded his edict after it *became public.* However, before the content of the letters was public knowledge, there was no disgrace, and the letters could certainly be redacted. However, the king explained that the letters could not be remanded under any circumstances, even before they had been opened, though in essence, all that would be rescinded in such a case would be the letters themselves, and not the royal orders. Therefore, in the end, he instructed them to write new letters.

– whether it is just or not, whether it is appropriate or not, whether or not the king now agrees to its content or has long ago changed his mind.

"And I am afraid that you have no one to blame for this situation but yourself!" the king went on, explaining his statement as follows, "I asked you many times to reveal your background to me. I begged you to tell me of your family origin, but you stubbornly refused! Had you revealed these details to me from the start, I would never have allowed that villain to send the first letters to begin with, and this whole problem would have been avoided!" the king claimed.[13]

Needless to say, concepts such as "Divine Providence," "repentance" and "Heavenly decrees" were absolutely foreign to him. He did not know that the decree had actually been sealed in the heavens, not in his earthly palace. Nor did he understand that until he passed his signet ring to Haman, the Jews were not roused to full repentance; only the removal of the ring from the king's finger accomplished what the prophecies of forty eight prophets could not![14] He could not grasp that he, Haman, and the advisors who cooperated in issuing the terrible decree were no more than a whipping rod in Hashem's Hand.

Nevertheless, the king sought to allay the queen's concerns. "Don't worry, Esther, nothing will happen to your people. Let me explain to you why," he announced, pulling Mordechai into the conversation in order to help him calm down the sobbing queen.[15]

---

[13] Targum Sheini
[14] Megillah 14a
[15] Yosef Lekach

"Why did I give you the 'house of Haman,' the enemy of the Jews?" the king asked. "And what were my reasons for hanging him on the gallows?"

He immediately answered his own questions, "When I gave you Haman's estate, Queen Esther, it was not because I wanted to bestow great wealth upon you. Had that been my goal, I did not have to give you Haman's *house* in particular; he has possessions that are worth far more than his house![16] Besides, the king's treasuries hold more than enough money to endow you and all your people with indescribable wealth for their entire lives!

"So why did I give you the 'house of Haman?' Because I wanted everyone to know what fate befalls someone *who tries to annihilate the Jews*, so that it will be perfectly clear to every resident of the royal provinces *what will be the end of anyone who starts up with the queen's people!*

"The same goal was behind my decision to hang him on the gallows. Both of these events are the type of tidbits that tend to gain publicity, and publicity is precisely what I wanted. Now," the king said to Mordechai and Esther, "you can send new letters to all the provinces, as you see fit, and write whatever you want there about the Jews, but without nullifying the first letters that were sent in the king's name.[17] In any case, you

---

[16] Ibid

[17] The Megillas S'sorim offers two additional explanations. According to the first, it indeed was not possible to recall the first letters. However, in the second missives, they wrote that the intention of the first letters was to *convert the Jews* – spiritual destruction. The king now commanded that the Jews be allowed to avenge themselves from those who sought to kill them. This, he implied, would cause them to become comfortable among the gentiles, leading them to assimilate. Mordechai agreed to this suggestion, since he was fully confident that this would never lead the Jews to

have nothing to worry about. No one will dare rely on the original letters and hurt the Jews; nobody wants to find himself hanging on the gallows, and his house and possessions given over to strangers!

"Further," the king added, "don't forget that the general populace knows nothing about the decree. All they know is that they have to be prepared on the thirteenth of Adar, but they haven't the vaguest notion for what. Therefore, what could be simpler than to send letters delineating what will take place on the appointed day – that the Jews are authorized that day to take revenge on their enemies!

"As for the officers and nobles who know about Haman's decree, have no fear. They certainly will not dare to let a word out for fear that they will suffer the same fate as Haman did for attempting to destroy the Jews," the king summed up.

---

leave their beliefs, certainly not at this point, after they had just witnessed Hashem's Divine Providence and the miraculous way in which they had been rescued from the hand of Haman.

According to the second approach, the first letters said that the *Jews* should be prepared for the thirteenth day of Adar, but they did not say for what purpose. Haman's intention was to see to it that the Jews would be in their homes on that day and would not go off to other countries where it would not be possible to locate and destroy them. The Jews understood his scheme all too well. In the second letters, the only information added was the *purpose of the preparations*, stating explicitly that the Jews had to be prepared to *take revenge from their enemies*. That changed the picture from one extreme to the other, without stating any significant diversion from the original meaning of the first letters.

The Minchas Erev writes that the king meant to say that in *Shushan the capital*, there was no need to fear, since the residents knew what had happened to Haman, and would surely not dare to raise a hand to hurt the Jews. However, in regard to all other places, the king advised them to write that permission was granted to the Jews to resist their enemies who rise against them; from that, everyone will infer that the king had changed his mind and would not touch the Jews. But Mordechai and Esther did not suffice with following the king's advice; they further explained the first letters as meaning that the nations should be prepared for this day upon which the Jews would take revenge from their enemies.

Mordechai and Esther accepted his opinion and immediately wrote out the new letters.[18]

It should be pointed out that not all opinions agree with the description mentioned above. Some say that even once the king agreed to allow Mordechai and Esther to send a second set of letters to the provinces, they could only write that permission was granted to the Jews to defend themselves against their enemies and to fight like two opposing armies.[19]

According to this approach, there was another tremendous miracle that took place[20] – that in a fierce battle between the

---

[18] The Malbim, following his approach, explains that the general population was indeed sent a second round of letters *explaining* the unclear first letters, as we explained. The nobles and officers were also sent new letters, in which an order was delineated that was precisely the opposite of what the first letter instructed them. However, just as they were forbidden to open the first letters until the thirteenth day of Adar, so were they forbidden to open the second letters until this date. That being the case, there would still remain a possibility that the officers, who would open both of the contradictory letters in one day, would prefer to obey the first ones and not the second. The king allayed Esther's fears on this point by explaining that once he had given over Haman's estate to Esther and hung the villainous Haman on the gallows, the officers would be afraid to follow Haman's lead, as they would understand that the first letters were not really the king's idea at all, but rather the devious invention of Haman's corrupt mind.

He also explains that Esther was concerned about two things. One – that the decree would be carried out on its appointed date, the thirteenth of Adar, and two – that the nations of the world would cause trouble and pain for the Jews even before that date. As we described in earlier chapters, some of the gentiles had already begun to harass the Jews and hurt them, on the assumption that they were destined to be killed anyway. In regard to these concerns, the king responded as we mentioned above, that once the nations saw that Haman was hung on the gallows and his estate given to Esther because of his malicious intentions towards the Jews, they would understand that anyone who would dare to threaten or hurt the Jews would suffer a bitter fate.

[19] Ralbag and others

[20] The Yosef Lekach challenges these opinions, since if they still needed an open miracle in order to prevail in the war, what was the point of all the rejoicing described later in the *megillah*? Besides, is there a need to *permit* a person to defend

Jews and the nations, between a lone sheep and seventy wolves, the Jews won![21]

In any case, according to all opinions, Mordechai and Esther wrote letters to all the nations in the provinces of Achashverosh's realm, marking the beginning of the Jews' deliverance.

---

himself? Had the second letters not been issued, would the Jews have gone to their deaths without fighting for their lives? He resolves this challenge by explaining that the joy was for the strong encouragement they felt once they knew that the king supported them and officially authorized them to defend themselves. This inner confidence boosted their strength and enabled them to resist their enemies with staunch heart.

[21] An additional opinion cited in the commentaries maintains that the substantial difference between the first letters and the second lay in whose side the king's armies would take. According to the first letters, they were meant to assist in annihilating the Jews, while according to the second letters, their role was to assist the Jews in their defense. However, according to this opinion, we are left with the question of why this would not be considered a revocation of the king's word.

THE SECOND LETTERS

"Then the king's scribes were summoned, on the
twenty third day of the third month – which
is Sivan. Everything Mordechai dictated was
written to the Jews and to the satraps and nobles
and the governors of all the provinces from
Hodu to Kush – one hundred and twenty seven
provinces, to each province in its own script and
to each people in its own language, and to the
Jews as well, in their script and language. The
letters, written in the name of King Achashverosh
and sealed with the royal signet, were sent with
mounted couriers, riders of swift mules born of
mares, and stated that the king had authorized
the Jews in every city to gather and defend
themselves, to destroy, slay and annihilate every
armed force of any people or province that harass
them, along with their children and women, and
to plunder their possessions, on a single day in all
the king's provinces, on the thirteenth day of the
twelfth month – which is the month of Adar. The
contents of the letter were to be distributed to all
provinces and publicized to all peoples, so that the
Jews should be prepared on that day to avenge
themselves on their enemies. The couriers, riders of
swift mules, went out in urgent haste by the king's
command, and the edict was given in Shushan
the capital.

Then Mordechai left the king's presence clad in
royal garments of blue and white, with a large
golden crown and a robe of fine linen and purple,
and the city of Shushan rejoiced. The Jews had
light and gladness and joy and honor. So too,
in every province and in each city, wherever
the king's command and his edict reached, the
Jews had great gladness and joy, feasting and a
holiday. Many of the people of the lands professed
to be Jews, because a fear of the Jews fell upon
them." (8: 9-17)

The second letters, sent by Mordechai to the Jews and authorizing them to defend themselves, or, alternately, interpreting the first letters in a manner which would be to their benefit, were dispatched on the twenty third day of Sivan.

We find that the sequence of events described in the main part of the *megillah* – beginning with the lots cast by Haman, continuing with his slanderous presentation to the king, the terrible decree, the dialogue between Mordechai and Esther, the three day fast, the queen's unsolicited appearance before the king, Esther's first and second banquets, the parading of Mordechai through the streets of Shushan with Haman heralding his honor, and even the hanging of Haman – all took place over the course of no more than four or five days in Nisan.[1]

---

[1] In the chapter "The Debate between Mordechai and Esther," dealing with Esther's fast, we explained that the authorities disagree regarding when exactly the three day fast commenced and on which date each event took place. In any case, it is clear that the maximum range was between the twelfth and the sixteenth of Nisan.

After Haman's ignominious end, there is a mysterious lull in the sequence of events. Suddenly, nothing was so urgent; a kind of indifference or apathy appeared to have set in. More than two months elapsed until couriers were dispatched with the new letters, though they were vital to deter potential damage to the Jews. What was the meaning of the lengthy delay in dealing with this burning problem?

Some maintain[2] that extensive mediation on Esther's part was necessary to convince the king to agree to send these second letters. As far as Achashverosh was concerned, he preferred to hide behind his excuse that "an edict which is written in the king's name and sealed with the royal signet cannot be revoked," and to leave the decree intact. Therefore, Esther had to endanger her life again and again, coming repeatedly to plead with the king, until finally, at the end of two months, he was willing to authorize the second letters, which were promptly dispatched that very day, before the fickle king would have a chance to change his mind.[3]

Others explain[4] that Esther's request was presented to the king immediately after Haman was hanged and Mordechai officially introduced to the king, i.e. around Pesach time. However, Mordechai intentionally put off *sending out* the letters since he wanted the same couriers who brought the first letters, sent by Haman, to bring *his* letters as well.

---

[2] Ibn Yichyeh, Ralbag

[3] Malbim. Though the Malbim agrees with the commentary of the Gra brought in the next paragraph, according to which the second letters were delayed until the first couriers returned, nevertheless, he maintains that the moment the letters could be sent out, Mordechai did so, since every day that passed posed the danger that the king would change his mind.

[4] Perush HaGra, Yosef Lekach

Mordechai was well aware that many gentiles would be sorely disappointed upon hearing that Haman's plot was foiled and the opportunity to kill out the Jews and plunder their possessions lost forever. He was concerned that these people would claim that the second letters were forged, their "proof" being that these letters were delivered by other couriers, not by the king's usual messengers.

In order to forestall such arguments, Mordechai preferred to wait patiently until the first couriers returned, and then to send the very same couriers out again with the new letters in their pouch, making it clear to all that the letters were absolutely authentic.

In Urgent Haste, by the King's Command

The second letters were definitely more specific than the first. They stated explicitly that the *Jews* should be prepared for the thirteenth day of Adar, and were sent especially to the Jewish subjects in every province. In regard to the second letters, we are told that the couriers were sent out *in urgent haste* by the king's command, as opposed to the first letters, where there is no mention of urgency, but only haste.

The purpose of these changes was to lend the second letters maximum authenticity, and to make it clear that the king had definitively and irrevocably retracted his original intention to annihilate the Jewish people. In order to accomplish that, it was necessary to emphasize in every way possible that the king attributed greater importance and urgency to these letters than he ever did to the first ones.

Indeed, Mordechai and Esther sent these second letters in the quickest way possible. In addition to demonstrating the special significance the king attributed to these letters, the urgency also flowed from their concern that their fellow Jews should not suffer fear and anguish a moment longer than necessary.[5]

According to those opinions maintaining that the second letters did not offer a substantial change to the first ones, but only authorized the Jews to come to their own defense, the necessity of informing the Jews of the matter as soon as possible is even more obvious, since they needed time to rally their forces properly in order to successfully stand up to their enemies on the fateful day.

Therefore, even the young ponies, which were not yet accustomed to running long distances, were drafted now for the cause.[6] Mules bred of mares,[7] the fastest and finest mules, also served the mounted couriers,[8] while the speediest camels in the king's possession galloped through the deserts, rushing to bring the news to the Jews in every corner of the empire.

Now there were no more secrets. In every place the couriers reached – and they reached every far-flung province[9] – joy broke out among the Jews. The Jews rejoiced that their lives had been saved in a most miraculous and inexplicable manner.

---

[5] Besides, they were also concerned about the harassment the Jews in the various provinces were suffering at the hands of the gentiles in the meantime.

[6] Ralbag

[7] The Targum explains that these were horses whose hooves and spleens were removed so that they would be able to run non-stop without tiring.

[8] This is how Ibn Yichyeh explains the words "*achashte'ranim benai haramachim*." However, Rashi writes that these words refer to especially speedy camels.

[9] Malbim

The people of the land rejoiced as well; they were gratified to see how truth had prevailed in the end.[10] They were also happy to discover that the new queen, who they now learned was of royal lineage - a descendant of Shaul the first king of Israel - befitted her lofty position.

The letters themselves were written in clear, plain language, that even a child could understand.[11] In addition to the dry order, they included comprehensive explanations, as had the previous letters.

We described earlier the lowly demagoguery used by Haman in order to intensify the hatred of the kingdom towards the Jews and cause them to eagerly anticipate annihilating them on the appointed day. Now, it was necessary to undo all traces of Haman's hateful slander.

Therefore, in the new letters,[12] Mordechai told of the God of the Hebrews, describing what Pharaoh had done to the people of Israel in Mitzrayim, as well as the evil that Amalek and his descendants had wreaked on the Jews through the ages. He delineated in great detail the recent sequence of events that had taken place in Shushan: How Mordechai had saved King Achashverosh from the conspiracy of Bigsan and Teresh, how the king wished to repay him, and how Haman fell into the trap and met his just end, on the very gallows he had prepared for the *tzaddik*.

The letters written by Mordechai and Esther in the king's name read as follows:[13]

---

[10] Ibn Ezra
[11] Ibn Yichyeh
[12] Targum Sheini, Ibn Yichyeh
[13] Targum Sheini

"To my dear subjects, residents of 127 provinces on land and sea, to the governors of the provinces and honored rulers, and to my armed forces in each land, may your well-being increase!

"I write to you in order to demonstrate my honor and glory, that even though I rule over land and sea, over numerous peoples and mighty empires, I have always conducted myself with humility, my foremost goal being to bring peace to the land – for your good and benefit, my dear subjects.

"I hereby wish to testify to the loyalty of the Jewish people to their king, and attest to the fact that they love all the people in the kingdom, render honor to the rulers, and deal kindly with all the government officials.

"Certain individuals of high rank, holding broad powers in the kingdom, deceived the king with their lies and machinations, and led me to write the letters that were sent to you, which were bad both in the eyes of God and man.

"These scoundrels wished to spill innocent blood and harm guiltless people, though they were devoid of deceit and even numbered among them righteous, precious individuals such as Queen Esther and Mordechai the Jew!

"Had I known that the subject of the slander was the loyal Jewish people, I never would have entertained the idea of destroying them – the people who are called 'the children of the God of heaven and earth,' the people whom the Creator of the world watches closely and whose affairs He lovingly directs.

"But I was duped, and the one responsible is Haman ben Hamedasa, the man whom I promoted and raised above the rank of all the other officers. But he did not know how to conduct himself with honor and glory; instead, he sought ways to do away with the king and usurp the throne, and therefore, he received his just deserts and was hanged on the gallows!"

Even though the wording of the letters did not explicitly state that the king rescinded the order given in the first letters, nevertheless, its content made perfectly clear that the Jews were not slated for death, and effectively countered the hatred that the earlier letters had churned up throughout the empire.

To Plunder their Possessions

There was an additional, more substantial difference between the first letters and the second. While in the first missives, Haman commanded all the peoples to destroy, slay and annihilate the Jews, young and old, women and children, *all in one day, and to plunder their possessions*, i.e., to conclude the slaughter all in a single day and then to begin the plunder afterwards, Mordechai instructed them to do otherwise.[14]

Actually, Mordechai felt that it would not be proper for the Jews to plunder their enemies' possessions at all. All they had asked of Hashem was that their lives be spared; why would they want to take a stranger's money and possessions? Therefore, Mordechai actually preferred that they would not touch the booty at all.

The problem was that, officially, the second letters were meant to interpret and elaborate on the first ones – not to

---

[14] Malbim

contradict them. That being the case, Mordechai could not simply omit details that were stressed in the original letters.

Mordechai found a simple solution. Instead of eliminating the phrase about the plunder, he simply changed the order. Instead of ordering that the annihilation be completed in one day, while the plunder would be allotted a special slot of time on the following day, he ordered that the plunder be completed on the same day the Jews were given to defend themselves – the thirteenth of Adar.

"The Jews will surely want to utilize every moment of this special day to avenge themselves from their enemies; they will not have time to waste plundering loot!" Mordechai said to himself. He expected the Jews to understand that this was his intention and refrain altogether from touching their enemies' possessions.

Haman, on the other hand, in the first letters, could not allow himself to formulate the language that way. He knew full well that the most effective way to get the masses out on the streets and motivate them to slaughter the Jews would be a monetary incentive. They would be more than happy to slay and destroy, in order to later plunder the victims' treasures.

Therefore, Haman made a point of emphasizing that the plunder could not be started until after the annihilation was complete. He knew that if a green light was given to begin the plunder before his extermination project was finished, the project would be doomed to dismal failure, since the gentiles would rather plunder valuable money and treasures than kill the Jews.

Now that the Jews were given the chance to defend themselves, a large number of gentiles chose to join up with the Jews in their battle. Not necessarily exceptional Jew-lovers, most of these gentiles were attracted by the opportunity to gain booty from the Jews' enemies.

In fact, this was one of the reasons that led Mordechai to permit plundering the possessions of those who were killed. Since the balance of power between the Jews and the gentiles was so heavily weighted in favor of the latter, Mordechai was interested in providing the Jews with reinforcements however possible.[15] If allowing plunder would provide the gentiles with the necessary motivation to join forces with the Jews, then so be it.

But many gentiles latched on to the Jews long before the time of the battle and its plunder arrived; they were simply afraid of the Jews and of Mordechai, whose rank in the palace was rising all the time.

The gentiles who asked to join the Jewish nation at that time are not considered *geirei emes,* true converts. They were not motivated by a sincere desire to adhere to the absolute truth and to the One Who spoke that truth, but rather by the fear that the Jews would kill them on the day when they were given permission to do so.[16] Therefore, these "converts"

---

[15] Perush HaGra

[16] The Ibn Yichyeh explains that those who adopted a Jewish identity out of fear of Mordechai were the Amalekites from among the gentiles, since the others had nothing to fear. Clearly, Mordechai never intended to kill harmless gentiles and nations who never raised a hand to the Jewish people. Only the Amalekites – against whom the Jews were commanded to conduct a holy war, and who, by their very existence, cause the throne of Hashem to be incomplete, so to speak - were terrified of Mordechai and tried to convert.

were never accepted as such, but remained with the title of *"mis'yahadim,"* "those who act like Jews." Although they followed Jewish customs, they never became a true part of the Chosen People.[17]

According to some opinions, these gentiles never wanted to join Hashem's people to begin with; they just wanted to masquerade as Jews in order to save their skin. Needless to say, these impostors would never be accepted in the Jewish community.

Mordechai Left the King's Presence

Whether or not the gentiles' intentions were sincere, the very fact that they sought to convert to Judaism gives us an idea of the general atmosphere that prevailed on the streets. The Jews, who until very recently had been persecuted and threatened, suddenly rose to greatness – they had a 'sister' in the palace! Their *rav* was the viceroy of King Achashverosh and nobody in the realm exceeded him in rank!

Mordechai Hatzaddik, who Haman had expected to hang on the gallows, had left the king's presence in majestic

---

The Ibn Yichyeh explains further that even though we were commanded in the Torah regarding Amalek, "Do not leave a single soul alive," this *mitzvah* was an instance of *hora'as sha'ah*, a temporary exception, applicable only when the Jews left Mitzrayim and again when Shaul went to war against Amalek by Hashem's command. At all other times, however, the Amalekites were able to convert to Judaism and there was nothing to prevent their acceptance into the Jewish community. He also explains that the Amalekites may not have revealed their origin, but rather followed the example of the Givonites and came deceitfully to the Jews in order to save their lives. Following this explanation, he points out that their conversion was certainly not accepted since it was only a superficial conversion. However, according to the first of his explanations, he seems to maintain that many of the people of the land actually did convert and were considered true, kosher Jews.

[17] Perush HaGra

style, while his enemy swung between heaven and earth. For Hashem humbles one person and raises the other; nothing is too difficult for Him.

The *megillah* describes Mordechai, who was considered "king of the Jews,"[18] as he emerged from the palace, "clad in royal garments of blue and white, with a large golden crown," which towered over his head like a canopy,[19] "and a robe of fine linen and purple."[20] The total value of Mordechai's royal clothing amounted to some four hundred and twenty golden talents.[21] The finery included a cotton shirt adorned with pictures of all the birds in the world, a valuable belt dotted with onyx stones, shoes studded with gold and diamonds, a dagger girding his hip with the form of Yerushalayim rebuilt engraved upon it, a golden crown upon his head, and above it, *tefillin* set in gold – so that everyone should know that this is Mordechai the Jew![22]

When Mordechai left the king's presence in these garments, a royal reception awaited him outside. The streets of Shushan had been adorned with myrtles, and the courts draped with fabrics of purple and fine linen. The *kohanim* blew trumpets in his honor and announced, "Whoever shall not seek the well-being of Mordechai and the Jews shall be killed, and his house plundered!"

The ten sons of Haman joined the impressive parade as they were led through the streets, their hands bound, grudgingly

---

18 Yalkut 1059
19 Ibn Yichyeh
20 According to the Ralbag, the *tachrich* was a turban for wrapping the head.
21 Targum
22 Ibid

singing Mordechai's praises, "Blessed is the God Who gives good reward to the Jews and grants the wicked their just deserts! Our father relied on his wealth and honor, and Mordechai the righteous Jew overcame him with his prayers and fasting!"

The Gra gives us a deeper insight into Mordechai's royal appearance. The true finery, as far as Mordechai was concerned, was the "royal garments of blue and white," the *tzitzis* he wore with its threads of blue and white. The "large golden crown" refers to the *tefillin shel rosh*, the head phylacteries, the "*tachrich*" is a reference to the *retzu'os*, the bands of the *tefillin* which are wound on the arm, and "fine linen and purple" alludes to the *tefillin shel yad*, the arm phylacteries.

At the apex of Mordechai's success, at the acme of his honor and wealth, he did not lose sight of the true glory. He knew that matters of this world are nothing but vanity, devoid of substance. True glory, true royalty is that which is suffused with spirituality and which draws its vitality from Torah and *mitzvos*!

It was not for naught that Mordechai merited such glory and splendor; it was in the merit of his devotion to his people, as the *megillah* describes the *tzaddik's* deep anguish over the decree. Now, in the merit of the sackcloth Mordechai wore in his concern for the Jews, he was clothed by Achashverosh in royal garments. In the merit of the ashes he placed on his head, he was adorned with a golden crown. In the merit of the clothing he tore in his distress, he was given fine linen robes. In the merit of the cry of anguish he emitted in the city square, the entire city of Shushan now rejoiced and cheered in his honor![23]

---

[23] Minchas Erev

Indeed, the city of Shushan rejoiced and was gladdened,[24] and the Jews had light, gladness, joy and honor. But Mordechai was not carried away by the prevailing spirit of joy. He knew, as is the nature of *tzaddikim*, that all the honor he merited could only detract from his immeasurably valuable merits in the World to Come. Besides, Mordechai was concerned that the Jews might become too sure of themselves and resume sinning, and next time, they might have to pay the full price for their transgressions.

Therefore, Mordechai did not openly exhibit his joy. He merely poured out his praise and gratitude to the Creator for saving His people from the hands of their enemies, and sufficed with that.

Now, all they could do was wait a few months and see how things would turn out: how the deliverance of the Jews would be carried out in practice, how they would prevail against their enemies, and how Hashem would take revenge from those who deserved His vengeance, as we shall see in the next chapter.

---

[24] The Gaon Rabbi Yitzchok Ze'ev Halevi explains that the rejoicing in Shushan commenced after they saw Mordechai's royal garments, since until the deliverance of the Jews was ensured, Mordechai would not remove his sackcloth nor halt his fasting. Even after his personal deliverance from Haman, he resumed his sackcloth and fasting. Now that the Jews saw that Mordechai left the king's presence in royal garments of blue and white, they concluded that the deliverance of the Jews was a reality, and therefore, Shushan rejoiced and was gladdened!

TURNED ABOUT

*"On the thirteenth day of the twelfth month
– which is the month of Adar, when the king's
command and edict were to be carried out, on the
very day when the enemies of the Jews expected
to overcome them, it was turned about and the
Jews overcame their enemies. The Jews assembled
in their cities throughout all the provinces of
King Achashverosh to strike at those who sought
their harm, and no one stood in their way, for
their fear had fallen upon all the people. All the
provincial officers, satraps and nobles and those
who conduct the king's affairs elevated the Jews,
because the fear of Mordechai had fallen upon
them. For Mordechai was prominent in the royal
palace, and his fame was spreading throughout
the provinces, for Mordechai the man grew
increasingly greater.
The Jews struck their enemies a blow by sword,
killing and annihilating them, and treating their
enemies as they pleased. In Shushan the capital,
the Jews killed and annihilated five hundred
people. They also killed Parshandasa, Dalfon,
Aspasa, Porasa, Adalia, Aridasa, Parmashta,
Arisai, Aridai and Vyzasa, the ten sons of Haman
ben Hamedasa, the Jews' enemy, but they did not
put a hand on the spoils." (9: 1-10)*

As we mentioned in earlier chapters, when Haman cast lots to choose a day on which the Jews' *mazal* was at a nadir so that he could successfully overcome and destroy them, the lot fell on the thirteenth day of Adar. However, even though this was the time when the Jews' fortune was presumably at its worst, Hashem overturned the forces of astrology and, on this very day, gave His people a great deliverance and a sweeping victory over their enemies![1]

This triumph was not a simple matter in the least. By nature, it was not at all certain that the Jews would prevail. In fact, in some of the districts, a fierce battle took place between the Jews and their enemies. It was only with Hashem's great kindness that the Jews reaped a clear and absolute victory.

The Jews Assembled in their Cities

The centers of population in Achashverosh's realm fell into one of two main categories: some were cities surrounded by a wall, while others were unwalled cities.[2]

The fortified cities, surrounded by a wall, were primarily occupied by the officers, dignitaries and rulers of the provinces. These cities also housed the nobles who received the detailed letter in which Haman explicitly commanded them to destroy,

---

[1] Malbim. However, we cited earlier other opinions which maintain that the Jews' *mazal* is never at a low point, since they are above *mazal*. Rather, the lot was cast to verify on which day Haman's *mazal* would be at a peak, so that he could stand up against them. According to these opinions, this *mazal* would no longer be of any significance once Haman was hanging on the gallows.

[2] The Yosef Lekach makes a different division. He differentiates between the *provinces*, which the second letters reached, and where there was no resistance to the Jews' battle, and the *villages*, where the second letters had not reached at all. The Jews there defended themselves, however, and their fear fell upon all the people because they heard of Mordechai's prominent position in the palace.

slay and annihilate all the Jews, the letter that was concealed from the general population.[3]

In these cities, no resistance arose against the Jews. Nobody stood in their way, and they were able to treat the Amalekites as they wished. Miraculously, none of the other gentiles intervened on behalf of the Amalekites. Nor did they attempt to arbitrate between the two sides and prevent the battle in which the Jews would settle accounts with those who sought to destroy them. Additionally, they didn't argue that they should not carry out the instructions in the second letters, that the king might retract this command in a short time, as was the case with the first letters.[4]

In addition, much of the general populace supported the actions of the Jews, or at least gave their silent assent.[5] This support stemmed from the Jews' public announcement that their intention was to strike at the Amalekites alone. The masses harbored a latent hostility towards the Amalekites, a hatred based on their envy of Haman the Amalekite, who had been promoted to such a lofty position in the palace, above all the other royal officers.[6]

---

[3] According to the Malbim's approach, the content of the letter was concealed from the nobles as well until the appointed day arrived. At that point, they opened both letters: the first one, in which the order to destroy the Jews was delineated, as well as the second one, where Mordechai and Esther wrote as they saw fit.

[4] Ibn Yichyeh. He adds that even those individuals among the general population who were related to the Amalekites from their mother's side did not intervene on their behalf.

[5] Megillas S'sorim

[6] Actually, Mordechai had also been promoted to a high rank. But, we can assume, the jealousy towards Haman was aroused by *his conduct after achieving his position*, i.e., his haughty command to all the people to prostrate themselves before him. Mordechai, on the other hand, even after he was promoted, remained humble, as we shall explain, and that may well be why no jealousy was aroused against him.

Besides, most of the general population had no idea that the decree was originally meant to be directed against the Jews, and that a change of some kind had taken place. They received the first letters commanding them to be prepared for the thirteenth of Adar, and then received the letters of Mordechai and Esther, clarifying to them that on this day, the Jews were authorized to avenge themselves from their enemies!

It is no wonder, therefore, that none of the masses found it necessary or wise to resist the Jews, who were acting with the king's endorsement, and who were directing their battle not against the general populace, but rather against the Amalekite nation in particular.

But the officers and dignitaries as well – who had received the detailed first letters and understood that the Jews were originally slated to be destroyed, and that even now, these first letters had not been nullified, rather permission had been granted to the Jews to resist their enemies – did not lift a finger against the Jews.

Not only did these officers refrain from averting the Jews' revenge, they did not even let a word out about the existence of the first letter, with its different content, "because the fear of Mordechai had fallen upon them."[7] They were afraid they would suffer the same end as Haman, who found his death as a result of his efforts to harm the *tzaddik*.[8]

Indeed, they had reason to fear. Mordechai, whose relationship to the queen was recently revealed to the king,

---

[7] Apparently, only the officers feared Mordechai, since it was clear that Mordechai would not involve himself with every private citizen, but rather with the "higher-ups" who would disobey his word and hurt the Jews.

[8] Malbim

grew higher in rank from day to day. While at first he had been appointed in charge of the king's household alone,[9] by the time a short period had elapsed, at the close of the *megillah*, we find him already serving as viceroy to the king. It is logical to assume that if anyone had attempted to hurt the Jews, Mordechai would certainly have brought him to account, using the new authority bestowed upon him.

In those cities where no resistance was posed, the Jews were somewhat restricted in their actions. They could not slay all their adversaries, only their *oy'vim* – those who were publicly known as enemies of the Jewish people and had actively sought to harm them.[10] However, the *son'im*, those who were known to be hostile to the Jews only in their hearts, escaped with their lives, though they too were humiliated and degraded.[11]

In the villages, on the other hand, the open cities where only the simple people lived, matters did not flow so smoothly. In these cities, there were no higher officials who were frightened of Mordechai, and there were no soldiers of the royal army to keep the peace. There, a genuine battle broke out, with the

---

[9] This is the opinion of the Yosef Lekach. However, the Malbim maintains that right from the start, Mordechai was in charge of three areas: the king's household, the various provinces, and the army whose job was to conquer more provinces. According to the Malbim, Mordechai became increasingly greater each day as a result of the third of these positions – as officer in charge of the conquering army. Each time he succeeded in capturing another province for King Achashverosh, his status rose yet more.

[10] The Targum Sheini explains that they killed those who harassed the Jews as a result of Haman's decree, saying to them, "In a few more days, we will kill you all, we'll even spill the blood of your children, and your carcasses, we'll throw to the ground!"

[11] Malbim. However, the Ibn Yichyeh explains that all the Amalekites were killed, while the worst Jew-haters among them were tortured as well.

Jews needing to defend themselves and fight fiercely against the gentiles.[12]

On the one hand, this meant that the Jews had to rely on miracles to overcome the enemies who tried to kill them. On the other hand, the Jews in these villages had an advantage over their brethren in the bigger cities; they were not restricted in which of their enemies they could slay. In the heat of battle, they could kill any Amalekite, even those whom they knew only hated Jews in their heart.

Not a Hand on the Spoils

In the wake of their victories, the Jews did not put a hand to the spoils. As we mentioned earlier, the decision to abstain from plundering the spoils was made by Mordechai Hatzaddik himself,[13] and it was hinted at in the text of the letters he sent

---

[12] The Malbim explains that only in the unwalled cities were the Jews aware of the open miracle that they had experienced, since they had fought – and won. Therefore, they set the date of their deliverance as a holiday even that first year. By contrast, in the larger provinces and walled cities, the Jews did not realize that a miracle had taken place. They thought there had been a misunderstanding of Haman's decree from the start, and that the Jews were never slated to be killed, or that the king had rescinded the decree, and no special miracle was necessary on the thirteenth of Adar which would justify designating it as a holiday. Only the following year, when Mordechai sent out letters clarifying that they had been under a real threat of annihilation as a result of Haman's letters, which had never been nullified, did the Jews in the big cities understand how great a miracle had been done for them, and they too set the fourteenth of Adar as a day of feasting and rejoicing. It should be pointed out, however, that many of the commentaries disagree with the Malbim, and maintain that even the Jews in the walled cities celebrated the first year, when the miracle took place.

[13] The Megillas S'sorim explains that the Jews simply *did not have a chance* to take spoils, since they were busy doing the *mitzvah* of eradicating Amalek and could not be bothered with such trivialities as plundering booty. According to his approach, it would seem that there was no explicit instruction from Mordechai regarding the spoils; just that in practice, the Jews did not take their enemies' spoils.

out to all the people. Several reasons led Mordechai to this decision.

First of all, he did not want to draw the rope the king had thrown him too taut. He knew that Achashverosh could accept with equanimity the slaughter the Jews would carry out to defend themselves, but he would not be able to tolerate the Jews making a monetary profit as an outcome of his order.[14] Therefore, Mordechai instructed the Jews to refrain from taking spoils, so as to appease the king and not cause his avarice of the Jews' money to rouse his hostility towards them.

Secondly, Mordechai wished to make it perfectly clear to the nations of the world that the Jewish people are not money-hungry. Avraham Avinu demonstrated this quality when he refused to accept from the king of Sedom "from a thread to a shoelace,"[15] and the Jewish people throughout the generations follow in his footsteps.[16]

It is reasonable to assume that this emphasis was especially vital in light of the slander Haman had tried to spread about the Jews. In his letters, Haman had reported in great length how corrupt, dishonest and thieving the Jews are. Therefore, Mordechai wished to emphasize that the reality is quite the opposite. The proof – the Jewish people did not lay a hand on their enemies' spoils, even though they were given explicit permission to do so.

Though the Jews did not touch the spoils, plundering did take place. However, the ones responsible for it were the

---

[14] Rashi
[15] Bereishis 14:23
[16] Ibn Yichyeh

gentiles who the Jews did not fight against. These gentiles took advantage of the opportunity and plundered the possessions of the Amalekites who were killed. Mordechai expected this to happen, and that is another reason why he told the Jews not to take their enemies' spoils, so that the gentiles would join forces with them to strike down the Amalekites.[17]

A Blow by Sword

The commentaries differ on the manner in which the Jews slew their enemies. Some maintain that the Amalekites who were not particularly malicious to the Jews were killed by the sword, while the known enemies, who had actively afflicted the Jews throughout the years, were subjected to a more painful, torturous death.[18]

Others state that the Amalekites were all struck at first with the sword, in a manner that would increase their suffering, and only afterwards were they finished off.

No mercy need be aroused towards these cursed Amalekites. Each and every one of them deserved a cruel and unusual death, since each one was happily willing to do his part in carrying out Haman's "final solution" for the Jews, and would eagerly have tortured any Jew that fell into his hand, had he been given the chance.

The Amalekites' bodies were not left intact, either. The Jews realized that if the bodies would remain it might bring to a drive

---

[17] However, the Yosef Lekach, following his approach, explains that in the villages – where Mordechai's letters never reached, and where the Jews defended themselves and were victorious as a result of the fear of Mordechai and of the Jews as a whole that fell upon the people – the Jews did take the spoils.

[18] Ibn Yichyeh

for revenge with an intentional disregard of the circumstances that led the Jews to kill their oppressors. Therefore, they decided to destroy the bodies, as was common practice at that time.

The only bodies that remained intact were those of the ten sons of Haman, who were left to swing from the gallows, so that all would hear and see what happens to those who rise against the Jews.

Here, too, the Jews followed the common practice of those days, according to which only the bodies of dignitaries and kings would be preserved intact to be publicly displayed, in order to instill a fear into the population.

THE EDICT WAS ISSUED IN SHUSHAN

"That day, the total number of those killed in Shushan the capital was presented to the king. Then the king said to Queen Esther, 'In Shushan the capital, the Jews killed and annihilated five hundred men as well as the ten sons of Haman. What did they do in the rest of the king's provinces? What is your petition now? It shall be granted to you. And what more is your request? It shall be done.' Esther replied, 'If it pleases the king, allow the Jews in Shushan to do tomorrow as they did today, and let the ten sons of Haman be hanged on the gallows.'
The king ordered this done. An edict was issued in Shushan the capital and they hanged the ten sons of Haman. The Jews in Shushan assembled again on the fourteenth day of the month of Adar, and killed three hundred men in Shushan, but did not lay a hand on the spoils. The Jews in the rest of the king's provinces assembled and defended themselves, gaining relief from their adversaries, and killing seventy five thousand of their enemies, and did not lay a hand on the spoils. That was the thirteenth day of the month of Adar, and they gained relief on the fourteenth day, making it a day of feasting and rejoicing. The Jews in Shushan assembled on both the thirteenth and the fourteenth, and gained relief on the fifteenth,

making it a day of feasting and rejoicing. That is why the Jewish villagers who live in unwalled towns make the fourteenth day of the month of Adar a day of rejoicing, feasting and festivity, and for sending delicacies to one another." (9: 11-19)

In Shushan the capital alone, the Jews killed 500 men, among them the 180 sons of Haman,[1] as well as the ten sons of Haman with whom we are familiar,[2] and who were all killed at the same time.[3]

At this point, the number of those killed in Shushan the capital was brought to the king's attention. The commentaries differ on how this information reached him.

Some commentaries[4] explain that the Amalekites killed by the Jews had many relatives among the higher echelons of the palace. It is logical to assume that Haman the Agagite, a member of the Amalekite nation, made sure to plant his relatives in key positions, just as he appointed his sons over various districts in the king's realm. When these dignitaries heard of the slaughter the Jews were carrying out on their kin, they immediately came running to the king to report and ask him to put a stop to the Jews' activities.

---

[1] Targum. However, another seventy sons of Haman escaped with his wife Zeresh. These were the sons who became beggars, as we mentioned above.

[2] The reason the *megillah* differentiates between the 500 men and the ten sons of Haman is that the 500 men were "killed and *annihilated*" by the Jews, i.e., their bodies were destroyed, as we wrote earlier, while the bodies of the ten sons of Haman were preserved to be hanged from the gallows, so that everyone would hear of their end and fear would be struck in their hearts (Yosef Lekach).

[3] Megillah 16b

[4] Ibn Yichyeh

According to these opinions, when the king called for Queen Esther and told her of the number of people killed in Shushan, he did not intend to imply that he was pleased by the situation. He actually wished to tell her, "Queen Esther, I'll have you know that I have already done far more than necessary for you. If the Jews have killed such a large number of people in the city of Shushan, where I myself reside and where the people ought to feel a tangible fear of the king, I cannot even begin to imagine what the situation is in other places!"

But since, in practice, the king authorized Esther to make any request she wanted, she ignored the tone of his words, and went on to ask that an edict be issued in Shushan allowing the Jews to continue slaying their enemies the next day too, as well as to hang the ten sons of Haman on the gallows. The king, whose affection for Esther outweighed his indignation, accepted her request and gave his approval, though his decision defied all logic.

However, other opinions[5] maintain that it was Mordechai who reported the number of people killed in Shushan to the king.

"Your Majesty the king," he said, "I want you to know that we only killed our open enemies, the ones who actively did evil and sought to kill us. Now just imagine, in Shushan alone there are 500 people who fall into this category – hence, there were 500 killed,"[6] Mordechai made it clear to the king.

---

[5] Malbim

[6] The Yosef Lekach agrees that Mordechai was the one to provide the king with the number of people killed, but he offers a different reason for this. He explains that Mordechai ordered the slaughter in Shushan stopped while it was still daylight, so as to show the king that he was not attempting to take advantage of his goodwill and carry on unrestricted carnage. Therefore, on *that day* Mordechai was already

Achashverosh was shocked. He asked Esther, "Tell me, Queen Esther, if so many people are seeking to attack you and your people, what can I do to help? If in Shushan, where the king's fear is upon the people, there are so many people working against you, I shudder to think what the situation must be in the other royal provinces!"

Esther grasped at the opportunity. "I request that the Jews be allowed to do tomorrow in Shushan as they did today – to kill more of their enemies, and to hang the sons of Haman on the gallows as a vivid lesson, making it clear to everyone that the king seeks the benefit of the Jewish people and is ready to punish anyone who dares threaten them!" she said, and the king acceded to her request.

As They Did Today

In response to Queen Esther's special request, the Jews in Shushan the capital were given an additional day to fight their enemies, and for a very important purpose.[7]

First of all, since there was already a precedent of letters sent out by the erstwhile viceroy, Haman Harasha, without

---

able to specify the number of those killed. The king understood that if so many were killed in Shushan, where the slaughter did not continue all day, how many more must have been killed in the other provinces, where the Jews took advantage of every single moment of the day.

The king was indeed impressed by the early halting of the slaughter, understanding that this had been done in his honor. Therefore, he asked Esther what else she would like to request. Esther asked that Achashverosh allow the Jews to complete tomorrow what they had not finished today, since they had stopped the battle early in the king's honor – a request that was granted, as we mentioned above.

[7] The Rishon Letzion explains that all the many enemies of the Jews gathered from the other provinces to Shushan, and hoped to destroy the Jewish people, relying on the content of the first letters. That is why Esther asked the king to authorize the Jews to fight against them on the fourteenth day of Adar as well.

the king's full knowledge, it was crucial to emphasize that the present order was issued with Achashverosh's full knowledge and wholehearted support.

In order to make this clear, Esther asked the king to give an oral command, allowing the Jews to do in Shushan on the fourteenth day of Adar as they did on the thirteenth – in other words, to add a day that was not mentioned in the letters sent by Mordechai. This command would prove that the king supports the entire process and that the Jews enjoy his full backing.

This clarification was also vital so that no grudge or concealed hatred would linger in the hearts of the gentiles. Once it would be perfectly evident that the Jews did not act on their own initiative, but rather at the king's bidding, the gentiles' ill will and latent hostility towards them would dissipate.

However, this clarification was necessary only in the walled cities, residence of the nobles who had received the first, secret letters sent by Haman, with their explicit delineation of the decree.

In the unwalled villages where the simple people lived, nobody had an inkling of the existence of the first letters and their content. Therefore, when the second order went out authorizing the Jews to defend themselves, it was accepted without challenge. It never occurred to them that the order might be the cunning work of an outsider, and could possibly have been written without the full knowledge of King Achashverosh himself.[8]

---

[8] Perush HaGra. He adds that this is why the unwalled cities celebrate Purim on the fourteenth day of Adar, the day the war was concluded, while the walled cities celebrate only on the fifteenth – because the walled cities needed the same permission the king gave to the Jews of Shushan, to fight for an additional day. This

In addition, Queen Esther also wished to make it clear that the king's beneficence was still extended to the Jews, and that he intended to take full revenge from their enemies. She wished to emphasize that the letters were not merely a one-time decision, but rather reflected the king's new attitude towards his Jewish subjects, the proof being that he granted them an additional day in which to avenge themselves from their enemies, even though the letters did not require him to do so.[9]

Furthermore, when the gentiles in the other provinces of the king would hear that the Jews continued killing in Shushan on the fourteenth of Adar, while in their areas the Jews had stopped

---

permission proved that the king stood behind the military organization of the Jews and that he indeed allowed them to do as they wished to their enemies.

The Malbim explains otherwise. He says that Mordechai instituted the rule that the unwalled cities should celebrate on the fourteenth of Adar because that was the day their battle was concluded, since no officers lived among them who had in their possession the first letters ordering them to destroy, slay and annihilate the Jews, and which were still in force, as we mentioned above.

However, in the larger, walled cities, danger still threatened the Jews on the fourteenth, since Haman, who sought to *destroy* the Jews, certainly intended to sanction killing any Jew, wherever and whenever. Even if a particular Jew would escape death on the thirteenth, he should be killed afterwards; no one was to rest until the entire Jewish people would be wiped out. In contrast, when the king authorized the Jews to defend themselves, it was clear that he did not give them a blanket authorization to kill out the gentiles until they were destroyed. Rather, he gave them limited permission for the thirteenth day of Adar alone. The proof is that Queen Esther had to make a special request to the king in order to enable the Jews in Shushan to kill their enemies even for one additional day!

It turns out, then, that on the fourteenth day, the validity of the king's order authorizing the Jews to fight their enemies had expired, while the validity of the letters held by the officers in the large cities was still very much in force. Therefore, there was still a concern that they would decide to carry out the order in the first letters and destroy the Jewish people! The fact that this concern was baseless only became clear on the fourteenth of Adar, when the officers did not take any measures that indicated an intention to harm the Jews. Thus, in the larger, walled cities, final and absolute relief came only on the fourteenth day, and that is why the day of celebration set for them for all generations was the fifteenth of Adar.

[9] Malbim

the slaughter already on the thirteenth, they would infer that the Jews in the rest of the world loved the neighboring gentiles and had mercy on their lives, and therefore would not bear a grudge against them for the slaughter they had already carried out in their province.

They Hanged the Ten Sons of Haman

And so, the first request of Esther – giving the Jews in Shushan an extra day to fight – was carried out. But, as we may recall, she had presented a second request as well – that the ten sons of Haman be hanged on the gallows as a lesson to all of the fate that awaits those who seek to harm the Jewish people[10] or who dare to destroy any people that is not guilty of a capital crime.[11]

Indeed, Esther's second request was also carried out that same day. Haman's ten sons, who had been killed on the first day of battle and their bodies left intact, were hanged, all at one time,[12] on the gallows that their father had prepared for Mordechai,[13] the same gallows upon which their father still swung, after almost a full year had elapsed.[14]

---

[10] Ibn Yichyeh

[11] Yosef Lekach

[12] Megillah 16b

[13] Aside from the inherent wickedness of the ten sons of Haman, as members of the Amalekite nation and as renowned Jew-haters, Chazal point out that they "merited" such "special" treatment, i.e., being hanged ignominiously on the public gallows, because they sabotaged the rebuilding of the *Bais Hamikdash*. As we mentioned at the beginning of the chapter "In the Days of Achashverosh," the ten sons of Haman were the ones who wrote the letter of indictment that was the direct cause of the halting of the construction work on the *Bais Hamikdash*.

[14] Haman was hanged on the sixteenth of Nisan of the previous year, while the calendar now stood at the fourteenth of Adar. See also Targum Sheini, where he explains that indeed, the decision to leave Haman hanging on the gallows for such a long period of time roused wonderment and grumbling on the part of the king's

Since the gallows towered to a height of fifty cubits, there was plenty of room for Haman and his ten sons, though they just exactly fit in. The Targum Sheini, detailing the order of places on the gallows, explains that Haman and each of his sons were allotted three cubits each from the height of the gallows.[15] Haman was hanged at the top, taking up three cubits, followed by a one cubit space, and after him was Parshandasa. Parshandasa occupied three cubits, followed by a one cubit space, and after that was Dalfon. The same pattern followed for the rest of the sons: Aspasa, Porasa, Adalya, Aridasa, Parmashta, Arisai, Aridai, and the last one – Vyzasa.

The Targum also explains that the gallows was imbedded three cubits into the ground, to give it stability, and that Vyzasa's feet were separated from the ground by four cubits.

We find, then, that the eleven bodies occupied thirty three cubits on the gallows, the space between them amounted to another ten cubits,[16] the distance between Vyzasa and the ground was four cubits, and when we include the three cubits sunken into the ground, the total height amounts to precisely fifty cubits.[17]

---

secretaries towards Esther. They claimed that she should act as the holy Torah commands (Devorim 21:23), "Do not leave a dead body on the gallows," but Esther gave them the answer they deserved, see ibid.

[15] Equivalent to about 1.8 meters or nearly six feet.

[16] There were only ten cubits of empty space between the eleven bodies, since Haman himself was hanged from the very top of the gallows, while after Vyzasa there was no more space beyond the four cubits mentioned specifically.

[17] I contrast, the Targum Yonasan states that there were three cubits of space from Haman's head to the top of the gallows, four and a half cubits from the foot of Vyzasa to the ground, three cubits allotted for each body, and a half cubit between the bodies. However, this approach brings the total height of the gallows to only forty eight and a half cubits, and needs further study. Perhaps the Targum Yonasan did not mean to say *precisely* a half cubit between bodies, but actually a bit more, which would make up the difference. The Yalkut (1059) brings another calculation, see ibid.

Mordechai Hatzaddik stood opposite the gallows from which the arch enemy of the Jews and his ten sons swung and proclaimed, "Woe to you, Haman Harasha! You schemed to harm the Jewish people, and the One Who knows everyone's innermost thoughts paid you your just deserts! But while you sought to eradicate us from beneath the protective wings of our Father in heaven,[18] the Creator did not pay you back in kind; He left your children under your wings – hanging from the gallows right below you!"

Wonder of wonders! Hashem delivered His beloved children from the vicious hand of their enemy Haman, paid him his just punishment and hanged him and his sons on the gallows. The panorama of events comprises a remarkably perfect system of miracles, devoid of even a single detail that can be attributed to "nature" or "happenstance."

In missives that he dispatched,[19] Mordechai recorded all these miracles and all the events that took place behind the scenes which demonstrated the manifold kindnesses of Hashem, all of which helped save the Jews from destruction. Esther followed suit and sent out detailed letters to the Jews,

---

[18] Targum Sheini. The apparent intention of the Targum is that Mordechai was referring to Haman's desire to cause the Jews to sin, so that they would leave their safe position "under Hashem's wings," so to speak, and He would stop protecting them. We see throughout the *megillah* that Haman tried to lead the Jews into transgressions, whether it was through the feast he thought up, or the false image he engraved upon his robe so that the Jews bowing to him would be guilty of idol worship, etc.

[19] The Yosef Lekach explains that Mordechai's letters were not specific, while Esther's letters were moe explicit. The Malbim, on the other hand, maintains that in Esther's letters she simply reinforced the validity of those sent by Mordechai, and added her request that the written synopsis of the miraculous sequence of events be included among the holy writings of Tanach. This written version, known to us by the name *Megillas Esther*, was included together with the letters she sent.

commanding them to observe the *mitzvos* of Purim – feasting and rejoicing, gifts for the needy, reading the *megillah* and sending delicacies to one another.

And indeed, the Jews accepted upon themselves, their descendants and all those who would join them in the course of future generations, to observe both of these days in their time as they were written, and confirmed that the memory of these days would never depart from the Jews, not even in the Days to Come.

All this is described to us in the *megillah*, as it writes:

> *"Mordechai recorded these events, and sent letters out to all the Jews in all of King Achashverosh's provinces, near and far, commanding them to observe the fourteenth day of the month of Adar and the fifteenth day of the month, each year, as the days upon which the Jews found relief from their enemies, and the month which had been transformed for them from sorrow to joy and from mourning to festivity. They were to observe them as days of feasting and joy, and for sending delicacies to one another and gifts to the needy. The Jews undertook to continue the practice they had begun, just as Mordechai had written to them.*
>
> *"For Haman ben Hamedasa, the Agagite, enemy of all the Jews, had plotted to annihilate the Jews, and cast a* pur *– that is, lots – to terrify and destroy them. But when she [Esther] came before the king, he commanded by means of letters that*

the wicked plot that he [Haman] had devised
against the Jews shall revert upon his own head,
and they hanged him and his sons on the gallows.
"For this reason, they called these days 'Purim,'
from the word **pur**. *Therefore, because of all that*
was written in this letter, and because of what
they had experienced and what had happened
to them, the Jews confirmed and accepted upon
themselves and their descendants and upon all
who might join them, to observe these two days
without fail in the manner prescribed, and at
their proper time each year. And so, these days
should be remembered and observed in each
generation, in each family, in each province and
each city. These days of Purim shall not depart
from the Jews and their remembrance shall not
cease from their descendants.

"Then Esther, the daughter of Avichayil, and
Mordechai the Jew wrote with full authority, to
enforce this second letter of Purim. Letters were
dispatched to all the Jews, to the one hundred
and twenty seven provinces of the kingdom
of Achashverosh, words of peace and truth, to
establish these days of Purim on their proper
dates, just as Mordechai the Jew and Queen
Esther had commanded them, and as they had
accepted upon themselves and their children the
matter of the fasts and prayer. Esther's statement
validated these regulations for Purim and it was
recorded in the book." (9:20-32)

GLOSSARY

Akeidas Yitzchok: Event when Yitchzok was prepared to be sacrificed by his father

Aron Kodesh: The holy ark

Bais Hamikdash, Mikdash: The Holy Temple

Bais Midrash: Torah house of study

Beis Din: Rabbinical court of law

Bnai Yisrael, Klal Yisrael: The Jewish people

Bracha: Blessing

Bris Milah: Circumcision

Chazal: The sages of the Talmud

Cheder: Young boys' Torah school

Chesed: Acts of kindness

Chilul Hashem: Desecration of God's Name

Chuppah: Wedding canopy

Chutzpah: Audacity

Daven: Pray

Drasha: Speech

Eretz Yisrael: Land of Israel

Esrog: Citron fruit used on Sukkos holiday

Gadol Hador, Gedolei hador, Gedolim: Greatest rabbinical leader(s) of the generation

Gemara: Talmud

Goyim: Gentiles

Halacha, Halachic: Jewish law, having to do with Jewish law

Hashem: God

Hashgacha: Providence

Kashrus: Kosher

Kesubah: Marriage contract

Kisei Hakavod: God's throne of glory

Kohen Gadol, Kehuna Gedola: The High Priest/Priesthood

Kohein, Kohanim: Priest(s) who served in the Temple

Kri'as Shema: Prayer of Shema proclaiming God's Oneness

Levi, Levi'im: Member(s) of the tribe who served the priests in the Temple

Livyoson: Sea animal that will be served in messianic times to the righteous

Luchos: Tablets that have the Ten Commandments written on them

Lulav: Palm branch used on Sukkos holiday

Maror: Bitter herbs

Mashgiach: Kashrus supervisor

Mashiach: the Messiah

Mazal: Astrological sign

Mefarshim: Commentaries

Mishkan: Tabernacle

Mitzvah, Mitzvos: Commandment/s of the Torah

Moshol: Parable

Navi: book of the Prophets

Nimshol: Meaning behind the parable

Oy: Woe!

Posuk, Pesukim: Verse(s)

Perek: Chapter

Rav: Rabbi

Rasha, Resha'im: Wicked man/men

Rebbe: Torah teacher

Retzu'os: Tefillin straps

Rosh Chodesh: First day of the new month

Ruach Hakodesh: The Divine Spirit

Sanhedrin: High court of the Jewish people

Sefer Torah: Torah scroll
Sefer: Book
Shabbos: Sabbath
Shamayim: Heaven
Shechina: God's Presence
Shlit"a: May he live a long, good life
Shofar: Ram's horn
Shul: Synagogue
Siyata Dishmaya: God's help
Tallis: Prayer shawl
Talmidei Chachomim: Torah scholars
Talmidim: students
Ta'anis Esther: The Fast of Esther
Tefillah: Prayer
Tefillin (shel rosh, shel yad): Phylacteries (of the head, of the arm)
Teshuva: Repentance
Tzaddik, Tzaddekes, Tzaddikim: Righteous man/woman/men
Yerushalayim: Jerusalem
Yeshiva, Yeshivos: House/s of study
Yisraelim: Israelites
Yom Tov: Holiday
Zechus: Merit

נר זכרון

לנשמתו הטהורה של עטרת ראשנו

מאור עינינו מורנו ורבנו

משיירי כנסת הגדולה נזר הרבנים בדורנו

גודר גדר ועומד בפרץ

יחיד ומיוחד בענוה

מרן הגאון הצדיק רבנו **יוסף צבי הלוי דינר** זצוקלל"ה

ראב"ד דהתאחדות קהילות החרדים באנגליה

זקן הרבנים שהאיר את שמי יהדות אירופה

והשיב דבר השם זו הלכה למעלה משבעים שנה

כמסורה שקבל מאבותיו ורבותיו גדולי אשכנז זי"ע

נלב"ע באור לארבעה עשר לחודש ניסן תשס"ז

ת.נ.צ.ב.ה.

לעילוי נשמת

האישה הכשרה ישרת הדרך

מרת **יהודית רוטנר** ע"ה

בת ר' חיים תרסנטי ז"ל

נלב"ע בי' בניסן תשס"ז

ת.נ.צ.ב.ה.

לעילוי נשמת

סבנו, האי גברא רבה, ידיו רב לו בתורה ובמעש"ט

הר"ר **יעקב יצחק** בהר"ר משה הכהן **קליין** זצ"ל

נלב"ע ה' טבת ה'תשנ"א

וזוגתו סבתנו הצנועה והצדקנית

מרת **מירל** ע"ה בת הר"ר שלום זצ"ל

נין הרב ר' שמעלקא מסעליש זי"ע בעל ה'צרור החיים'

נלב"ע א' באדר ה'תשמ"ג

ת.נ.צ.ב.ה.

לעילוי נשמת

סבתנו אצילת הנפש, אשת חיל עטרת בעלה

מרת **ציפורה אסתר וייס** ע"ה

בת הגאון הצדיק רבי רפאל בלזם זצ"ל

בעל ה'נחלי אפרסמון'

נלב"ע ג' ניסן ה'תשס"ג

ת.נ.צ.ב.ה.

לעילוי נשמת

אבי מורי ישר הדרך, רודף צדקה וחסד

עמירם בן ישעיהו **למברסקי** ז"ל

נלב"ע י"ב סיון ה'תשס"א

ת.נ.צ.ב.ה.

לעילוי נשמת

האי גברא רודף צדקה וחסד, אהוב על הבריות

אשר נזדכך ביסורים קשים וגדולים

הרב **רפאל אשר** זצ"ל בהר"ר צבי **טאוסקי** שליט"א

נלב"ע י"ב אייר ה'תשס"ב

ת.נ.צ.ב.ה.